THE TRAFFIC IN NARCOTICS

THE TRAFFIC
IN NARCOTICS

by
H. J. ANSLINGER
United States Commissioner of Narcotics

and
WILLIAM F. TOMPKINS
United States Attorney for the District of New Jersey
Former Chairman, Legislative Commission to Study
Narcotics, General Assembly of New Jersey

FUNK & WAGNALLS COMPANY, INC., NEW YORK

[1953]

$Repl.$

8

HV 5825
.A 75

11 / 24 / 64

023

PREFACE

THAT THERE IS A PRESENT PROBLEM IN NARCOTICS IS WELL EVI-
denced by the continued stream of stories that appear in the
daily press and in other journals—stories of teen-age addiction,
of smuggling rings, of brutal crime with narcotics and drugs as
a concomitant. The reports are in fact not particularly new in
substance, nor are they peculiarly an attribute of our own times.

But there has been too long an attitude of withdrawal from
discussion of unpleasant topics on the part of the general public
resulting, most unfortunately, in an almost total unawareness of
many serious social problems. That attitude has undergone a
notable change with a generation that has been embroiled in two
world wars and that has felt the tremendous impact of the tech-
nological advances reflected in the art of modern communication,
whether used with objectivity or as propaganda. No longer does
the general public reject discussion of problems that it recognizes as a true part of its social responsibility. It has come to feel
that what benefits the whole must inherently benefit the individual, that what has become a problem for the individual may well
become a serious problem for the community. One of these
problems of which there is an awakening social awareness is that
of narcotics.

One of the recognized ways of solving a basic problem is to
endeavor to understand it. *The Traffic in Narcotics* is an attempt
to present the facts, to review, if you will, the evidence, and to
reach some conclusions that may help in establishing sane, pro-
gressive, and healthy public attitudes and public action.

It is earnestly hoped that those in the professions who are
often personally concerned with one or another aspect of this

problem will find here helpful information and perhaps a wider appreciation of just what they have to contribute to the eventual control and amelioration, if not complete elimination, of this source of human degradation.

Perhaps a word will be useful on the manner in which this study has been arranged. A brief account of the history of the use of narcotics—the opium that has a long arm and no conscience—points out its antiquity and that its economic, political, and social ramifications are rooted deep in the course of history. To paraphrase Shakespeare, the world has been and is its stage.

That the reader may gain an understanding of the terms involved and just what the narcotic drugs are, their origins and principal characteristics are reviewed in a generally non-technical but sufficiently detailed way. Included, of course, are the various derivatives and the synthetic drugs which have made their appearance from the laboratory.

There follows discussion of the international scene. This is of major importance in any understanding of the subject, as it covers some forty-four years of international efforts, going back to 1909. No discussion would be complete without this survey, which is reflected in the body of laws operative in the United States, Canada, and many other countries in the pattern of international cooperation. To highlight the political factor inherent in the narcotics traffic, excerpts from several recent official discussions of the Commission on Narcotics of the United Nations illustrate points of conflict as well as present for review a public record not often accessible to the general reader.

Other chapters present the national, State, and local levels of control and law enforcement. Case histories are primarily used to characterize the scope of the traffic in its economic and social implications, both for the individual and for the community.

Particular attention is called to the account of the medical aspects and of the treatment of the addict. Both the general reader and the general medical practitioner will find here, it is believed, much that is genuinely informative and encouraging in the broad sense. The authors are grateful in being able to present the outstanding work of their colleagues in tangent fields of research and public service.

For the legislators in the various governmental units and for those in positions of authority the presentation of the Uniform Narcotics Drug Act will prove helpful in furthering the cause of narcotics control and interstate cooperation. This model law is reprinted in its entirety for reference in the Appendix.

It has been with genuine regret that any discussion of the role of education has not been found possible in this book. It would appear that as yet no consensus has developed among educators that would indicate any discernible trend for or against inclusion in the curricula or cocurricula. However, that there is here a subject of sufficient import to the community and to the individual suggests that the problem will bear careful watching and consideration by those who guide the youth of the nation in their formative years, their susceptible years.

In this connection it is to be observed that the United Nations Commission on Narcotic Drugs in 1951, following a League of Nations report of 1936, recommended "that propaganda in schools" could be used in certain areas of addiction and that "in other countries where it is of more sporadic character (Europe and North America), such measures would be dangerous . . ."

Throughout *The Traffic in Narcotics* the fact that there is a grave moral problem involved is clearly in evidence. It need not be labored here. Whether it is political, economic, or social morality the reader will quickly decide for himself. But that it is some man or woman, some child, who is the victim, is an inescapable conclusion. And it is this individual who must never be lost sight of in the consideration of the broader aspects of the problem.

The fact that millions of sufferers have had their pain assuaged throughout the ages by the opiates lessens not one whit the importance of a full understanding of the problem of narcotics and of the dissipation of public and individual ignorance. This understanding involves a knowledge of how the trafficker in narcotics operates, of what is being done to stop him and what still remains to be accomplished, and of why the citizen must not turn aside and rely on another to be the good Samaritan. For drug addiction is murder on the instalment plan.

The authors are convinced that though the situation today is disquieting despite forty-four years of striving for a system of international control, it would have been disastrous without those years of effort. It is a little known and too seldom mentioned fact that there is one important field of international diplomacy in which the United States Government has for several decades met with amazing and continuing success. There have been few more dramatic or more fruitful efforts at international collaboration than those in the field of the control of narcotic drugs. The results obtained are outstanding.

In this book three essentials have been stressed: international cooperation, compulsory hospitalization for the addict, and stringent penalties for the trafficker in narcotics. These are immediate steps toward the final goal.

It should be said by way of dedication that this study is presented with the sincere hope that it might contribute something of genuine value to an alerted general public and to those organizations within it which strive so consistently in the public weal: to the lawmaker who faces the problem of establishing public policy; to the law enforcement officers on all levels who serve to protect the public as well as to apprehend the criminal; to the physician in whose hands lies the gravest responsibility of use and abuse and of beneficent cure; to the pharmacist who dispenses the drugs for good or evil; to the social worker who must process his "cases" with humanity and broad understanding; to the educator who shares the responsibility in the guidance of youth; to the scientist whose researches are so important; and to all those who labor in the field of international cooperation.

THE AUTHORS

June, 1953

ACKNOWLEDGMENTS

GRATEFUL ACKNOWLEDGMENT FOR ASSISTANCE IS EXTENDED TO:

Dr. Nathan B. Eddy, National Institutes of Health

Dr. Lyndon F. Small, National Institutes of Health

Dr. Harris Isbell, Director of Addiction Research Center, U. S. Public Health Service Hospital, Lexington, Kentucky

Dr. Pablo Wolff, Expert Committee on Drugs Liable to Produce Addiction, World Health Organization

Honorable William T. McCarthy, Federal Judge, Boston, Massachusetts

Honorable Twain Michelsen, Superior Court Judge, San Francisco, California

Mr. R. S. S. Wilson, former Superintendent of the Royal Canadian Mounted Police

Mr. Herbert L. May, President, Permanent Opium Board, United Nations

Colonel C. H. L. Sharman, President, Supervisory Body, United Nations

Dr. Tsungming To, Dean, Faculty of Medicine, National Taiwan University, Taipei, Formosa

Detective Leonard J. Iatesta, Narcotic Squad, New Jersey State Police

Mr. D. Knowlton Read, Chairman, Narcotics Commission, American Prison Association

Congressman Hale Boggs of Louisiana

Congressman Gordon Canfield of New Jersey

Congressman Cecil R. King of California

CONTENTS

xi

THE TRAFFIC IN NARCOTICS

THE PATTERN OF MAN'S USE OF NARCOTIC DRUGS

THE POPPY, THE SYMBOL OF SLEEP AND DEATH, IS AGE-OLD IN THE lore of antiquity. On the clay tablets of the Sumerians it was recorded that the juice of the poppy was "collected in the early morning," perhaps before the Eastern sun should have tempered its anodyne. This people of the land of Sumer in lower Mesopotamia—now the Arab kingdom of Iraq—cultivated the poppy plant five thousand years B.C. in order to extract its juice; *gil* was the name they gave it which translated means joy or rejoicing, and this name is still used today for opium in some parts of the world.

It was the Babylonians, inheritors of the Sumerian civilization, who, with their expanding empire, spread the knowledge of the poppy's medicinal properties eastward to Persia and westward to Egypt where its use as a remedy for human ailments was known as early as 1550 B.C. The Greeks, too, early learned its uses, for it is from their word, *opion*, juice of the poppy, that our Latinized word comes. The poppy was old in Greek legend before Homer in the *Iliad*, recounting a decoction of it used by Helen of Troy, said that it had the power of "inducing forgetfulness of pain and the sense of evil." In the fourth century B.C. Hippocrates of Cos thought well of it and recommended "drinking the juice of the white poppy mixed with the seed of the nettle."

From then on many well-known writers extolled with enthusiasm the virtues of confections containing opium, and the use

1

of the therapeutic drug spread quickly through the Roman world, with itinerant quacks the means of popularizing it for a variety of lesser ailments.

The rise of Mohammedanism provided another stimulus with its concept of the separateness of the spiritual and physical nature. This doctrine permitted a freer approach to scientific observation and analysis, much less trammeled by the philosophic and religious mores of their contemporaries. Arabic doctors, both Moslem and Christian, were prodigal in the use of opium in their cures; among others, it became used as a specific for diarrhea and scores died of overdosage of the drug. It can be said, in passing, that until the twelfth century the use of opium was largely confined to medicinal purposes.

It was during the tenth century that knowledge of the famed Arabic pharmacopoeia was taken to China by Arab traders and traveling physicians and with them went the drug itself. In China, too, it was first used as a remedy for dysentery. Later its use became wide-spread when it was found that it enabled a teeming people to exist on very little food during times of famine, a problem current throughout Chinese history.

Eastward from its ancient home through Persia to India was another road the poppy traveled to become naturalized. That it thrived there is evidenced by the Portuguese Barbosa, companion and friend of Magellan, who in 1511 could write of the "opium which the most of the Moors and Indians eat." It is also thought that, because their religion forbade the use of alcohol, the Brahmin priesthood of India became users of opium as a sublimating substitute. To India Chinese junks sailed the long, arduous voyage around the Malayan peninsula to secure the opium that became the beginnings of the "traffic" as we use the word today. As the eighteenth century approached, a rapid increase in the importation of opium began through the hands of the Portuguese, and still later through the agency of the famous—or infamous—East India Company.

Opium was not unknown in western Europe. A famous physician climbed the proverbial ladder of success in the 1500's as a result of his bold dosages of the drug for his patients. That the drug would resist poison, deafness, asthma, coughing, colic, jaundice, fever, leprosy, female troubles, and melancholy was among the claims of these practitioners of the healing arts. Turner, first English herbalist, in 1551 says of the poppy, "how excellent is that flower in the disease of the pleurisie." And again quaintly says of an over-dosed patient, "put stynkynge thynges unto hys nose," to awaken him.

FOREIGN MUD

At first used medicinally in China, opium was no serious social problem—with the exception of the unaccounted-for deaths from overdosage—until a Manchu emperor from the North conquered Amoy, in Fukien Province on the coast, and the island of Formosa in 1683, and his soldiers learned of the "delight" of opium smoking from the inhabitants there. Still it was not a serious menace to Chinese civilization until European traders began their work of exploitation.

Portuguese traders from their footholds in India were the first of these Western traffickers; their initial freight of 200 chests in 1729 increased fivefold within the ensuing forty years. Increasing use of the drug created a widening demand for it among the Chinese and eventually the wall of Chinese isolation was broken through by the British who secured the open-door policy for trade. The British-chartered East India Company and its successors (1600-1874) sold freely to Chinese merchants. By 1796— a short sixty years—the welfare of the Chinese people was menaced seriously by what, a century before, had been considered "a minor article of domestic commerce." The Emperor Yung Chen was the first to issue an edict against the habit-forming smoke. His proclamation, initiating a series of laws against opium smoking, said nothing, however, about the steady tide of opium flooding China from foreign ports. Finally, in 1800, the problem waxed grave in China, and the importation and the cultivation of the opium poppy were prohibited. But in spite of the law, the opium trade continued, growing unabated.

"How much foreign mud [opium] do you have on board?"

The speaker—a corrupt Chinese port official; the person to whom the inquiry was directed—the captain of a British clipper; the year—

1834; the place—the deck of the clipper, anchored some five hundred yards off Swatow.

This scene was repeated innumerable times at ports up and down the China coast in the early 1830's. It was not long before the foreign mud became the *casus belli* for the Opium War between Great Britain and China which was terminated by the Treaty of Nanking in 1842. A résumé of the first great traffic in opium and its impact upon subsequent events provides an excellent backdrop for the situation today.

BACKGROUND FOR WAR

In the early days of the eighteenth century the British, following the venturesome Portuguese, Dutch, and Spanish had established a trading base at Canton where they soon outstripped in activity their European competitors. From the beginning and, in fact until the Treaty of Nanking abrogated them, the trade of the British, together with that of other Europeans, was restricted by regulations devised by the Chinese to keep the foreigners at arm's length, yet permitting the Chinese to continue to export their teas and silks and to receive desired English goods. The export of Chinese commodities far exceeded the imports of British goods and this resulted in an adverse cash balance to the British traders. Initially these debits had been discharged by silver payments, but by the close of the nineteenth century there was found a new commodity that balanced the books and ultimately provoked a war; that commodity was opium.

The East India Company had exercised a controlling government-sponsored monopoly of all British-Asiatic trade since the early 1600's. The cultivation of opium in India was included in this monopoly. The entire Indian crop was sold to independent merchants at the famous Calcutta auctions. In turn, these firms shipped opium to the China coast where, with the aid of dishonest Chinese officials, it was smuggled into the country. This illicit opium traffic, it has been estimated, was several times as great as all the legal trade combined.

A clear picture is presented by relating how Anglo-Chinese

trade operated around the 1830's. Imported into China through legal channels were chiefly cotton and woolen goods worth approximately three million dollars. British interests, however, were exporting from China almost five times that amount in tea and silk and, in addition to and despite this adverse trade balance, were actually exporting Chinese silver, whereas normally they should have been importing it to pay the trade balance between their exports and imports. By what device was this accomplished? The opium traffic provided the means. Under the aegis of the East India Company the independent trading companies would export a few million dollars worth of tea and import many times that amount in opium, thus acquiring large silver balances in their favor. These firms then gave to the East India Company the use of these balances and in return received payment in London. Thus, because the trade balance was tilted in their favor by the opium revenue, British interests were enabled to export considerable silver from China.

The East India Company had obtained virtually a world monopoly of opium due to their control of its cultivation in India, and the funds derived from the yearly auctions at Calcutta comprised a very large and important part of Indian state revenues. This government-granted monopoly was thus the source of a vicious traffic, which the Crown could have effectively delimited, had it so desired, by limiting cultivation in India and prohibiting export. This course, however, would have seriously impaired Indian revenues.

In addition to Indian revenues, the opium trade provided the wherewithal to finance the tea and silk exports from China, and all this was what the mercantile group had carefully encouraged and nurtured and which *ultimately was to open up China to free trade*. Speaking of the merchants, while their main avowed intent was to open up China to free trade without burdensome restrictions, the fact remained that such a result could only be, and ultimately was, a *real boon to the opium traffic*, a fact which should not escape unnoticed.

Following minor outbreaks and incidents and futile attempts to compromise the situation, the whole problem really started to localize in early 1839. The Chinese Emperor conferred with one

Lin Tsê hsü, the governor-general of a neighboring province, a completely honest official who had been most successful in suppressing the traffic within his own jurisdiction. The Emperor, concerned both because he received no customs income from the illegal traffic in Indian opium and also because too much silver was leaving the country, was most receptive to the Lin plan for terminating the opium traffic.

Lin's solution was twofold: first, to use whatever pressure was necessary, and second, in order to prevent further traffic in opium, to compel the British to submit to the jurisdiction of the Chinese courts and to accept the death penalty upon conviction if any merchant was found to have violated the Chinese opium laws. Unfortunately for Lin, he grossly underestimated both the rising power and the reaction of the British Government to the idea of being forced to terminate its opium traffic without gaining any other compensating concession. The Emperor was convinced, however, that it was the correct course to pursue and accordingly appointed Lin commissioner to Canton with the powers necessary to stamp out the opium traffic.

Immediately after Lin's arrival at Canton he issued an edict which required that all opium stocks be surrendered within three days, and furthermore that bonds be posted guaranteeing no future imports of opium, and, if any were imported, that the offending individual submit to a Chinese court trial and death by strangling on conviction; the penalty for non-compliance— the closing down of all trade with China plus the use of force by its army and navy. The pressure was on; a crisis had arrived.

There was considerable demurring on the part of the merchants; additional sanctions by Lin; an attempt to bargain by the merchants; and finally, threats of death to some members of the mercantile community. To this gradual and effective pressure the chief superintendent of the British Colony, a Captain Elliot, finally succumbed since he feared for the lives and safety of the resident merchants and their families. He, therefore, was forced to order that all of the opium be surrendered with the promise that the British Government would then indemnify the merchants for their loss. The opium was turned over and destroyed. This act, of itself, undeniably constituted complete and full recognition by the British Government of the illegality of the opium traffic. However, this act of recognition only rounded out the picture because Parliament at London had already been studying the problem and concluded it was unwise to abandon this important and lucrative source of revenue.

THE OPIUM WAR, 1840-1842

Such was the situation when the Foreign Minister, Lord Palmerston, prepared to debate the strained Chinese situation in Parliament. Palmerston, under the tutelage of William Jardine, the greatest and most influential of the opium smugglers, expressed a desire that the China market remain open and that he was prepared to employ military force to accomplish it. However, such a war could never be sold to the British people on the basis of Lin's seizure of the opium. The only tactical ground would be a flag-waving appeal to Britain's honor with the hope that all mention of opium would be suppressed. Furthermore, the Chinese could then be forced to reimburse for the opium (which Lin had seized and for which Captain Elliot had agreed, in the name of his Government, to indemnify the British merchants), for it was a certainty that this indemnity consisting of several million pounds sterling, would never be approved by the man in the street if it were to come from his own pockets. Suffice it to say and without relating the intricacies of the parliamentary debate, Palmerston prevailed by a narrow margin and the war was on.

No purpose is served by describing the war itself, which resulted in an overwhelming victory for the English, who then proceeded to dictate the Treaty of Nanking, of August 29, 1842. Under the terms of the treaty five ports, Shanghai, Canton, Foochow, Amoy, and Ningpo, were opened to free trade; the Chinese were required to pay for the opium which Commissioner Lin had seized; Hong Kong was ceded to England; and the Chinese were compelled to bear the cost of the British expedition.

The merchants' group had now succeeded. China was opened to free commerce, and the opium traffic continued to flourish because of its tremendous benefit to Indian revenues. Within ten years after the war its volume increased almost threefold, and until the traffic was finally terminated by an agreement of May 8, 1911, it continued to be an important source of revenue.

NOT WITHOUT FAULT

While British policy in connection with this pernicious traffic was inexcusable and indefensible, the fact should not be over-looked that the policy of American officials and merchant-traders in the Far East greatly paralleled that of the British. Commodore Kearney, visiting Hong Kong in 1842, found abundant evidence of American participation in the opium traffic. Two American companies, Russell & Company and Augustine Heard & Company, both of Boston, were large participants, as were other Americans.

While American merchants condemned the opium traffic during the critical period of 1839, by 1853 American traders were again enmeshed in the traffic. The United States Commissioner to China, Humphrey Marshall, was shocked at "the wholesale system of smuggling that is carried on both under the English and American flags, almost in view of Chinese ports, and which in my opinion amounts to a gross and abominable violation of our treaties (in their spirit) with this government [China]." William B. Reed, in 1858, calculated that approximately one fifth of the opium entering Shanghai was carried by American ships. It is thus patent that Americans were as well involved in this disgraceful business, and accordingly must share the onus with the British.

TOOL OF WAR

Opium has become an effective and subtle tool of war. The second time China was impregnated with it was before World War II, when Japan was preparing for its invasion of the Chinese mainland and correctly had estimated the power the drug had of undermining the Chinese people, both morally and physically. The Japanese had coldly calculated its devastating value as fore-runner to an advancing army; long before the steel missiles began to fly, opium pellets were sent as a vanguard of the military attack.

Thus there was carried on what can be called a "chemical" warfare against the Chinese. It was the invasion of the country by drugs which some say is just as destructive as a whole series of successful bombing raids. Drugs can all too thoroughly demoralize a nation and expedite its conquest.

Its effectiveness was visible wherever the Japanese army had been. A systematic attempt was undertaken to undermine the Chinese population by making new addicts and by encouraging participation again by those who had once been addicted. Poppy cultivation was re-introduced and followed up by the establishment of a drug factory. The Japanese left no effort unattended.

The story of opium was not a new one to the Chinese and with it they could perhaps deal, but heroin and morphine were different. The first hypodermic syringe of morphine can easily lead to addiction for life. A few whiffs of heroin may be the start of a deadly habit.

To cope with the new problem, the Nanking Government passed a law in 1936 declaring that addicts must present themselves for a cure within a year or suffer the death penalty. Remedial work was accomplished during this period. But when the Japanese set up the Peace Preservation Council in Tientsin in 1937, the Nanking law, it was announced, would no longer apply to the district. The drug habit spread and the function of the anti-narcotic hospital, set up under the law, ground to a halt. Japanese drug-joints sprang up almost in the streets. The proprietors, Japanese and Koreans, were not allowed to sell to the Japanese, but open offers of drugs were made to foreigners and to the Chinese. Tientsin became a drug-ridden city.

During the Japanese occupation, huge quantities of Iranian opium were arriving at Shanghai for consignment to the Japanese army and to Japanese companies. This was in 1938. The explanation the Japanese gave for the importation was that the opium was being shipped into China for use by a large heroin factory at Shanghai.

In Nanking four groups were chiefly responsible for opium circulation. They were the Special Service Section of the Japanese army, the so-called Reform Government of Nanking, independent Japanese and Korean drug runners, and Japanese firms. In 1938, one eighth of the Chinese in Nanking were slowly being poisoned by drugs. Foreign observers, medical men, journalists, and missionaries had reported a year earlier that the drug situation there was steadily worsening, for the Chinese local officials and magistrates were unable to prevent its sale.

The Japanese did much to insure the merchandising of drugs. Well-lighted and attractive clinics were opened. Some of them displayed a deceptive red cross. Illuminated street signs led victims from the highways, byways, and side streets to the opium stores and dens. Newspaper advertisements told of the various diseases the drug would allegedly cure. Patients entering a clinic were given a cursory examination by a quack doctor or drug dispenser and then they were listed as sufferers of some disease the cure for which was drugs. Thereafter, as often as they wanted it, heroin or morphine was sold to the patients and in amounts unlimited.

THE TABLES TURN

The Report was dated March 10, 1952; it was from the United States Representative to the United Nations Commission on Narcotic Drugs; it showed that the tables had turned. The title of that report was "The Source and Extent of Heroin Traffic in Japan." The Communists were smuggling opium and heroin from China into Japan, the United States, and other countries. Again, the policy of trying to weaken an enemy by subsidizing addiction was at work. This time the free people of the world, fighting against communism and its spread, was the objective, with an enemy who was spreading addiction to swell its coffers and finance a war.

Studies clearly show that the major illicit sources of the world's narcotic supply today are Communist China, Burma, Malaya, India, Japan, Turkey, Thailand, Iran, Syria, Lebanon, Italy, and Mexico.

Beginning in 1951 investigations conducted in Italy proved that Italian heroin has been smuggled into the United States and elsewhere since 1948. Five licensed factories there diverted one ton of heroin into illicit channels for smuggling. The Italian Government, recognizing this shocking situation, has undertaken certain remedial measures. In October 1951 the Italian Commission of Public Health passed a decree indefinitely suspending the further production of heroin. It is apparent that further production of heroin in Italy is unwarranted and unnecessary since possibly only 20 kilograms of heroin of the annual production of 200 kilograms were used or needed for Italian medicinal consumption. Twenty kilograms is about 44 pounds.

The pattern of the criminal investigations conducted in Italy by agents of the United States Bureau of Narcotics with the cooperation of the Italian police has been consistent. Gangsters had a virtual monopoly over all of the diverted Italian heroin which they were supplying to the organized narcotic gangs of principal east-coast, midwest, and west-coast American cities. Internationally notorious deportee gangsters in Italy are in control of this traffic.

The foregoing facts, brief and with little detail, supply but the background, since this book is not intended to be a history of the opium traffic. But that history does point up the fact that the present wave of drug addiction in the United States, Canada, Turkey, Egypt, England, Germany, Japan, and in fact, all countries is not something previously unknown to mankind. The misuse of opium has occurred since its discovery. If it weren't for the boon it has afforded in medical therapy, decent people everywhere would certainly never have tolerated its continued existence.

For centuries the poppy has been the symbol of a dangerous instrumentality—of traffic fraught with evil, of unprincipled men who satisfied by it their lust for wealth and power, of amoral nations who compromise for economic reasons and of a potent weapon of aggression. And today it is the Communists of Red China who are exploiting the poppy, who are financing and fostering aggressive warfare through depravity and human misery.

Drug addiction is a cold, calculated, ruthless, systematic plan
to undermine by creating new addicts while sustaining the old.
It requires all-out action on all levels of government, local, state,
and national, as well as by international cooperation. It will take
that kind of concerted effort to stamp out drug addiction.

THE ANATOMY OF NARCOTIC DRUGS

THE DESCRIPTION AND DISCUSSION THAT IS PRESENTED IN THIS CHAP-
ter will provide the reader with a survey of the narcotic drugs
and, it is believed, with a better understanding of the problems
to be discussed in later chapters. While not exhaustive in detail,
sufficient information is given to establish clearly the various
characteristics of the drugs that contribute to what is in this book
called the traffic in narcotics.

OPIUM AND ITS DERIVATIVES

The use of opium in medicine and surgery is indispensable.
The famous English physician of the seventeenth century, Syden-
ham, once wrote, "Among the remedies which it has pleased Al-
mighty God to give to man to relieve his sufferings, none is so
universal and so efficacious as opium." There can be no doubt
that opium is a blessing when properly utilized; but, as has been
indicated earlier, a vast illicit use for it has unfortunately been
prevalent through the centuries and probably will always continue.

The term opium is defined by the United States Pharmacopoeia
as the "air-dried milky exudation obtained by incising the unripe
capsules of *Papaver somniferum* Linné, or its variety *album* De
Candolle (Fam. *Papaveracea*)." Opium is obtained from the
poppy plant, which is an annual herb, and in commerce must
be cultivated. The plant is probably indigenous to Asia Minor;
it is now most widely grown in China, India, Turkey, Macedonia,
Yugoslavia, Bulgaria, and Iran.

By the middle of the sixteenth century, the use of opium was both accepted and fairly well understood by the physicians and pharmacists of Western Europe. Paracelsus first used the term *laudanum* in 1537, and in the eighteenth century Le Mort made the first preparation of *paregoric*. In 1805, a German pharmacist named Sertürner first isolated *morphine* from opium. This was the beginning of modern alkaloidal medicine. In 1832 Robiquet isolated *codeine,* and sixteen years later Merck discovered *papaverine.*

The alkaloids, comprising about 25 percent by weight of opium, represent its pharmacologically active constituents, and the most important of these are morphine, codeine, and papaverine. Other natural alkaloids of lesser import are thebaine (1835), narcotine (1803), and narceine (1832). Additionally, there are many derivatives of morphine, among which are heroin, dionin, codeine, dilaudid, and dicodid.

There are two preparations of opium which are therapeutically employed today, laudanum and paregoric. These compounds, however, have been used with decreasing frequency since the isolation of morphine, and today the customary use of paregoric is with children and in the treatment of diarrhea.

There follows a brief description of the principal opium derivatives.

MORPHINE

The most commonly used and best known of the alkaloids is morphine, the principal medical function of which is the relief of pain. Its greatest drawback is the danger of addiction. It is usually prescribed in the form of its salts and the two most familiar of these are morphine sulfate and morphine hydrochloride. Morphine may be given orally or by subcutaneous injection, and under emergent conditions it is given intravenously. Dosage, of course, depends upon the patient, the nature of the illness, and varying other factors of diagnosis.

The therapeutic uses of morphine may be summarized as follows: *

* *Pharmacologic Principles of Medical Practice,* by John C. Krantz, Jr. and C. Jelleff Carr.

1. The principal use is to relieve pain. Its use here is indicated only when those analgesics which do not produce addiction have failed.
2. It is useful in checking diarrhea.
3. It is valuable in the treatment of dry non-productive coughs which have failed to yield to codeine.
4. It is excellent for pre-operative medication.
5. It is indicated in surgical hemorrhage, whereby the blood pressure is reduced and bleeding diminishes.
6. It is useful as a hypnotic when pain interferes with the ability to sleep and when potentially less harmful narcotics have failed to induce sleep.

HEROIN

Heroin (diacetylmorphine), which is about five times as potent as morphine, can produce a most vicious addiction. Because of this potency, together with the concomitant strong euphoric effects, this drug is always in great demand by addicts, and, accordingly, it has become the foundation of the illicit traffic. In view of the fact that its value from a therapeutic standpoint is no greater than that of morphine and since its toxicity is higher and objections to its use greatly outweigh its advantages, the United States prohibits the importation, manufacture, or sale of heroin. Some fifty nations now prohibit the manufacture of heroin.

DILAUDID

Dilaudid (dihydromorphinone hydrochloride), used mainly as a substitute for morphine, is also more potent than morphine. It has a much greater analgesic effect, but of shorter duration, than morphine. Both tolerance and addiction to dilaudid occur.

DIONIN

Dionin (ethylmorphine hydrochloride) generally has the same pharmacological qualities as codeine. Formerly used as a cough remedy, its use is presently mainly employed in treatment involving the eyes.

CODEINE

Codeine, widely used and frequently prescribed in the phosphate or the sulphate form, is a derivative of morphine, and tolerance and addiction to it can occur as well. While it is employed in several ways, its primary use is in the treatment of cough. It is much less potent than morphine and, for that reason together with the fact that it generally fails to produce euphoria, is rarely used by drug addicts.

PAPAVERINE

Papaverine hydrochloride is the salt of an alkaloid contained in opium and as such is embraced within the scope of the Federal narcotic laws and regulations. It is unlike morphine both pharmacologically and chemically, and has only a mild analgesic effect.

COCAINE

Cocaine is obtained from the leaves of the *Erythroxylon coca* Lamarck, and also from other species of *Erythroxylon,* a shrub indigenous to Peru and Bolivia. Peru provides the bulk of coca leaves for the commercial trade. But the species are grown successfully elsewhere in tropical regions. Their leaves can be harvested from two to four times annually depending on climatic and other growing conditions.

There are four principal uses of coca leaves: (1) in medicine; (2) for the manufacture of cocaine; (3) for the manufacture of non-narcotic flavoring extracts; (4) for chewing.

The Incas of ancient Peru believed that coca-leaf chewing both diminished hunger and lessened fatigue, and thereby enhanced their endurance and they considered it of paramount importance in connection with high-altitude labor, particularly in the Andes mountain regions.

Coca-leaf chewing, or *coqueo* as it is called, is habitual in several South American countries, notably in Peru and Bolivia, but it is also prevalent in Colombia, northern Argentina, and Brazil. While many local factors probably are involved, coca-leaf chewing has been considered in some areas a practical necessity in overcoming the effects of climate, altitude, and nutrition. Recent studies, however, indicate that neither climate nor altitude has been a determining factor since the practice occurs in varying climates and in widely differing altitudes. Coca-leaf chewing, by inhibiting the sensation of hunger, maintains a constant state of malnutrition, ultimately undermining the health and stamina of the user. The conclusion, therefore, is clear that in its effects it is injurious and not beneficial.

The discovery of cocaine is usually credited to Nieman, who reported it in 1859. It has been claimed, however, that the real credit belongs to Gardeke, who produced it under the name of erythroxyline in 1855. Subsequent to its introduction, toward the close of the nineteenth century its growth as a local anesthesia drug in medical practice increased tremendously. However, as its use spread, it became evident that it was not only very toxic but also habit-forming.

Cocaine may be classed in the stimulant or excitant group of drugs as far as its effects on the nervous system are concerned. It is patent, therefore, that its very nature makes it a most dangerous drug, particularly so when the user has a maladjusted personality. The drug causes mental deterioration; and, physically, nausea, digestive disorders, sleeplessness, loss of appetite, emaciation, and tremors result from its continued use.

In medicine, cocaine is used principally as a local anesthetic. It produces desensitization of the sensory nerve endings and because of this is often employed as a nasal, oral, or ocular anesthetic before treatment or surgery. Due to its dangerous characteristics, however, it has been replaced in medicine by preparations, such as procaine and Novocaine. Because of its toxicity, it is rarely used hypodermically, inasmuch as less toxic compounds are readily available for the purpose of injection.

Addicts prefer to sniff the drug, absorbing it through the mucous membranes of the nose. The cocaine powder used in this way is commonly known as snow, and its continued sniffing can cause the nasal septum to become perforated.

Cocaine is very scarce on the illicit market because the international movement of coca leaves is strictly controlled. Peru, it might be mentioned, has closed all cocaine factories.

MARIHUANA

Delving back through the centuries, we find references to the hemp plant as early as three thousand years ago in China—about 1200 B.C.—hence its description as a drug of the New and Old World is apt. It is probable that central or southern Asia was its original habitat. Today it is found growing either wild or under cultivation in wide areas of India, the Shan States of Burma, Turkey, Syria, Lebanon, Greece, Brazil, Mexico, the United States, and in Africa. In Western European countries only small quantities are grown.

Because of its wide-spread distribution, it might be helpful to identify some of the names by which it is known throughout the world. The name *marihuana*, of Mexican-Indian origin, has become the general term in North and South America. In the United States the word *reefer* has through popular usage come to mean a marihuana cigarette. In England, which is experiencing an increase in its illegal use, it is popularly known as *Indian hemp*. Then there is the *hashish* of the Middle East, which is sometimes used in the United States. In Morocco and Algeria it is called *kif*; in Tunisia, *takrouri*; in South Africa, *dagga*; in India, *bhang*, *charas*, and *manzoul*. It is the *maconha* and *djamba* of Brazil, and the *esrar* and *manzoul* of Turkey.

What is this substance and whence does it come?

Marihuana, to use its popular name, belongs to the genus *Cannabis*, of which there is only a single species, *Cannabis sativa* L. Varieties, grown in different sections are botanically described as *Cannabis indica* (Indian hemp), *Cannabis mexicana*, and so forth. Since the bulk of the resin is contained in the flowering tops, the term marihuana has been relatively limited to those portions of the plant, while hashish refers to a special form of recovered resin of the plant. Commercially the plant, aside from its drug-producing properties, is used in the production of textiles, cord, and twine; depending on climate and soil, plants in different areas will have a greater or lesser commercial value due to the relative softness or hardness of the fibers.

Numerous products are made from the hemp plant that are used by drug addicts. *Bhang* is obtained from the leaves, the whole substance of which is reduced to a powder. The powdered leaves are frequently mixed with spices, honey, or water. It is eaten or drunk as well as smoked. *Ganja* consists of the flowering tops of the plant and is prepared by crushing it into a sticky mass. It is for the most part smoked in pipes or as cigarettes, but on occasion is eaten. From the resin extracted from the tops is secured the *charas* of India and central Asia; the *chira, chiras* of Egypt, Syria, and Greece; the *hashish* of Egypt, India, and Syria. The raw resin extracted from the tops is either kneaded into sticks or reduced to powder.

In discussing its use, one fact should be emphasized at once. Whereas the opiates can be a blessing when properly used, *mari-huana has no therapeutic value*, and its use is therefore *always* an abuse and a vice. This important fact should never be forgotten, and pharmacopoeias throughout the world have generally expunged it.

At present the consumption of hemp is allowed by law in only three countries, namely, India, Tunisia, and Morocco. The oral consumption of bhang has always been permitted in India and the smoking of ganja is still permitted in many Indian states, but all states have now decided to restrict progressively the consumption of Indian hemp. Only Indian hemp mixed with tobacco is permitted to be used in Morocco. Hemp in the form of *takrouri* is legally consumed in Tunisia.

Hemp is either smoked or taken orally depending upon the individual, the place, or local customs. By absorbing it through the digestive tract, some experts feel that the effect is stronger. However, smoking is undoubtedly the most prevalent method of use in the Americas and in England. Cigarettes are prepared from the tops and leaves of the plant, and they are typically about the size of an American king-size cigarette, but somewhat thinner and more loosely packed. A cheaper grade is also prepared from the leaves and other parts of the hemp plant which, since the resin content is less, results in a product less effective for the smoker.

Marihuana is grown illegally in some States of the United States. While the Mexican variety, some of which is smuggled over the Texas border, is preferred by some smokers, there is always a ready market for all types. It is cheap compared to the price of heroin and cocaine since the price of a cigarette on the illicit market averages from fifty cents to one dollar.

The user of marihuana, unlike the heroin addict, seems to prefer to pursue his vice in groups or, in the vernacular, at tea parties. He (and here it might be interjected that men far outnumber women in this vice) has been well termed by one authority as a "gregarious addict." Like all narcotic addicts, any reasonable conception of hygiene on the part of the smoker is sorely lacking. At gatherings a cigarette is passed from lip to lip. Cupping the hands to prevent the loss of the fumes, the greatest amount of smoke possible is deeply inhaled and retained for a maximum length of time. At times several consecutive short puffs are taken, and on occasion the smoke is swallowed. And so it goes until eventually the cigarette is entirely consumed.

As a result of this habit, the inveterate smoker will have the same tell-tale stains of any heavy smoker of ordinary cigarettes— the yellow or dark brown stains accompanied by a hardening of the skin of those portions of the fingers which have held the cigarette.

EFFECT ON THE INDIVIDUAL

What are the physiological and psychological effects of the use of marihuana? What does it do to the individual? First of all, marihuana does not create physical dependence as do the opiates. Habituation occurs in the average case, but experts have observed the development of a special tolerance in instances of prolonged and excessive use. Collaterally, the danger of progression to the use of and addiction to the opiates always lurks in the background for the user of marihuana. A further distinction between the opiates and marihuana has been touched on before but bears repeating. While opium can be a blessing or a curse, depending on its use, marihuana is only and always a scourge which undermines its victims and degrades them mentally, morally, and physically.

Medical experts agree on the complete unpredictability of the effect of marihuana on different individuals. A small dose taken by one subject may bring about intense intoxication, raving fits, criminal assaults. Another subject can consume large amounts without experiencing any reaction except stupefaction. It is this unpredictable effect which makes of marihuana one of the most dangerous drugs known. Moreover, every individual will react in a different degree to the same dosage of this narcotic, depending on his physiological and emotional constitution.

Certain physical effects appear to be present in the majority of cases of marihuana intoxication. The first reactions appear, an hour or so after consumption, in the form of muscular trembling, increased heartbeat, acceleration of pulse. This is accompanied by a ringing in the ears, an intense feeling of heat in the head, dizziness, and sensations of cold in the hands and feet. Constrictions in the chest, dilation of the pupil of the eye, and muscular contraction follow. The physical reactions increase in intensity until either vomiting or complete stupefaction occurs. Initially the individual is excited, restless, and boisterous, over-garrulous and uninhibited. Next comes a period of dissociation of ideas and exaggeration of emotions. Judgment and concentration are impaired; the subject shows a marked inability to judge both time and space; perceptions are distorted; in short, mental confusion occurs, accompanied by hallucinations. Marihuana sharpens the sensibilities, and in this stage the addict is prone to suggestion, violent or otherwise. The intense overexcitement of the nerves and emotions leads to uncontrollable irritability and violent and irresponsible acts due to irresistible impulses of suggestive origin. The last stage might include hallucinations, varied and often terrifying. Restless sleep, accompanied by bizarre phantasmagoria, then overcomes the victim.

In the earliest stages of intoxication the will power is destroyed and inhibitions and restraints are released; the moral barricades are broken down and often debauchery and sexuality results. Where mental instability is inherent, the behavior is generally violent. An egotist will enjoy delusions of grandeur, the timid individual will suffer anxiety, and the aggressive one often will resort to acts of violence and crime. Dormant tendencies are released and while the subject may know what is happening, he has become powerless to prevent it. Constant use produces an incapacity for work and a disorientation of purpose. The drug has a corroding effect on the body and on the mind, weakening the entire physical system and often leading to insanity after prolonged use.

BY WAY OF ILLUSTRATION

The following are summaries of a few of the many cases recorded in the files of the U. S. Bureau of Narcotics which illustrate the homicidal tendencies and the generally debasing effects arising from the use of marihuana:

Oklahoma City, Okla. 1943. While under the influence of marihuana, twenty-seven-year-old Carl J. M., hotel bellboy, shot and killed elderly J. S. S., guard in the Federal Building at Oklahoma City, Oklahoma. He was convicted for the crime and sentenced to serve 10 years. Another bellboy, who was arrested in the case, confessed that he and M. had smoked marihuana in a hotel room before the crime was committed. M. then left the hotel and walked to the Federal Building. On the street he met three sailors, one of whom he bit on the neck. He struck a small boy whom he met on the sidewalk. M. then went to the Federal Building and took charge of an Army Recruiting Office. When Mr. S. . . . , the building guard, was called to remove M., a fight ensued. M. seized a gun from the guard and shot and killed him instantly. M. then placed the gun on a chair and walked down the hall singing. He engaged in another fight, but was finally subdued and placed in jail. Two days later M. was still unable to think or talk coherently. He talked about trying to get on the top of an automobile where he could reach a telephone wire and swing himself to the top of the hotel and from there he could get to heaven. Later, at a hearing, M. stated that he had smoked marihuana several times; that he did not remember leaving the hotel, nor the fights nor the shooting of Mr. S. . . . ; he did not remember his arraignment and stated the first he knew about the matter was after he came out of the stupor when someone told him he had shot and killed a guard at the Federal Building. M.'s employers stated he had always been quiet and sober, and had never caused trouble of any kind.

The effects he experienced are characteristic, particularly with regard to the distortion of space and lack of restraint or memory by individuals of their own actions while under the influence of marihuana.

Clarksburg, W.Va. 1937. Lewis H., twenty-six years of age, arrested for rape of nine-year-old girl while under the influence of marihuana.

Baltimore, Md. 1936. The chief engineer of a vessel arriving at Baltimore complained to the Federal narcotic office that the crew of his vessel were using some unknown narcotic that was so virulent in its effects on the men that the officers were obliged to protect themselves by carrying blackjacks to ward off attacks. The narcotic agent ascertained that a fireman, aged twenty-two, was a marihuana user, and that two of the seamen on the ship had purchased a bag of dried marihuana while ashore in the Canal Zone and smuggled it aboard ship, where it was consumed by members of the crew. Officers of the steamship said these men were "under the influence of this narcotic throughout the trip to Baltimore and that their conduct bordered on the mutinous."

Cleveland, Ohio. 1948. James B., who was arrested by police for the murder of a sixty-year-old widow, admitted that he and an accomplice had participated in brutal attacks on sixteen women for the purpose of robbing them of their money. He said he wanted the money to buy wine and reefers which he consumed at the same time. Before committing their atrocious crimes, B. and his accomplice always fortified themselves with wine and marihuana.

Spokane, Washington. 1940. Joseph M., shortly after having smoked two marihuana cigarettes, brutally murdered a seventy-four-year-old retired railroad worker. According to testimony brought out at his trial for manslaughter, M. had never before seen his victim and could assign no reason for having murdered him other than that following the smoking of the marihuana cigarettes he had become obsessed with an idea that he was being pursued and upon encountering the aged man he attacked and killed him. M. was sentenced in October, 1940, to serve twenty years in the Washington State Penitentiary.

Del Rio, Texas. 1940. One Eleutero G. while allegedly under the influence of marihuana, shot to death two women and then committed suicide by literally slicing himself to bits about the abdomen, heart, and throat, in a manner which indicated that he was bereft of all reasoning. Law enforcement officers believed that G. was under the influence of marihuana at the time of the double murder and suicide and that he had previously used marihuana. It was the opinion of the doctor who saw G. just before he died that no one could so mutilate himself unless he was unable to feel "shock" and the only thing he knew that would produce such a condition, to such a degree, is marihuana. G. had wandered around in the fields for hours after the killing and after his self-mutilation.

The following cases were taken from police records of several cities:

Investigating a disturbance in a café in a southern Ohio city, police officers saw Anthony E. pointing a loaded revolver at patrons. E. resisted arrest, and after a severe struggle the officers subdued him. Earlier, E., with the use of his revolver, had robbed Abe L., driver for the W. Bakery Co., of $5.00. At the time of the arrest, the defendant was completely under the influence of marihuana and a quantity of marihuana was found in his possession.

On a Saturday evening in November, 1945, a pretty seventeen-month-old baby girl was left in the family car while her parents went in search of a relative. When they returned to the car less than ten minutes later, the baby had disappeared. The next afternoon, scarcely 200 yards away, the body was found in the furrow of a cotton field. The baby was naked except for one small white shoe and a red-knitted bonnet. She had been violated. Teeth marks covered her body. Her tiny contorted face had been shoved into the mud and particles of dirt in her lungs showed that she had been alive at the time and suffocated later.

Police arrested a twenty-five-year-old cotton picker, Paul G., who readily admitted kidnapping the child and "spanking her a little bit." G. stated that on the Saturday evening in question he had been drinking when a friend offered him a reefer which he accepted and smoked. Further intoxicants followed. Then G. went to a dance hall, from which he departed because no one would dance with him in his condition. As he left, he heard the child crying in a car. Annoyed, he picked up the infant and spanked her, but remembers nothing further except he "guesses he just went crazy." His next recollection was when he came to in his cabin the following morning with mud and blood on his clothes.

For what the district attorney described as "the most horrible, the most brutal crime in the history of the area," Paul G. was sentenced to death. The final words of his counsel are well worth remembering: "The real criminal in this case is marihuana!"

On January 10, 194–, Robert F. assaulted Mrs. Mildred Y., stole a gun, and held up his former employer. On January 15, he entered a salesman's car while it was stopped in traffic, and when the salesman didn't follow directions, shot him in the stomach. On January 21, he broke into a home, stole some money, and beat a seventy-eight-year-old woman severely. On January 22, he entered a cleaning shop, attempted to rape the clerk, and stole $75. An aroused police force tracked him down, and cornered him. F. shot one officer and then seeing that he was trapped, shot himself. Each of these crimes was attributed to marihuana intoxication.

One summer evening Moses M. bought his first two marihuana cigarettes for twenty-five cents each. After smoking them, he said, "I felt just like I was flying." Moses, crazed with marihuana, went through the window of his hotel room, dropped eighteen feet to the roof of the garage next door in his bare feet, and then went through the window of K.'s room crying, "God told me to kill this man." Seizing K. by the throat, Moses beat him to death with his fists after which he broke a chair over his victim's head. Then screaming that he was pursued by Hitler, Moses went out through the window, and dropped his two hundred pound frame to the alley thirty feet below. In court Moses had no recollection of the killing and asserted, "I didn't want to hurt him." "Twenty years," said the Court.

THE SOCIAL ASPECTS

In addition to showing a link between the use of marihuana and crime, these cases emphasize the serious social menace to the community which results when an individual with criminal tendencies uses this narcotic. Many times the false courage to commit overt crime has been supplied by marihuana, and often violence is perpetrated without the culprit being able to recall anything about it. Pathetic cases have been reported wherein the offender fancied an approaching member of his family as an enemy and killed him. Because the narcotic affects the judgment of speed and distances, a man under its influence at the wheel of an automobile is capable of leaving a trail of fatal accidents in his wake. One can readily see the menace a marihuana-user would present wherever the safety of others depends upon the proper discharge of his duties. It takes but little imagination to picture the chaos and injury which might occur if the user were a locomotive engineer, for example, or the operator of steam or electrical equipment.

Since the enactment in 1937 of Federal control legislation, considerable progress has been made towards a solution of the nation-wide marihuana problem. In the first five-year period, the Federal Bureau of Narcotics, cooperating with State and municipal enforcement agencies throughout the country, conducted a program of eradication in which approximately 60,000 *tons* of marihuana were destroyed. In addition, the Bureau has seized large amounts of marihuana, both bulk and as cigarettes, in the illicit traffic, and has arrested about 1,000 persons annually for violations of the Federal marihuana law. Due to the ease with which it grows, marihuana presents a continuing problem. Numerous police departments have educated their personnel to recognize the plant and have initiated local campaigns to eradicate it from vacant lots and roadsides in localities where it has been found growing. Many State and city officers throughout the country have been quick to realize the dangers of the drug and to assist in its suppression.

The fact that the price of marihuana cigarettes is not prohibitive like that of other drugs makes it a definite menace to the youth, who seem to be its chief victims.

SYNTHETIC NARCOTIC DRUGS

Demerol was the first drug produced synthetically and designed for analgesic use as a substitute for the pain-relieving opium derivatives. The new drug bore no chemical relationship to morphine. When the result of official tests indicated that the new drug possessed addiction-liability similar to morphine, the Bureau of Narcotics proposed and obtained enactment of a special statute, approved July 1, 1944, making the Federal narcotic laws applicable to the new drug under the statutory designation *isonipecaine.*

However, it was known that other new synthetic drugs being

developed had comparable analgesic properties and might be found to possess addiction-liability. The Bureau of Narcotics recommended successfully the enactment of a statute, effective March 8, 1946, which established a general procedure for the expeditious application of control measures to any drug found to be dangerous from the addiction-liability standpoint. Under this statute, the Federal narcotic laws are made applicable to any drug found by the Secretary of the Treasury (after due notice and opportunity for public hearing) to have addiction-liability similar to morphine and cocaine, and proclaimed by the President to have been so found by the Secretary. The Secretary, in making such findings, and the Bureau of Narcotics, in determining general questions of policy where chemistry and pharmacology of narcotics or marihuana are involved, receive invaluable cooperation by way of scientific research, and advice, and technical service, from the United States Public Health Service and the Committee on Drug Addiction and Narcotics of the National Research Council.

Eleven of the new synthetic analgesic drugs have been made subject to narcotic control by this procedure, but only a few of these drugs have been made available for general medical use, examples being Methadon (Dolophine or Adanon), Nisentil and Dromoran.

THE PROTOCOL OF 1948

The U. S. Representative on the United Nations Narcotic Commission proposed an international agreement in the nature of an addition to the 1931 Convention, which was adopted and became effective as the Protocol of 1948. This Protocol establishes international procedure, analogous in principle to that established in the United States by the Act of March 8, 1946, whereby new drugs found to have dangerous addiction-liability are promptly brought under control imposed by the 1931 Convention, the definite finding in this case being made by the World Health Organization. Up to the present time, the findings of the Secretary of the Treasury under the national law and the findings of the World Health Organization under the 1948 Protocol, with respect to addiction-liability of the same new drugs, have been in accord.

By August 1952, thirty-nine nations had signed the Protocol of 1948.

III

PROGRESS IN INTERNATIONAL
COOPERATION—PART ONE

THERE HAVE BEEN FEW MORE DRAMATIC OR MORE SUCCESSFUL EF-forts at international collaboration than those in the field of the control of narcotic drugs. The results obtained are outstanding.

The present study surveys not only the historical development of the international control of narcotic drugs under the various treaties, but also explains in detail the somewhat complex administrative, advisory, and policy-making machinery. It reviews the new problems which have arisen and the new solutions which have been sought. The study also deals with such questions as the development of synthetic drugs, the efforts to control opium production and the progress toward streamlining the international control machinery.

THE SHANGHAI CONFERENCE—1909

The first step in the international campaign against narcotic drugs took place in 1909 when an International Opium Commission met in Shanghai on the initiative of the United States Government which had become seriously concerned over the problem of addiction in the Philippines.

Representatives of thirteen governments—Austria-Hungary, China, France, Germany, Great Britain, Italy, Japan, The Netherlands, Persia, Portugal, Russia, Siam, and the United States—participated in the conference.

RESOLUTIONS ADOPTED

The United States Delegation proposed the immediate prohibition of opium smoking, but the conference was not prepared to go further than the following resolution:

Be it resolved:

That in view of the action taken by the Government of China in suppressing the practice of opium smoking, and by other Governments to the same end, the International Opium Commission recommends that each delegation concerned move its own Government to take measures for the gradual suppression of the practice of opium smoking in its own territories and possessions, with due regard to the varying circumstances of each country concerned.

Nine resolutions were adopted unanimously. The representatives recognized that "the use of opium in any form otherwise than for medical purposes is held by almost every participating country to be a matter of prohibition or for careful regulation;" that "the unrestricted manufacture, sale, and distribution of morphine already constitute a grave danger, and that the morphine habit shows signs of spreading; the International Opium Commission therefore desires to urge strongly on all governments that it is highly important that drastic measures should be taken by each government in its own territories and possessions to control the manufacture, sale, and distribution of this drug, and also of such other derivatives of opium as may appear on scientific inquiry to be liable to similar abuse and productive of like ill effects;" . . . that "it is also the duty of all countries to adopt reasonable measures to prevent at ports of departure the shipment of opium, its alkaloids, derivatives, and preparations, to any country which prohibits the entry of any opium, its alkaloids, derivatives, and preparations;" that "all governments possessing concessions or settlements in China, which have not yet taken effective action toward the closing of opium divans in the said concessions and settlements, to take steps to that end as soon as they may deem it possible;" . . . and that "each delegation move its government to apply its pharmacy laws to its subjects in the consular districts, concessions, and settlements in China."

THE HAGUE CONVENTION OF 1912

The United States considered it important that international effect and sanction should be given to the resolutions of the International Opium Commission which had met in Shanghai in 1909, and to this end its Government proposed that an international conference be held at a convenient date, at The Hague or elsewhere, composed of one or more delegates of each of the participating powers, and that the delegates should have full powers to conventionalize the resolutions adopted at Shanghai. The date of the assembling of the conference was finally fixed by The Netherlands for December 1, 1911.

The Hague Convention as finally agreed upon contains a number of general principles which remain as the foundation and mainspring of all drug control. Even the rules for domestic control—vague as they were in some instances—have stood the test of time and are still the basis of domestic control, although amplified by later conventions. The Convention incorporated the principles adopted at the Shanghai Conference and imposed an obligation on the parties "to use their best endeavours" to put these principles into practice. Its main defect was that it created no administrative machinery for the implementation of the agreed principles. While the production and distribution of raw opium was to be subjected to control, no limitation was placed on the quantity to be produced or distributed except indirectly by means of restricting exports in accordance with the legal requirements of the importing countries, nor were any measures indicated as to how control over production and distribution was to be effected.

The Hague Convention bound the contracting parties to adopt provisions of control and regulation for raw opium, prepared opium, and the manufactured substances—medicinal opium, morphine, diacetylmorphine (heroin), and cocaine. The production of raw opium was to be controlled and its distribution regulated. Import or export should be made only by duly authorized persons, and each contracting party was required to limit the number of towns, ports, or other places through which export or import was to be permitted. Export to countries prohibiting the import of raw opium was to be prevented, and controlled to countries which restricted its import.

The manufacture, internal traffic in, and use of prepared opium were to be gradually suppressed, while imports and exports were to be immediately prohibited. In countries where prohibition of exports was not immediately practicable, however, prohibition should take place as soon as possible. In these countries exports were to be restricted in the ways provided for raw opium; the exporting country was required to adopt the measures necessary for complying with the regulations in force in the country of import.

The manufacture, sale, and use of morphine, cocaine and their respective salts was to be limited to medical and legitimate uses only. The parties "shall use their best efforts to control all those who manufacture, import, sell, distribute and export morphine, cocaine and their respective salts, as well as the buildings where such persons exercise that commerce."

The parties were to examine into the possibility of enacting laws making the illegal possession of raw opium, prepared opium, morphine, cocaine and their respective salts liable to penalties.

The Hague Convention did not come into general application until after the end of World War I. On February 11, 1915, the convention came into force for the United States of America, China, and The Netherlands, which were the first three countries to agree to apply its provisions. The original ratification article required that all states which had participated in the conference of 1912 should have ratified the convention before it could come into force. There was considerable delay and for this reason a subsequent special protocol was needed. Many countries became parties to the convention through the Peace Treaties signed at the end of World War I, and all of which contained an article under which ratification of the peace treaty should "be deemed in all respects equivalent to the ratification of that Convention [Hague Convention] and to the signature of the Special Protocol . . . for bringing the said Convention into force."

By August, 1952, seventy countries had become parties to the Convention.

THE GENEVA CONVENTION OF 1925

The International Opium Conference which sat at Geneva from November, 1924, to February, 1925, and was attended by delegates from thirty-six countries, adopted a new Convention. The aims of the convention are stated in the preamble, which notes that the Hague Convention produced results of great value, but that illicit traffic in and abuse of narcotic substances still continued on a large scale, and that it was necessary to examine "with a view to the conclusion of an agreement, the question of the limitation of the amounts of morphine, heroin, or cocaine and their respective salts to be manufactured; of the limitation of the amounts of raw opium and coca leaf to be imported for that purpose and for other medicinal and scientific purposes; and of the limitation of the production of raw opium and the coca leaf for export to the amount required for such medicinal and scientific purposes . . ."

The joint resolution, adopted by the Congress of the United States on May 15, 1924, authorizing participation in the Conference, quoted these principles and stipulated "that the representatives of the United States shall sign no agreement which does not fulfil the conditions necessary for the suppression of the narcotic drug traffic as set forth in the preamble."

After prolonged sessions, neither the plans for the direct limitation of quantities of drugs on the basis of estimated requirements as proposed by the United States Delegation, nor for the limitation of the production of raw opium and coca leaves to amounts required for medical and scientific needs were accepted, and under these circumstances the Delegation of the United States had no alternative other than to withdraw from the Conference. The Chinese Delegation also withdrew because of the refusal of the governments in whose territories the use of prepared opium was still legal to agree to its suppression.

Abandoning attempts directly to limit the production of raw materials and the manufacture of narcotic drugs, the Conference concentrated on the control of trade and commerce. By the terms of the Convention, the contracting parties agreed to establish control of the manufacture, sale, and movement of dangerous drugs, and to report annually the quantities manufactured, consumed, stocks on hand, etc., and every three months the quantities exported and imported. Thus governments are made responsible for the legitimacy of exports and imports, and any attempt to divert drugs in transit can be detected. The most important advance was the establishment of the system of compulsory import certificates and export authorizations. Under this system the exporter must obtain from his government an export authorization which will only be issued on production of the copy of an import certificate issued by the government of the importing country, stating that the drug in question is needed for medical purposes.

The creation of the Permanent Central Board to supervise the statistical system initiated by the Convention represented another important step in international narcotic control. Under the Convention the parties undertook to furnish to the Permanent Central Board estimates of the quantities of each of the substances covered by the Convention to be imported into their territory for internal consumption during the following year, but one of the chief shortcomings of the Convention was its failure to provide a method of determining each country's and the world's total legitimate need of narcotic drugs, as well as binding obligations to keep within those limits.

The Geneva Convention of 1925 came into force on September 28, 1928. By August, 1952, sixty-two countries had ratified the Convention.

THE 1931 CONVENTION FOR LIMITING THE MANUFACTURE AND REGULATING THE DISTRIBUTION OF NARCOTIC DRUGS

Reference has been made to the fact that the Geneva Opium Conference which concluded the 1925 Convention did not accept proposals for the effective limitation of the manufacture of dangerous drugs. In a document published by the Secretariat of the League of Nations, it was revealed that between 1925-29 approximately 100 tons of morphine passed into the illicit traffic. Six tons of cocaine escaped into the illicit traffic in the same period. The total annual requirements of these drugs were estimated at 39 tons. As knowledge of this situation spread, public opinion in certain countries demanded limitation of manufacture, and in 1931 an International Conference was convened at Geneva to conclude a convention for this purpose.

The system of limitation embodied in the Limitation Convention of 1931 is based upon estimates which each contracting party undertakes to provide, with non-contracting parties also asked to furnish estimates, of the quantities of drugs required during the ensuing year. Each estimate is based solely on medical and scientific requirements, and must be submitted by August 1st of the year preceding that for which the estimate is made. These estimates are examined by an international body of experts—the Supervisory Body—which was set up by the Convention. If a contracting or non-contracting country fails to return an estimate, the Supervisory Body is entrusted with the duty of drawing up an estimate for it. This far-reaching provision is absolute in respect of contracting parties.

The estimates for each country, which may be followed by supplementary estimates accompanied by an explanation for their necessity, are required to show for each of the drugs covered by the Convention, whether in the form of alkaloids or of salts or of preparations of the alkaloids or salts:

1. The quantity necessary for medical and scientific needs (this includes the quantities required for the manufacture of preparations for which export authorizations are not required, whether intended for domestic consumption or not);

2. The quantity necessary for conversion whether for domestic consumption or export;

3. The amount of the reserve stocks which it is desired to maintain;

4. The quantity necessary for the establishment and maintenance of any governmental stocks.

The Supervisory Body forwards to every government of the world an annual statement containing the estimates for each country.

The estimates system introduced by the Limitation Convention of 1931 differs from that contained in the Geneva Convention of 1925 in that the estimates under the Convention of 1931 are required for the total quantities necessary for consumption within the country, and are binding, whereas those which the parties agreed to submit under the Convention of 1925 relate only to imports for medical, scientific, and other purposes, and are not binding.

Under the Limitation Convention of 1931 controls are applied to all stages between manufacture and ultimate consumption of manufactured drugs. This Convention marked a great advance in international supervision of the drug traffic and also of international law. World manufacture was effectively limited, as were also the supplies available for each country. The Convention achieved its purposes, and it is generally recognized that it has been completely successful in its application.

The following opinion on the 1931 Convention was expressed by the Assembly of the League of Nations:

The Convention marks an entirely new and highly important development in international cooperation, since this is the first time that an industry has been brought under international regulation, and that manufacture in its economic aspect has been wholly subordinated to higher humanitarian and moral aims. Thanks to the system established by this Convention and the Geneva Convention, there will be at the headquarters of the League itself a sort of central counting-house for the world traffic in drugs.

Noteworthy from the point of view of international law is the fact that a government not a party to the Convention and which has not furnished its estimates, may be prevented from importing drugs from a country which is a party, due to an embargo issued by the Central Board under Article 14, paragraph 2, of the Limitation Convention on account of excess over the estimates for the non-party state furnished by the Supervisory Body.

The 1931 Convention came into application in its entirety as from January 1, 1934. By August, 1952, seventy-three countries had ratified the Convention.

THE CONVENTION OF 1936 FOR THE SUPPRESSION OF THE ILLICIT TRAFFIC IN DANGEROUS DRUGS

The object of the 1936 Convention is stated in the Preamble to be: "to strengthen the measures intended to penalize offenses" contained in the previous international conventions and "to combat by the methods most effective in the present circumstances the illicit traffic in the drugs and substances covered by the Conventions." The experience gained since 1912 had shown that the illicit traffic could not be effectively suppressed unless there were equally severe penalties in all countries, and also effective measures to make it possible to bring to justice traffickers who escaped from the country where they had violated the drug laws, or who directed illicit traffic in one country through another country.

The 1936 Convention stipulated that offenses defined therein should be included as extradition crimes in any extradition treaty to be negotiated between the contracting parties. In countries where the extradition of nationals is not recognized, the parties undertook to prosecute a national who had returned to his country after committing an offense abroad which came within the terms of the Convention. These provisions were designed to prevent narcotic traffickers from escaping prosecution because the laws of the country in which they resided did not cover smuggling offenses committed abroad. The Convention also provided that the contracting parties should set up a central office to supervise and coordinate all operations necessary to prevent the illicit traffic.

The United States refused to sign the 1936 Convention on the ground that it covered trade in and distribution of manufactured drugs only and did not include raw materials or smoking opium; it would afford no constitutional basis for Federal control of the production of cannabis, opium, and the opium poppy; and furthermore, while in some countries its enforcement might result in improvement in efforts to prevent the abuse of narcotic drugs, the provisions of the Convention would weaken rather than strengthen the effectiveness of the efforts of the American Government to prevent and punish narcotics offenses and to obtain extradition therefor.

The 1936 Convention came into force in October 1939, one month after outbreak of World War II. By August, 1952, nineteen countries had ratified the Convention.

THE PROTOCOL OF 1946

The supervision of operation of the several narcotic Conventions had been performed by the Opium Advisory Committee of the Council of the League of Nations, which went out of existence upon the organization of the United Nations. In February, 1946, the Economic and Social Council established the Commission on Narcotic Drugs, and the U. S. Commissioner of Narcotics was appointed the United States Representative on this Commission. He proposed an agreement which was adopted as the Protocol of 1946, whereby all functions assigned under the several conventions to organs of the defunct League of Nations were transferred to corresponding organs of the United Nations. Thus the new Commission on Narcotic Drugs assumed the functions of the old Opium Advisory Committee.

SINGLE CONVENTION ON NARCOTIC DRUGS

The Commission on Narcotic Drugs has devoted considerable time to discussion and modification of a draft prepared by the UN Secretariat, of a so-called Unified Convention, that is, a convention designed to include all of the operative provisions of the existing international conventions and protocols controlling the traffic in narcotic drugs including marihuana. In addition to the usual divergence of views as to the necessity of a given provision, or the appropriateness of a proposed method of reaching a desired aim, there was the difficulty that one or more of the existing international agreements, considered essential for incorporation into the single convention, had not been adopted by some of the high contracting parties to other conventions.

The object of the proposed unification is not only to combine the eight international agreements on the subject but also to revise and strengthen these agreements, closing loopholes, and rejecting obsolete provisions. It is obviously most desirable to revise these international agreements, one of which dates back to 1912, and to incorporate them if possible into a single agreement which will provide reasonably effective control over the production of opium, coca leaves, and cannabis, over the manufacture of the dangerous or potentially dangerous products of these substances as well as of synthetic substitutes for them, and over the distribution of such raw material and of the manufactured products or synthetic substitutes.

THE PERMANENT CENTRAL BOARD

The Permanent Central Board,* a semi-autonomous organ, was created by the Geneva Convention of 1925, and its main function was defined as continuously to "watch over the course of the international trade in narcotic drugs." Its duties have been discharged without interruption since 1928.

The Permanent Central Board consists of eight persons who, by their technical competence, impartiality, and disinterestedness, command general confidence. Originally the members of the Board were appointed by the Council of the League of Nations. Since the amendments to the 1925 Convention contained in the Protocol of December 11, 1946, came into force, the Economic and Social Council of the United Nations is the appointing authority.

The 1925 Convention laid down certain conditions for the appointing authority. The membership of the Board must include in equitable proportion persons possessing a knowledge of the drug situation both in the producing and manufacturing countries and in the consuming countries.

It was also stated in the Convention that the members of the Central Board, who are appointed for five years, should not hold any office which put them in a position of direct dependence on their governments. This provision, which was inserted in order to make it possible for the Board to carry out certain semijudi-

* Generally referred to as the Permanent Central Opium Board.

cial functions under the Convention, has created problems in the selection of its personnel. It was pointed out at the first session of the Commission on Narcotic Drugs that changing social systems in various countries might make it difficult for these governments to propose candidates who fulfilled these conditions. At the second session the Commission adopted a resolution concerning the meaning of this provision which was approved by the Economic and Social Council at its sixth session.

According to this resolution, it is possible for the Council to elect members who, although they might originally have been in a position of direct dependence on their government, undertook to relinquish their government office during their term of duty with the Permanent Central Board, provided that they also agreed not to act under the instructions of their governments while exercising their functions as members of the Board. It was also agreed that it was possible for the Council to elect professional men and women in academic positions, from universities or other institutions supported by the state.

In 1925 it was decided that the Hague Convention of 1912 should be reinforced, because its provisions and the national laws governing the movement of drugs did not prevent illicit traffic, in large part because of the lack of an administration or the machinery to supervise the traffic. The Permanent Central Board fills this need. The High Contracting Parties were convinced, says the 1925 Convention, that contraband trade and abuse of narcotic drugs could not be suppressed without more effective control of production or manufacture and closer supervision of the international trade. Accordingly, the parties undertook to institute certain measures for the internal control of narcotic drugs and the raw materials from which they are made, pledging themselves to institute legislation to limit exclusively to medical and scientific purposes the manufacture and distribution of narcotic drugs.

Precise and definite obligations were imposed by the 1925 Convention. The participating countries agreed to set up a system of issuing import certificates and export authorizations. They were also to submit annual estimates of the quantities of narcotic drugs which they needed to import each year for medicinal and scientific purposes. Further, they undertook to furnish statistics of the production of raw materials, of the manufacture, consumption, export, import, and stocks of narcotic drugs, and the amount seized on account of illicit import.

The international body which was created to receive these statistics was the Permanent Central Board. In order that it should be able to carry out its duties in a truly impartial manner, careful provision was made in the Convention that it should be constituted in such a way as to be completely independent of governments.

In addition to the functions mentioned, the Board was vested with the power of recommending sanctions against a country importing or manufacturing narcotic drugs in excess of its legitimate needs. Several sanctions have been enforced. Each year the Board publishes a report showing the statistics it has received under various headings and stating whether any countries have exceeded their estimates. In this way, the parties to the Convention are kept informed of any undue accumulation of drugs in any particular country and can act on this information for their own protection.

An instance of the effectiveness of the work of the Board was exemplified when it reported, prior to the 1931 Convention, that a Central American country had imported one hundred times its medical needs, or a supply of narcotic drugs sufficient for one hundred years. American authorities immediately began investigating, and found that narcotics were leaving that country and were being smuggled into the United States in exchange for arms and ammunition which were being sent for use in a revolution. When the Director of Health of the country then refused to issue licenses for the release of narcotics, he was assassinated. After a civil investigation, the entire gang of smugglers was rounded up and sentenced to long terms of imprisonment.

The 1925 Convention worked satisfactorily in regard to trade, but it was found that the provisions relating to the manufacture of narcotic drugs had to be strengthened. It was to achieve this that a new Convention, a Convention to supplement the provisions of those of 1912 and 1925, was negotiated in 1931.

DRUG LIMITATION CONVENTION

Under the 1931 Convention, a more rigorous system of submitting estimates was instituted to bring about a strict limitation of the amounts of narcotic drugs to be manufactured in each country. It had been found that knowledge of the movements and quantities of narcotics was not sufficient to control the illicit traffic. The new estimates submitted to the Permanent Central Board were to be examined by a Supervisory Body especially created for the purpose, and, once approved, were to be binding. It was, however, given to the Permanent Central Board to supervise the extent to which the parties to the Conventions carried out their obligations in respect of their estimates. Under Article 14 of this Convention, if the import and export returns show that the estimates of an importing country are or will be exceeded, the Board is under an obligation to inform all the High Contracting Parties "who will not during the currency of the year in question authorize any new exports to the country except in the special circumstances set forth in the Convention."

At the entry into operation of the 1931 Convention, information at the disposal of the Permanent Central Board under the 1925 Convention could be used more effectively. The Board now not only published statistics and recommended sanctions, but by comparing its statistics with the estimates approved by the Supervisory Body, it could ascertain if any country was violating its obligations under the 1931 Convention by exceeding its estimates.

The Board admitted that the degree of the success of international control varied from one narcotic drug to another. In the case of raw materials falling under the Convention of 1925, the control was vitiated by the inability of some of the most important producing countries to report their production accurately. In the findings of the annual report of the Permanent Central Board summarizing the work of the Board in 1951, it was noted that the Iranian Government had, for the first time in seventeen years, sent statistics for raw opium, so that it was possible to strike a balance, for the year 1950, of the quantities disposed of and available. According to this balance, 333 tons of raw opium disappeared in Iran in 1950. (This is an example of the searching scrutiny of the Permanent Central Board.)

The Board then asked the Iranian Government for an explanation. It was pointed out by the Board that so long as such incidents occur and remain unexplained, the situation must continue to be most disquieting.

In the case of manufactured drugs, the chief aims of the 1925 Convention (a complete account of the supplies available) and of the 1931 Convention (the limitation of the manufacture to medical and scientific requirements) had, the Board felt, to a large extent been achieved. Broadly speaking, the Board described the satisfactory elements in the situation as being the wide extent of the control, which demanded a high degree of cooperation between governments, and the general reduction in drug addiction, of which there is considerable evidence. The Board, however, did not hesitate to criticize certain technical aspects of the submission of estimates and statistics.

One of the chief advantages derived from this method of control seems to be that governments do not resent the fact that a board is continuously checking them. During World War II, the offices of the Permanent Central Board were moved to Washington, and Germany and her satellites continued to permit their narcotic agencies to function and to submit figures to this Board, an indication that even in time of war this Board has been able to function. The attitude of the Board has always been that it is helping governments to fulfil their voluntary obligations. This point of view has set an interesting precedent.

In its quasi-judicial capacity, the Board supervises fulfillment of certain obligations voluntarily assumed by governments, specified in the following provisions of the 1925 and 1931 Conventions:

GENEVA CONVENTION OF 1925

Article 24

1. The Central Board shall continuously watch the course of the international trade. If the information at its disposal leads the Board to conclude that excessive quantities of any substance covered by the present Convention are accumulating in any country, or that there is

a danger of the country becoming a centre of the illicit traffic, the Board shall have the right to ask, through the Secretary-General of the League, for explanations from the country in question.

2. If no explanation is given within a reasonable time or the explanation is unsatisfactory, the Central Board shall have the right to call the attention of the Governments of all the Contracting Parties and of the Council of the League of Nations to the matter, and to recommend that no further exports of the substances covered by the present Convention or any of them shall be made to the country concerned until the Board reports that it is satisfied as to the situation in that country in regard to the said substances. The Board shall at the same time notify the Government of the country concerned of the recommendation made by it.

3. The country concerned shall be entitled to bring the matter before the Council of the League.

4. The Government of any exporting country which is not prepared to act on the recommendation of the Central Board shall also be entitled to bring the matter before the Council of the League.

If it does not do so, it shall immediately inform the Board that it is not prepared to act on the recommendation, explaining, if possible, why it is not prepared to do so.

5. The Central Board shall have the right to publish a report on the matter and communicate it to the Council, which shall thereupon forward it to the Governments of all the Contracting Parties.

Article 26

In the case of a country which is not a party to the present Convention, the Central Board may take the same measures as are specified in Article 24, if the information at the disposal of the Board leads it to conclude that there is danger of the country becoming a centre of the illicit traffic; in that case the Board shall take the action indicated in the said Article as regards notification to the country concerned.

Paragraphs 3, 4 and 7 of Article 24 shall apply in any such case.

DRUG LIMITATION CONVENTION OF 1931

Article 14

1. Any Government which has issued an authorization for the export of any of the drugs which are or may be included in Group I to any country or territory to which neither this Convention nor the Geneva Convention applies shall immediately notify the Permanent

Central Board of the issue of the authorisation; provided that, if the request for export amounts to 5 kilogrammes or more, the authorisation shall not be issued until the Government has ascertained from the Permanent Central Board that the export will not cause the estimates for the importing country or territory to be exceeded. If the Permanent Central Board sends a notification that such an excess would be caused, the Government will not authorize the export of any amount which would have that effect.

2. If it appears from the import and export returns made to the Permanent Central Board or from the notifications made to the Board in pursuance of the preceding paragraph that the quantity exported or authorised to be exported to any country or territory exceeds the total of the estimates for that country or territory as defined in Article 5, with the addition of the amounts shown to have been exported, the Board shall immediately notify the fact to all the High Contracting Parties, who will not, during the currency of the year in question, authorise any new exports to that country except:

(i) In the event of a supplementary estimate being furnished for that country in respect both of any quantity over-imported and of the additional quantity required; or

(ii) In exceptional cases where the export in the opinion of the Government of the exporting country is essential in the interests of humanity or for the treatment of the sick.

THE SUPERVISORY BODY

COMPOSITION—APPOINTMENT

The Supervisory Body was created by the 1931 Conference for the Limitation of the Manufacture of Narcotic Drugs. It was composed of four members, of which one was to be appointed by the Permanent Central Board, one by the Advisory Committee on Opium and Other Dangerous Drugs, one by the Health Committee of the League of Nations, and one by the Office International d'Hygiene Publique. The Protocol of December 11, 1946 substituted the Commission on Narcotic Drugs for the Advisory Committee, and the World Health Organization for the Health Committee and the Office International d'Hygiene Publique, as appointing bodies.

PERSONAL QUALIFICATIONS OF MEMBERS

The 1931 Convention does not expressly establish any requirements as to the personal qualifications of the members of the Body. A study of the minutes of the 1931 Conference reveals, however, that the framers of the 1931 Convention thought of the members of the Body as independent experts, some of whom should have the medical knowledge necessary for the performance of the functions of the Body.

TENURE

No provisions were made as to the period of tenure of office of the members of the Body. This omission would perhaps justify the interpretation that it is left to the appointing bodies to determine the period, and by agreement between them, it was fixed at three years when the first appointments were made in 1933. Later renewals made during the lifetime of the League of Nations were also made for the same period. The Commission on Narcotic Drugs, at its third session, recommended that the terms of office of the members of the Supervisory Body should be five years, and accordingly, in 1948 the members were appointed for a period of five years.

SECRETARIAT

The Secretariat of the Supervisory Body shall be provided by the Secretary-General of the United Nations (formerly, by the League of Nations). The Secretary-General shall ensure close collaboration with the Permanent Central Board.

FUNCTIONS

The Supervisory Body, by examining estimates submitted by countries and framing estimates for states which have not submitted them, guarantees that each country and territory may obtain drugs sufficient (but not more than sufficient) to meet medical and scientific needs. It limits, through the estimates, world manufacture and international trade. The task is delicate and responsible, for upon the accuracy of the final estimates will very largely depend the practical success or failure of the principle of limitation. An overestimate may permit the manufacture of surplus drugs, which will inevitably find their way sooner or later into the illicit trade.

FIRST, the Body is required to examine the estimates furnished by various governments and has the right to demand, if it thinks fit, further information or details from a government with regard to the latter's estimates. (The estimates must be furnished in accordance with Articles 2 and 5 of the Convention.) With the government's consent, the Supervisory Body may amend any estimate in accordance with the information obtained. With the independent information already at its disposal, through the work of the Commission on Narcotic Drugs and the Permanent Central Board, the Body is in a position to check the figures in the national estimates for each drug and to form an idea of their relationship with the known needs of different countries. The Body can only request further information with regard to the national estimates actually presented. It cannot go beyond this and request information on any other basis or relating to matters which are not directly connected with the fuller explanation of the figures shown. It has no competence to infringe upon the more general sphere of activity of the Commission on Narcotic Drugs.

SECOND, the Body itself as far as possible draws up estimates (a) for those territories to which the Convention applies but for which estimates are not furnished in accordance with Articles 2 and 5 of the Convention, that is, when no estimates at all are furnished by the given date, August 1st, preceding the year to which they refer, or when the estimates are in an imperfect or incomplete form, as, for example, when separate figures are not shown for each drug; (b) for those territories to which the Convention does not apply, including both non-contracting countries and colonial areas for which the metropolitan state has not accepted the obligations of the Convention.

Recently the Supervisory Body has found it necessary to provide estimates for Russia, Romania, Poland, Albania, Afghanistan, China and the German Democratic Republic. It may be noted that Article 5, paragraph 7, refers without qualification "to the determining by that Body as provided in Article 2 of the estimates for each country or territory on behalf of which no estimates have been furnished." In such cases, nations must surrender sovereignty to this international body. The system of limitation of manufacture on the basis of estimated needs would be seriously impaired if estimates could be neither requested nor prepared for territories for which a government was unwilling to accept the obligations of the Convention.

Estimates made by the Body itself are in every way indistinguishable from estimates furnished by the countries themselves to the Permanent Central Board. A country can, of course, attempt to modify them by submitting a supplementary estimate.

THIRD, the Body is required to draw up a statement consisting of the estimates furnished by governments or, in their absence, by the Supervisory Body, of requirements for medical and scientific needs. The statement of the Body is a plan for the world's drug industry for the coming year. The responsibility of the Body is clear when it is remembered that this statement is not merely a guide to the industry and the trade. The function which it is called upon to fulfil invests it with a more solemn character. It constitutes, on the date of its communication to governments, a statement of obligations binding upon the contracting governments and, eighteen months later through the international accounting system of the Permanent Central Board, a standard by which the action of governments in observing their obligations will be judged. Thus the essential function of the Supervisory Body is to ensure that the estimates are kept within reasonable limits.

RESULTS

The machinery established by the Supervisory Body emerged from its initial trial in 1933 with considerable success. Estimates were received that year for 45 countries (including 14 countries which had not ratified the Convention) and for 83 colonies, protectorates and territories. The Supervisory Body was called upon to provide estimates for 23 countries and 31 colonies for which no estimates had been furnished. For 1952, estimates were furnished by 73 governments and 78 territories, and the Supervisory Body was called upon to provide estimates for only 10 countries and 6 territories.

The effectiveness of the Supervisory Body is attested to by the fact that in the first year of its existence, it succeeded in reducing the total amount of morphine required for all purposes (in 1934) by more than *three tons*.

MANDATE OF THE SUPERVISORY BODY

Extract from Article 5 of the International Convention of July 13, 1931, as amended by the Protocol of December 11, 1946:

6. Estimates will be examined by a Supervisory Body . . . The Supervisory Body may require any further information or details, except as regards requirements for Government purposes, which it may consider necessary.

7. After examination by the Supervisory Body as provided in paragraph 6 above of the estimates furnished, and after the determination by that Body as provided in Article 2 of the estimates for each country or territory on behalf of which no estimates have been furnished, the Supervisory Body shall forward, not later than December 15th in each year, through the intermediary of the Secretary-General of the United Nations, to all the Members of the United Nations and non-member States referred to in Article 28, a statement containing the estimates for each country or territory, and, so far as the Supervisory Body may consider necessary, an account of any explanations given or required in accordance with paragraph 6 above, and any observations which the Supervisory Body may desire to make in respect of any such estimate or explanation, or request for an explanation.

THE OPIUM ADVISORY COMMITTEE

Although international cooperation in the drug field was begun before the League of Nations came into being, supervision by special international bodies did not exist in the pre-League days. This supervision was created by the League of Nations.

Under the Versailles Peace Treaty, the Opium Convention of 1912 was automatically put into effect; and through the insertion of Article 23 (c) in the Covenant of the League of Nations, which stated "in accordance with the provisions of international Conventions existing or hereafter to be created, the members of the League . . . will entrust the League with the general supervision over the execution of agreements with regard to . . . the traffic in opium and other dangerous drugs," the League was entrusted with the execution of this Opium Convention. On December 15, 1920, the first Assembly of the League of Nations passed a resolution creating an Advisory Committee which was to be appointed by the Council "to exercise a general supervision over the traffic in opium and other dangerous drugs and to secure the full cooperation of the various countries in this field." The Council of the League actually appointed the Advisory Committee on the Traffic in Opium and Other Dangerous Drugs in 1921 and included in accordance with the provisions of the Assembly Resolution representatives from the Netherlands, United Kingdom, France, India, Japan, China, Siam, and Portugal, as the countries specially concerned. The Assembly Resolution had provided that the Council should be authorized to add to the Advisory Committee, in the capacity of member or assessor, a representative of any non-member State specially concerned in the traffic which had ratified The Hague Convention, and to send a special invitation to the United States of America, which sent an observer after 1923.

DUTIES—EFFECTIVENESS

The Secretariat of the League of Nations was charged by the Assembly with the duty of collecting information concerning the arrangements made in the various countries for carrying out the Hague Convention, and concerning the production, distribution, and consumption of narcotic drugs which was of great assistance to the Advisory Committee in presenting its annual report to the Council on all matters regarding the execution of agreements concerning the traffic in opium and other dangerous drugs. The Advisory Committee performed the functions of a policy-making body for the international control system, under which great advance was made in the control of the legal trade in narcotics and in reducing illicit traffic and drug addiction.

In the early years of the activities of the Opium Advisory Committee of the League, much time was devoted to discussions of policy. At the outset the Opium Advisory Committee was largely composed of representatives of opium-producing countries, the great manufacturing countries and those countries which maintained opium-smoking monopolies in certain Far Eastern countries and territories, and this aroused certain suspicions and misgivings in the minds of those who had the drug problem at heart. Under the impact of this situation the Advisory Committee was repeatedly enlarged and from 1930 it was really representative of all countries which were affected by the drug problem as producers of raw materials, as manufacturers, as consumers, or as victims of illicit traffic and drug addiction.

The Advisory Committee was enabled to strengthen the administration of the system of control at several of its weakest points as the authority for the discussion of the annual reports which the governments of States-members undertook to send in to the Secretariat and as the clearing-house for all information about seizures. It incessantly urged governments to impose stricter internal regulation and in particular to adopt what has now become one of the most effective weapons of control, the import-certificate system. Through the information gradually collected by the Committee, the disquieting fact began to emerge that the amount of dangerous drugs manufactured was several times the quantity required for the medical and scientific needs of the world.

As the result of the Opium Advisory Committee's turning the pitiless spotlight of the world press on specific narcotic conditions from time to time, it was able to drive the illicit traffic from France, Switzerland, Holland, Bulgaria, and Yugoslavia. It repeatedly exposed the manner in which loose controls over manufacture, and lack of effective laws had encouraged the building up of large scale illicit trafficking in these countries.

The Advisory Committee, by revealing the extent of the abuses and by gaining recognition as a highly efficient instrument for guiding and encouraging the collaboration of governments in this field, prepared the ground for advance to the second phase reached in 1925 when the First and Second Geneva Opium Conferences met.

Under the terms of the Geneva Convention of 1925, which came into force on September 28, 1928, a strict check was made possible over the international trade in narcotic drugs. In its review of the general situation concerning the manufacture and trade of drugs between 1931 and 1935, the Advisory Committee stated that it was in a position to calculate the legitimate needs of the world for manufactured drugs and that up to the year 1931 there had been considerable discrepancy between the amounts manufactured and legitimate needs. It showed that in 1929, 58 tons of morphine for all purposes had been manufactured, and that in the period 1931-35 the legitimate needs of the world averaging 29 tons a year had been completely satisfied by an annual production of that amount. In 1929, 3.6 tons of heroin and 6.4 tons of cocaine had been manufactured, and in 1935, only 674 kilograms of heroin and 3.9 tons of cocaine, which represented a reduction of 82 percent in the manufacture of heroin and about 40 percent in the manufacture of cocaine. In 1929, 6 tons of morphine, 850 kilograms of heroin, and 2.2 tons of cocaine had been exported. In 1935, the export of morphine and heroin was only a quarter of this amount and the export of cocaine one half, without any resulting damage to medical requirements.

The Advisory Committee estimated that in the period 1925 to 1930 at least 90 tons of morphine had escaped into the illicit traffic. It emphasized that since 1931 there was no surplus of legal manufacture to supply the illicit traffic. The review of the period between 1931 and 1935 showed that the application of the Geneva Convention of 1925 had not only considerably reduced the manufacture of narcotic drugs, but had stabilized the quantity at the level of the world's medical and scientific needs.

By 1939, the international cooperation for the control of narcotic drugs was firmly established and was showing real results. Order had been brought out of comparative chaos, and in most countries there was an effective system of national control. In its report to the Council on the work of its twenty-fifth session the Opium Advisory Committee pointed out that every effort should be made to prevent the achievement of twenty years from being jeopardized by the war. It was clear that special measures would have to be taken to prevent a repetition of the chaotic conditions which followed World War I, and to enable the international bodies concerned with the control of narcotic drugs to continue their work. Through the courtesy of the Government of the United States, branch offices of the Secretariats of the Supervisory Body and the Permanent Central Board were opened in Washington in February of 1941. The Conventions were not impaired by World War II: while some domestic controls disappeared or were disorganized, the majority of controls survived the war, and continued in operation even in countries subjected to enemy occupation. This in itself was a striking tribute to the vigor and effectiveness of the international control.

In the same manner that the United Nations Commission on Narcotic Drugs does today, the Opium Advisory Committee afforded a world forum where the problem of the illicit traffic in narcotic drugs was publicly discussed every year, and where any government whose territory was used as a base for the illicit traffic was without fear or favor publicly asked to account for its stewardship. Most of the progress made has been due to publicity, and the value of this Committee as an instrument of publicity was widely recognized, and in some quarters, feared.

OPIUM SMOKING

The beginning of the modern movement for the suppression of the opium traffic may be said to date from the action of the United States Government in 1905 in forbidding the use of opium in the Philippine Islands, where opium smoking was a widespread evil. That Government had appointed a committee to investigate thoroughly not only the Philippine opium problem but the entire problem as it then existed in the Far East.

When the Shanghai International Opium Commission met in 1909, the United States Delegation proposed the immediate prohibition of opium smoking, but the conference was not prepared to go that far.

The Convention of 1912 established the duty of gradual suppression of the opium-smoking habit as a principle of international law.

Two Agreements * of the countries having territories in which opium smoking constituted a serious problem attempted to advance the process of suppression by such measures as establishing opium monopolies providing for government ownership of retail shops selling smoking opium, licensing and rationing of smokers, prohibition of sale to minors, educational measures, etc. None of these measures proved adequate, however, and when war broke out in 1939, the smoking of opium was still legalized in The Netherlands Indies, British Malaya, the Unfederated Malay States, Brunei, Formosa, Kwantung Leased Territory, Sarawak, Burma, India, Ceylon, British North Borneo, Hong Kong, French Indochina, Thailand, Kwangchow-wan, Macao, and Iran. Much of this territory in the Far East was occupied by Japan during World War II, and curtailment of the opium traffic there became a matter of immediate concern to the United States in view of its military operations in the Far East and the large number of young troops deployed in that area.

From the standpoint of the health and safety of the men of the Armed Forces of the United States, the Government was convinced that it was imperative immediately upon the occupation by the United States forces of a part or the whole of any one of the Japanese-occupied territories to seize all drugs intended for other than medical and scientific purposes. American expeditionary forces under American command were therefore instructed to close existing opium monopolies, opium shops, and dens. That was the immediate problem. The long-range problem was what should be done in regard to the opium monopolies and the opium problem in general. Another question was, "What will happen if the British or the Chinese alone should reoccupy Burma, for example?" Would the British license the sale of opium for nonmedical needs, while the Chinese refused to license the opium smokers?

The competent authorities of the United States were of the

* Agreement concerning the Manufacture of, Internal Trade in, and Use of Prepared Opium, signed at Geneva, February 11, 1925; and Agreement for the Control of Opium-Smoking in the Far East, signed at Bangkok on November 27, 1931; generally referred to as 1925 Agreement and 1931 Agreement.

opinion that there would be an increase in addiction among Americans after the war because of the close association of their troops with opium in the Far Eastern areas. This opinion was based on the knowledge that drug addiction springs from association with drugs and addicts; a person easily falls a victim to such addiction through association and contacts; the opium smoker should be regarded as a focus of infection for susceptible individuals; also that experience in the past proves that wars tend to give rise to drug addiction. As long as opium smoking was permitted in the Far Eastern war theater, it was probable that troops would acquire addiction and that drug smuggling would continue from countries in the Far East to countries in the West, unless some counter action was taken. It was pointed out that the Americans had never allowed the sale of opium in the Philippines and that when the Japanese moved in the United States would not likely have gotten the support which it did get from the Filipinos if the United States Government had been selling the Filipinos opium for a generation as had been done, for instance, in Far Eastern territories under control of European governments.

Beginning on January 13, 1943, a series of informal meetings were held in the Treasury Department office of the Commissioner of Narcotics in Washington, attended by representatives of Great Britain, Canada, Australia, New Zealand, The Netherlands, and China; also by representatives of the State Department and the Foreign Policy Association, regarding the question of what should be done in case some island or territory where a smoking-opium monopoly existed was occupied by the military forces of the United Nations.

At the conclusion of the informal discussions it was apparent that the representatives of governments present were in agreement as to the final objective to be reached, viz., total prohibition of opium smoking, and that any differences of opinion expressed concerned only the methods to be applied to attain this objective. It was pointed out that monopolies did not reduce the number of smokers; that international cooperation would be the solution of the problem; and that the production of opium had a bearing on the control of the monopolies. It was emphasized that opinion in America was crystallizing against the opium monopolies because they feed the illicit traffic in the United States and elsewhere; that if the American Navy were to capture Hong Kong, for instance, under the status quo the official opium stores would probably be reopened immediately; that the American Navy could not indirectly license the opium trade abroad when it is condemned at home.

It was suggested that the other countries represented start discussions with a view to formulating policies to be pursued, as the United States had a clear-cut policy on the matter under discussion.

The observation was made that in some countries the command might shift from the Americans to the British and that in such event the Americans did not want a situation to arise in which some other country would say that opium was in and the Americans would say it was out; therefore it was desirable that agreements be reached.

As a result of these discussions the United States Government on September 21, 1942, addressed an aide-memoire to the British, The Netherlands and other interested governments on this subject. On November 10, 1943, the British and Netherlands governments announced their intentions to abolish the legalized sale of opium in their Far Eastern territories, and similar action was later taken by the governments of France and Portugal. Opium smoking has now been declared illegal in all parts of the world except in Thailand.

This action by the United States Government was a long step in advance, and brought about a quick solution to the troublesome opium-smoking problem which had been under discussion for settlement since 1905, and for which numerous international conferences and agreements had failed to evolve a satisfactory solution.

COMMISSION OF ENQUIRY ON THE COCA LEAF

In compliance with requests made by the governments of Peru and Bolivia, the Economic and Social Council sent a Commission of Enquiry to these countries in 1949 to investigate the effects of chewing the coca leaf. The Commission in the conclusions of its report declared that this habit induces harmful effects and decided in favor of the possibility of suppressing it gradually, as well as of the possibility of limiting the production and of controlling the distribution of the coca leaf.

The Commission on Narcotic Drugs considered the report during its seventh session (1952), and recommended: (a) that the Council request the technical assistance services of the UN to study the possibility of undertaking certain experiments under their program in Bolivia and Peru; (b) that the Council request the governments of Bolivia and Peru to take steps to limit immediately the production of coca leaves to licit consumption and manufacture; and (c) that the Council urge the governments of Bolivia and Peru to take measures to prevent coca leaves and cocaine from entering channels which could supply the illicit traffic in narcotic drugs.

LIMITATION OF OPIUM PRODUCTION

Since 1912 the United States has sought to obtain an international convention for limiting the production of opium to the world's medical and scientific needs, in the belief that such limitation will be of immeasurable benefit in the reduction of drug addiction and the curtailment of the illicit drug traffic. In 1912 we failed in our attempt to have an effective provision included in the Hague Convention. In 1925 our Delegates withdrew from the conference because it refused to consider this subject. In 1931 our Delegates presented an amendment to the Convention but the question was ruled as not within the scope of the conference as prescribed by the League of Nations Assembly.

In 1939 the Opium Advisory Committee of the League of Nations began studies for the purpose of preparing a convention to solve the problem of effective limitation of opium production, but its work was interrupted by the war.

The United Nations Commission on Narcotic Drugs decided to tackle the problem by stages, the first and most important stage being to secure the accession of the principal opium-producing countries to the necessary agreements for the limitation of production. It was for this purpose that the Economic and Social Council approved a proposal by its Commission on Narcotic Drugs for a meeting of the Ad Hoc Committee of the principal opium-producing countries, which met at Ankara in 1949, the Governments of India, Iran, Turkey and Yugoslavia being represented. They elaborated in some detail the proposed structure for an interim agreement under which the Governments would have been enabled to put into effect their intention of limiting the production of raw opium to medical and scientific requirements. They agreed on allocation of shares in the world production of opium as follows: approximately 50 percent for Turkey, 25 per cent for Iran, 14 percent for Yugoslavia, 6 percent for India; the balance undetermined.

At meetings of the principal drug-manufacturing countries and the principal opium-producing countries held in Geneva in 1950, a tentative agreement was reached on the general principle of limiting the production of opium. The plan contemplated the establishment of an international opium monopoly to which the producing countries would sell their opium and from which consuming countries would purchase their opium requirements. This plan presented many complicated problems, two of which were that the producing countries refused to permit international inspection, and there was disagreement on the prices at which the proposed monopoly should conduct its opium transactions. Discussions were held at several sessions of the United Nations Commission on Narcotic Drugs until 1951, when the Commission concluded that it would be advisable to forgo further discussion of the monopoly plan at the time.

The French Delegate to the Commission, however, proposed another plan based on the 1931 Convention for Limiting the Manufacture and Regulating the Distribution of Narcotic Drugs. The Commission decided to make the French proposal the basis for further discussion. A protocol was signed at the United Nations June 23, 1953.

INTERNATIONAL POLICE COOPERATION

In addition to receiving cooperation under the various provisions of international treaties, the American Government has concluded administrative arrangements with twenty-two governments which provide for the direct informal exchange between the Commissioner of Narcotics at Washington and the heads of their respective enforcement agencies of police information concerning the illicit traffic. This system has been found of inestimable value. In some cases, the Bureau of Narcotics has been able to reach around the world to prosecute international traffickers either by bringing the offender within United States jurisdiction from foreign lands or by securing his prosecution under the laws of his own country. For example, in the celebrated Louis (Lepke) Buchalter-Katzenberg case the Bureau was able to bring back to this country and prosecute defendants who attempted to take refuge in Greece and France. The famous Elie Eliopoulos Ring which controlled the world's illicit narcotic supply was broken through this arrangement.

NARCOTICS CONTROL PATTERN SUGGESTED
FOR ATOMIC ENERGY AND DISARMAMENT

The marked success achieved in the international narcotic drug control program has prompted numerous suggestions that some of its principles be used as a pattern for control in other fields such as atomic energy and disarmament.

Studies of the analogies between control of the traffic in narcotic drugs and that of the trade in and manufacture of arms have been made since 1932, by League of Nations experts and more recently by the United Nations. When the Conference for the Reduction and Limitation of Armaments met in Geneva in 1933, it was suggested in the Council of the League that attention be given to the results obtained in connection with the supervision of the traffic in narcotic drugs. The Secretariat prepared a memorandum on the subject which was submitted to the Conference under the title "Analogies between the Problem of the Traffic in Narcotic Drugs and That of the Trade in and Manufacture of Arms." An article entitled "Narcotics Control—A Pattern for Disarmament" was published in the *United Nations World* magazine for September, 1947.

A study entitled "Narcotic Drugs and Atomic Energy-Analogy of Controls" has been published by an international drug expert, Mr. Herbert L. May.

THE UNITED NATIONS AND THE INTERNATIONAL CONTROL OF NARCOTIC DRUGS

The United Nations Conference on International Organization met in San Francisco on April 20, 1945. In instituting the Economic and Social Council, the Conference anticipated that it would be concerned with the control of the traffic in and suppression of abuses of opium and other dangerous drugs.

THE COMMISSION ON NARCOTIC DRUGS

By a resolution adopted on February 16, 1946, the United Nations Economic and Social Council established the Commission on Narcotic Drugs to:

(a) Assist the Council in exercising such powers of supervision over the application of international conventions and agreements dealing with narcotic drugs as may be assumed by or conferred on the Council;

(b) Carry out such functions entrusted to the League of Nations Advisory Committee on Traffic in Opium and Other Dangerous Drugs by the international conventions on narcotic drugs as the Council may find necessary to assume and continue;

(c) Advise the Council on all matters pertaining to the control of narcotic drugs and prepare such draft international conventions as may be necessary;

(d) Consider what changes may be required in the existing machinery for the international control of narcotic drugs and submit proposals thereon to the Council;

(e) Perform such other functions relating to narcotic drugs as the Council may direct.

COMPOSITION

The Council stated that the Commission should be composed of fifteen Members of the United Nations which are important producing or manufacturing countries or countries in which illicit traffic in narcotic drugs constitutes a serious social problem. Finally the Council requested the governments of Canada, China, Egypt, France, India, Iran, Mexico, Netherlands, Peru, Poland, Turkey, and Union of Soviet Socialist Republics, the United Kingdom, the United States, and Yugoslavia to designate one representative each to constitute the Commission. The Commission holds annual sessions.

TENURE OF MEMBERS

The resolution of February 16, 1946 provided for a tenure of three years for the fifteen members of the Commission. The Economic and Social Council, at its 8th session, amended this provision, and decided that ten countries should serve for an indefinite period and five countries for three years.

DUTIES

The Commission on Narcotic Drugs is the direct successor of the Advisory Committee on Traffic in Opium and Other Dangerous Drugs of the League of Nations, and under the Protocol of December 11, 1946 all the functions formerly exercised by that body are now its responsibility. It is both the advisory organ to the Economic and Social Council in its task of applying and supervising the application of the various international instruments on narcotic drugs, and at the same time the policy-formulating body on all questions relating to the control of narcotic drugs. It is responsible for making the preliminary studies and drafts for new international agreements. In addition, the Commission has certain supervisory functions.

Under the 1931 and 1936 Conventions the governments undertake to submit to the Secretary-General annual reports on the working of the Conventions in their countries. The Commission is responsible for drawing up the form of these reports and in practice reviews them at each of its annual sessions. From the

Opium Advisory Committee the Commission also inherited the task of examining the seizure reports submitted under Article 23 of the 1931 Convention. The Commission on Narcotic Drugs is a governmental commission. In this capacity it affords a meeting place for many of the officials who are directly responsible for the control of narcotic drugs in their national administrations. Their regular collaboration in this Commission is of enormous service in coordinating the policies of the various governments in this field.

The Commission is, moreover, the appointing authority for one member of the Supervisory Body and one of the three experts appointed from time to time under the 1931 Convention to decide on the control of substances which are capable of being converted into habit-forming drugs.

IMPORTANT RECOMMENDATIONS

Some of the more important recommendations the Commission has made are the following:

That the legalized use of opium for smoking be prohibited;

That countries submit statistics of drugs brought under the 1925 Conventions whether synthetic or not;

That governments which have not submitted annual reports be urged to do so;

That the Secretary-General be instructed to draft a protocol, in accordance with principles approved by the Commission, to bring under international control drugs outside the scope of the 1931 Convention;

That a Commission of Inquiry be sent to Peru to study the effects of coca chewing and investigate the possibilities of limiting the production and regulating the distribution of coca leaves;

That the Secretariat be authorized to begin work on the draft of a single convention to replace the eight existing instruments relating to narcotics, including provisions for limiting the production of narcotic raw materials;

That all countries be urged to submit reports of seizures;

That the United Nations publish a periodical on narcotic drugs;

That synthetic drugs be placed under international control.

These recommendations were approved by the Economic and Social Council.

During the sixth session of the Commission, the United States Delegation reported on illicit heroin traffic in Italy, Turkey, Greece, and China and also illicit opium traffic in Thailand. As a result of this report, the Commission requested the Secretary-General of the United Nations to ask Italy to discontinue the manufacture of heroin and to take punitive measures to bring about cessation of this traffic. Turkey placed restrictions on chemicals required in the manufacture of heroin. As a result of the disclosures regarding Thailand, Burma asked for a United Nations Commission to give guidance to Far Eastern territories in the control of opium.

The Italian situation, which gave rise to wide-spread criticism and anxiety owing to the escape from that country of heroin into the illicit traffic, was confirmed by the fact that, whereas the stock of the drug in Italy at the end of 1950 should have been 306 kilograms, the Italian Government reported a stock of only 142 kilograms, and declared that this disappearance of 164 kilograms was in the course of investigation in the national territory and in the Free Territory of Trieste. Italy temporarily discontinued new production of heroin until the stocks should be disposed of and supervision over the trade in that drug intensified. At least 600 kilograms of diverted Italian heroin was smuggled into the United States and elsewhere from 1948-1952.

During the seventh session of the Commission, the United States Delegation reported a menacing situation in the wholesale smuggling of opium and heroin from Communist China. At the previous session, the United States Delegation had reported that there was offered for sale in Hong Kong 500 tons of opium then in China. This was made the subject of a Resolution by the Economic and Social Council requesting the organs entrusted under the international treaties with the control of narcotic substances to ascertain, if possible, the origin of this opium, the period in which it was collected, the total stocks of opium in China, and whether the cultivation of the opium and the export of opium are still prohibited in China.

An example of the type of discussion held at the United Nations Commission on Narcotic Drugs will be found in the following chapter.

EXPERT COMMITTEE ON DRUGS LIABLE TO PRODUCE ADDICTION

WORLD HEALTH ORGANIZATION (WHO)

CONTROL OF NEW DRUGS

Article 10 of the Convention of 1925 provided for recommendations of the Health Committee of the League of Nations in order to place additional drugs under control. These recommendations, however, are binding only on such countries as expressly accept them. The Health Committee was also authorized to exempt certain preparations containing narcotic drugs from control.

Article 11 of the Convention of 1931 established also a procedure by which new drugs, obtained from the phenanthrene alkaloids of opium or the ecgonine alkaloids of the coca leaf, could be placed under control without requiring consent from the contracting parties. The Paris Protocol of November 19, 1948, created a procedure for placing other drugs, whether synthetic or natural, under international control without requiring consent.

The aforementioned responsibilities of the Health Organization of the League of Nations under the International Conventions of 1925 and 1931, as well as the responsibilities under the Protocol of 1948, for technical consultation on the suppression of drug traffic devolved upon the World Health Organization, a specialized agency of the United Nations. To meet this responsibility, a Committee of five experts technically qualified in the pharmacological and clinical aspects of drug addiction was appointed to advise the WHO on any technical questions concerning this subject which may be referred to it. This Expert Committee is available to the Narcotics Commission of the Economic and Social Council to advise it on technical matters within the competence of WHO. At its fifth session, the executive board decided to change the name of the Expert Committee on Habit-Forming Drugs to Expert Committee on Drugs Liable to Produce Addiction.

FUNCTIONS RELATING TO THE SUBSTANTIVE SCOPE OF CONVENTIONS

The WHO (as formerly the Health Committee of the League of Nations) is authorized:

1. To exempt certain preparations, that cannot give rise to drug addiction on account of the medicaments with which their narcotic components are compounded, and which, in practice, preclude the recovery of the narcotic substances, from the application of the 1925 Convention;

2. To recommend to the parties to the 1925 Convention to place additional narcotic drugs under the control provisions of the Convention; and

3. To decide whether any phenanthrene alkaloid of opium or any ecgonine alkaloids of the coca leaf, which were not in use on 13 July, 1931, are capable of producing addiction or convertible into a drug capable of producing addiction.

The Health Committee had to consult the Permanent Committee of the Office International d'Hygiene Publique before taking these decisions. The WHO, replacing the Health Committee in this capacity, has to consult the Expert Committee on Drugs Liable to Produce Addiction appointed by the Organization, by virtue of the Protocol of 11 December 1946. This expert committee, therefore, takes the place of the former Permanent Committee of the Office International d'Hygiene Publique.

FUNCTIONS UNDER THE 1948 PROTOCOL

The World Health Organization was designated by the 1948 Protocol to decide whether a drug, outside the scope of the 1931 Convention, is capable of producing addiction, or of conversion into a product capable of producing addiction, and, therefore whether this drug should be placed under the regime laid down in the 1931 Convention for drugs of Group I or Group II of this Convention. This authority of the WHO is added to the above-mentioned powers originally possessed by the Health Committee and transferred to the new organization.

It should be pointed out that under the procedure of the 1931 Convention—in contradistinction to that of the 1948 Protocol— the WHO, like the Health Committee before it, cannot always decide the regime under which a drug, that is not by itself addiction-forming but convertible into an addiction-forming drug should fall, is decided under this procedure by a body of three experts of whom one member is elected by the Government which initiated the procedure, another member by the Commission on Narcotic Drugs (formerly by the Advisory Committee on Opium and Other Dangerous Drugs) and the third by the two members so selected.

POWER OF APPOINTMENT

The Health Committee of the League of Nations and the Office International d'Hygiene Publique each had the right to appoint one member of the Supervisory Body. The WHO, replacing the Health Committee and the Office International d'Hygiene Publique, has therefore the right to appoint two members of the Supervisory Body. [Article 5 (6) of the 1931 Convention (original and amended versions).]

SPEED IN CONTROLLING NEW DRUGS

Speed in extending international control to new drugs is essential. Otherwise addiction may be established in various parts of the world and additional stores of dangerous drugs, not accounted for, may be piled up before effective measures of protection can be taken. The procedure by which the WHO (or formerly the Health Committee of the League) examines the properties of a new drug which is suggested for international control, is, of necessity time consuming. Therefore, provisional measures are necessary. The so-called May proposal aimed at preventing manufacture or trade in a new drug (which might be likely to cause addiction), until it should be decided whether to place it under international control. The Convention of 1931 adopted the idea underlying this proposal, by providing that, pending the decision of the Health Committee of the League of

Nations (or, at present, the WHO), control would apply to a new drug obtained from any of the phenanthrene alkaloids of opium or ecgonine alkaloids of the coca leaf.

The new Protocol of 1948 dropped the limitation to certain groups of alkaloids and abandoned the automatic character of these provisional measures. Article 2 authorizes the Commission on Narcotic Drugs to decide whether such measures should be applied. The Commission is the only organ of the United Nations, other than the Security Council and the International Court of Justice, entitled to adopt decisions that are binding on individual Governments—excepting, of course, "corporate" decisions within the jurisdiction of the General Assembly, such as allocation of financial contributions.

DEFINITION OF DRUG ADDICTION

At the request of the Commission on Narcotic Drugs for a definition of "drug addiction," the Expert Committee on Drugs Liable to Produce Addiction drafted the following:

Drug addiction is a state of periodic or chronic intoxication, detrimental to the individual and to society, produced by the repeated consumption of a drug (natural or synthetic). Its characteristics include:

1. An overpowering desire or need (compulsion) to continue taking the drug and to obtain it by any means;

2. A tendency to increase the dose;

3. A psychic (psychological) and sometimes a physical dependence on the effects of the drug.

DEFINITION OF ADDICTION-FORMING DRUGS

The committee was of the opinion that the expression *addiction-forming* and its related grammatical forms should be replaced by *addiction-producing*, etc. The committee then adopted the following definition: *An addiction-producing drug is one which produces addiction as defined.*

The committee wished to emphasize that all available evidence at the present time indicates that any substance which will sustain an established addiction—that is, which will adequately replace the drug which has produced the addiction—must be considered as also capable of producing an addiction.

DEFINITION OF HABIT-FORMING DRUGS

A habit-forming drug is one which is or may be taken repeatedly without the production of all of the characteristics outlined in the definition of addiction and which is not generally considered to be detrimental to the individual and to society.

The committee was of the opinion that the expression *habit-forming* in the sense of *addiction-producing* should be eliminated from all texts.

FUNDAMENTAL STRUCTURE OF AN ADDICTION-PRODUCING DRUG

The committee was of the opinion that the fundamental structure of an addiction-producing drug is that particular arrangement of atoms within the molecule which is responsible for the addiction properties of the drug. In the present state of our knowledge it is not possible to say what part of the molecule of a drug is responsible for its addiction properties. Nevertheless, it is known that certain drugs having, in the main, a common structure produce in some degree a similar addiction. Therefore other substances which have a similar structure must be liable to suspicion as being addiction-producing. It is such analogues which are referred to under Section 1 of this report. Examples of common structure with relation to addicting-production include the groups of which morphine, pethidine, Methadon and cocaine are members. The committee would emphasize that this list is not complete and that probably new compounds of different structure will be developed which are also addiction-producing. Therefore the question of the relation of chemical structure to addiction-producing properties must remain open.

The definition of drug addiction drafted by the committee has been the subject of controversy in the Narcotics Commission and in other quarters.

IV

PROGRESS IN INTERNATIONAL
COOPERATION—PART TWO

THE PRESENTATION OF A MANY-FACETED SUBJECT SUCH AS THE theme of this study is often best accomplished by supplementing analysis and summary by illustration. The reader can then readily correlate the abstract and theoretic with the actual situation as it is found by those whose administrative concern it is. Documenting the preceding chapter, there will be found here examples of the discussions of the UN Commission of Narcotic Drugs which clearly illustrate the political aspects of the subject. There is also presented A Report of the United States Representative on the UN Commission which factually analyzes and details the present situation in a world area that is of first importance in any study of the narcotics problem.

UN COMMISSION ON NARCOTIC DRUGS

EXCERPTS FROM THE SUMMARY RECORDS OF THE HUNDRED
AND EIGHTY-SECOND MEETING, HEADQUARTERS, NEW YORK,
MAY 5, 1952

The CHAIRMAN recalled that at the previous meeting the USSR representative had made certain comments on the United States Government's annual report, with particular reference to the smuggling of narcotics from North Korea and the People's Republic of China. The United States representative had reserved the right to reply to those comments and had expressed the desire to do so at that meeting. He called on the United States Representative.

MR. ANSLINGER *(United States of America)* submitted to the Commission a report dated 10 March 1952 which had been sent to the United States Government by the Supreme Commander for the Allied Powers in Japan.

According to that report, investigations, arrests and seizures in Japan during 1951 proved conclusively that the Chinese Communists were smuggling heroin into Japan. According to the statements of arrested traffickers, profits from the smuggling were used to finance the activities of the Communist Party and to obtain strategic raw materials. All the heroin seized in Japan came from Communist China; it was brought into the country either through Hong Kong or through North Korea. However, only 50 percent of the heroin seized in 1951 bore an indication of origin.

The total amount of heroin seized in Japan in 1951 was 8.783 kgs. and 2,208 traffickers had been arrested. Of these arrested, 377 were Chinese Communists and 269 North Koreans—29.2 percent of the total, although nationals of the People's Republic of China and the Korean People's Republic formed only 2 percent of the total population of Japan.

The heroin seized in Japan was from 83 to 98 percent pure. In the illicit traffic, the price of a bag containing one English pound had risen from $1,861.11 at the beginning of 1951 to $3,611.11 at the end of the year. The price per gram had risen from $9.72 to $27.77, and the retail price paid by addicts was about twenty times higher. At that stage in the retail traffic the purity of the heroin varied between 30 and 70 percent.

The traffic in smuggled heroin had attracted the authorities' attention for the first time at the end of 1947. During 1948, it had increased and in 1949 had attained considerable proportions. In 1950, 1,978 grams of heroin had been seized at Konosaki, on the Japanese coast. It had been brought into Japan by a group of North Korean Communists, with the help of Japanese accomplices. At the same time, 729 grams of heroin bought from a Communist company at Genzan, in North Korea, had been seized at Niigata, also on the coast of Japan. The total of heroin seized in 1950 had been 10 kgs., or three times the amount seized in 1949.

The chief of the Communist Party in Kyushu, implicated in one of the seizures, had said the heroin had been given him by a North Korean called Kyo Son, a member of the central committee of the Communist Party of Rashin (North Korea).

The part played by Kyo Son and the relation between Communist

Party activities and narcotic smuggling had become clear with the arrest of a Japanese called Akira Ito. According to his own statement, Ito at the end of the war joined the army of the People's Republic of China. In September 1947, while he was a member of the crew of a smuggling ship belonging to a Chinese shipowner, Ito had gone to Japan and delivered secret messages to a member of the central committee of the Communist Party and to a notorious trafficker from Formosa who, when arrested later, was found to be in possession of 8.9 grams of heroin. After being arrested in Tokyo in November, 1947, for armed assault and sentenced to ten months' imprisonment, Ito had escaped and rejoined the Chinese Communist army. He had then been given special political training in China and sent to Rashin in North Korea where, after the outbreak of hostilities, he was put in charge of Communist propaganda. In September, 1950, he had again been sent to Japan to find one of the chiefs of the Chinese Communist Party and bring him back to North Korea. The ship in which he traveled had had a cargo of heroin, opium, and santonin, which had been exchanged for textiles, dynamite, and optical lenses.

On 31 August, 1951, during another voyage to Japan, the ship in which Ito was traveling had discharged thirteen cases at Sanrihama, eight of which contained santonin, and had loaded sixteen cases containing dynamite and fuses.

Replying to the USSR representative's statement at the previous meeting that it was absurd to claim that smuggling of narcotic drugs could be carried on in wartime while the coasts of the People's Republic of China were under a very tight blockade, he said that it seemed as if the USSR representative was unaware of the activities of the smugglers; contrary to what he thought, they found war conditions very favourable. A reference to the cases mentioned in the report of the Supreme Commander for the Allied Powers, which all concerned the traffic in heroin between Communist China and North Korea on the one hand and Japan on the other, would confirm that fact. To those cases should be added the large seizure of heroin made at New York on board a Norwegian ship coming from the Far East. The covering of the packages definitely showed that it was of Communist Chinese origin. The case of the traffickers whom agents of the United States Bureau of Narcotics had recently arrested at San Francisco and on whom large quantities of heroin of Hong Kong origin were found might also be mentioned.

The facts mentioned in the SCAP report showed that all the heroin seized in Japan came from Communist China. The heroin seized in

North Korea was of the same type as that seized in Japan, and he referred in that connection to page 27 of document E/CN.7/232/Add.2, which stated that the island of Tsushima was an important relay point in the smuggling of heroin from North Korea to Japan.

As regards the opium traffic, it should be noted that the Hong Kong authorities had seized large quantities of opium originating in Communist China and that a large amount of raw opium of the same origin had been seized in Thailand.

It was obvious from what he had said that the traffic in narcotic drugs in Communist China was increasing all the time and was a serious menace. The Commission should appeal to the authorities in Hong Kong to increase their vigilance and to governments to intensify the campaign against the illicit traffic.

Mr. Zakusov *(Union of Soviet Socialist Republics)* said that the United States Representative's statement was intended to divert the Commission's attention from the problem before it—the campaign against the illicit traffic. His speech contained slanderous assertions, intended to make the problem political, and merely took up the accusations of the United States press that Communist China was trafficking in narcotic drugs with Japan and South Korea in order to undermine the morals of United States troops and to obtain funds for the purchase of war material. . . . They (U. S. troops) used poison gases and bacterial warfare to such an extent that the war in Korea had become organized genocide. It could therefore be easily understood why the United States representative made slanderous attacks against the People's Republic of China. He was vainly trying to divert the attention of world public opinion from the horrors committed by the United States Armed Forces.

Mr. Anslinger *(United States of America)* said he would raise a point of order if the discussions continued on a plane so far removed from the question of narcotic drugs. The USSR representative had violently attacked the United States Government, which had merely communicated to the Commission accurate, detailed facts, supported by irrefutable proofs, on the traffic in narcotic drugs carried on by Communist China. The USSR representative claimed that the information given was inaccurate, but could not prove that. The Commission was waiting for him to produce statistics, documents and reports proving that his accusations were well founded and stating how the production, manufacture and illicit trade in narcotics in Communist China was organized. Instead of submitting such facts, he had merely tried to hide the truth under a mixture of half-truths, lies and offensive words. It was not slanderous to state that Communist China was at the present time the biggest source of the illicit traffic in narcotic drugs in the world; it was a true statement, as would be seen from a study of document E/CN.7/234. Moreover, China was not the only country where drugs entered the illicit traffic. When the Commission had studied the reports of other countries where such traffic was being carried on, their representatives had not made insulting remarks. They had merely given all the explanations requested, said what their governments were doing, and described the measures taken to combat the traffic. The USSR representative's attitude showed that he was unable to refute the facts the United States Government had communicated to the Commission.

The CHAIRMAN recognized that the Commission was an international body, in which all representatives had the right to be heard and to explain their governments' points of view, but it was solely a technical organ which, under its terms of reference, should deal exclusively with questions concerning narcotic drugs. If a representative departed from the one subject with which the Commission was competent to deal, he would be obliged to interrupt the debate and call that member to order.

MR. HSIA (China) recalled that on several occasions at previous sessions he had tried to warn the Commission of the danger to humanity of the change in the Chinese authorities' attitude to narcotic drugs. His statements had been interrupted by points of order on the ground that they had nothing to do with the debate. He could give the Commission many interesting details of the way illicit cultivation and export of opium were being carried on officially in Communist China. As soon as the Red armies occupied a sector, the Communist authorities reorganized opium cultivation. They were not concerned with domestic consumption, but were especially interested in discovering foreign markets. Any merchant who wished to export opium had to obtain a permit from the police—the special trade office—and thus became a legal shipper of opium. The authorities of the special trade office and all the other authorities gave him the assistance he needed to get rid of his opium by illicit means. Smuggling was carried on mainly over the south-eastern frontier. Motorized junks carried the drug to the ships and loading took place at sea. Opium was not, however, the only substance carried in that officially organized smuggling. A morphine factory had been set up in Western China under the auspices of the military authorities. It employed two Japanese experts and two hundred workers and produced 300 lbs. of morphine a day, the major part of which was destined for Japan or the Philippines. By thus officially organizing contraband in narcotic drugs the Communist authorities were trying to obtain foreign exchange in order to buy arms and war material. The Commission would realize the extent of the traffic when it knew that one shipment alone had been valued at U.S. $20,000,000.

MRS. MELCHIOR (*Poland*) was sorry that the question of the representation of the People's Republic of China had been deferred to the next session. It was contrary to all reason that a country with 500 million inhabitants should not be represented on the Commission and thus be able to defend itself against slanderous attacks.

MR. ZAKUSOV (*Union of Soviet Socialist Republics*) wished to know why the Commission considered his protests against the lying accusations against Communist China as political considerations that were not within its competence, but refrained from applying the same criterion when the representative of Nationalist China accused the Communist Chinese authorities of promoting illicit traffic.

He drew the United States representative's attention to the fact that all his information was drawn from the United States press; if the United States representative challenged the evidence in the United States press, that would indicate that the press was not telling the truth.

The USSR Government had been accused of failing to transmit any information on illicit traffic in narcotic drugs for some time; the Permanent Central Opium Board, however, was in a position to testify that the USSR had transmitted such information, although there might have been some delay since the terminology did not exist in Russian. The charge that the USSR had failed to transmit information had perhaps been made by certain countries where drug addiction was rampant and which were envious of the fact that that evil was non-existent in the USSR.

MR. ANSLINGER (*United States of America*) recalled that at a previous meeting, the Chinese representative's statement on the official organization of illicit traffic in Communist China had been cut short by a point of order raised by the USSR representative.

In his country the press was completely free; it was not subjected to any government control and could discharge its duty of informing public opinion without the slightest restraint.

With regard to absence of drug addiction in the USSR, he pointed out that the last prewar report submitted by the USSR in 1937 had mentioned the seizure of several hundred tons of opium for smoking on the Manchurian frontier. That seemed to be a sign that drug addiction did exist in the USSR, unless, of course, the USSR Government did not consider the habit of smoking opium as addiction.

MR. MAY *(Permanent Central Opium Board)* recalled that the Government of the People's Republic of China had not so far replied to his letter of 6 November, 1951, asking for information on the control of narcotic drugs and of opium in particular.

MR. VAILLE *(France)* considered that the USSR representative had pushed propaganda rather far when he had said, implicitly but clearly, that the United States had attacked Communist China. He could not let such an accusation pass uncontested since the United States, far from being an aggressor country, had come to the assistance of South Korea when the latter had fallen victim to aggression by Communist forces from North Korea. As long as strong nations felt it their duty to assist weak nations when the latter were attacked, the world would have reason to hope.

The CHAIRMAN reiterated that members of the Commission were entitled to state their point of view on the illicit traffic in narcotic drugs and on respect for the international obligations assumed by governments, provided that they kept within the limits of courteous discussion. The best example of the procedure that should be followed was that of the investigation that had been undertaken in Peru and Bolivia: the Commission had been asked for a scientific opinion and had been able to study the facts freely because its examination had dealt solely with the coca leaf and political considerations had not supervened. The Commission was a technical body, and it was not competent to discuss political questions or to consider the status of governments. He also reminded the Polish representative that the Commission had decided by 10 votes to 3, with 1 abstention, to defer the question of the representation of China to its eighth session. The discussion would therefore be confined to the question of illicit traffic in narcotic drugs. Regardless of who was speaking, any statement which was not to the point would be ruled out of order and any speaker who failed to comply with the ruling would be interrupted immediately.

MR. SHARMAN *(Canada)* unreservedly approved the Chairman's ruling. He recalled that a number of states, including Canada, made no attempt to hide the fact that drug addiction was a problem in their country. In Chapter V of its annual report (E/CN.7/232), the Canadian Government had indicated the scope of the problem and had stressed that, because large amounts of heroin were reaching Canada, addiction, which must be considered infectious among criminal psychopaths, was on the increase. In reply to a question, he had explained that the narcotic drugs brought illicitly to Canada came from the same source as those which were smuggled into the United States. His delegation shared the United States representative's views and warmly supported his clear and objective statement.

THE ILLICIT NARCOTICS TRAFFIC IN THE FAR EAST

REMARKS OF THE UNITED STATES REPRESENTATIVE AT THE
EIGHTH SESSION OF THE UN COMMISSION ON NARCOTIC
DRUGS, APRIL 15, 1953

After the debate on May 5, 1952, in this Commission on the situation in relation to the smuggling of narcotic drugs from Communist China, the Russian delegate circulated a statement, document E/2233 dated May 27, 1952, by the Ministry of Foreign Affairs of Communist China. The statement alleges that the report submitted by the representative of the United States Government contained the slanderous assertion that Communist China is engaged in the illegal sale of heroin to Japan, and was a baseless fabrication from start to finish; that from the date of its formation, Communist China has consistently and resolutely pursued a policy of the strictest prohibition of opium and other narcotic drugs.

Instead of giving this Commission a factual report on conditions as other governments have done, the Chinese regime delivered a diatribe of abuse to the Commission for listening to the truth, calling it "malicious slander," "shameless dissemination of lying rumors," intrigue and fabrication and endeavored to shift responsibility for the traffic to other governments.

In view of this challenge, I shall furnish the Commission with additional facts on the situation.

The 1950 organization of the Chinese regime for the sale of opium and other narcotics has been carried over into 1953 with the exception that some of the lesser officials have been changed with the top officials remaining the same as before.

At the time the Communists occupied Shensi the district was barren and unproductive so the Communists depended on the cultivation and sale of opium to finance their vast military administration. As a result the organization for the sale of opium and the Communist financial organization were closely correlated, and in the areas dominated by the Communists the free sale of opium and opium-smoking were acknowledged facts and opium was termed a special item.

As soon as the Communists advanced to Manchuria with the support of the Soviets, they put a stop to the free trade of opium in the areas under their domination, but encouraged such trade in areas controlled by the National Government as a strategem.

When the Communists occupied the whole of China, opium-smoking was prohibited in the land by order of the Communist Administrative Department, but it soon became known that traffic in narcotics would be permitted if it was contrived behind the scenes so those who wished to export opium applied to the government organization controlling special items and received licenses to export opium which amounted to a license to buy and sell opium and heroin.

Tientsin and Canton are the chief opium and heroin export centers in China.

Within the Communist government there is the Opium Prohibition Bureau of the Peoples' Government. Within this Bureau the responsible persons are: Po I Po, Chief of the Finance Division; Yie Chih Chuang, Chief of the Trade Division; and Wang Feng Chi, who as Chief of the Hwapei Opium Prohibition Bureau is the actual person in charge.

The Opium Prohibition Bureau amounts to a government monopoly which, in the Tientsin district, is known as the Yuta Concern which is located at 5, Aomen-lu, 10 Ward, Tientsin. Wang Tsu Chen is the head of this concern, Li Tsu Feng is the managing director, and Sung Han Chen is an active partner. Wang is a native of Nanking and was formerly a bandit; Li is a leader of bandits of the Tseng Jen Wang clique; and Sung is a famous opium dealer in Tientsin.

The opium business in the Canton district is monopolized by the South China Trade Bureau under the name of "Lin Chi Hang." Wang Jui Feng, a senior Communist leader, is in charge.

In Hankow stockpiling and transportation are carried out by the

Hankow Agency of the Central and Southern District Tobacco Bureau. The person in charge is Lo Wen, Chief of the Accounting Department of the Central and Southern Army District.

The opium stored in the Shihkiachwang Warehouse, with Kuo Hua Yuen in charge, includes the stockpile of opium which was accumulated before the Communists took charge of the government.

The person in charge of the Northern Shensi Warehouse is Kung Liang who is responsible for the planting, harvesting, and processing of opium in the northern Shensi district.

The Jehol Agency, the original name was the Jehol Agency of the Central Tobacco Bureau Superintendent's Office, is headed by Wu Chih Ho who is in charge of the seeding, harvesting, and processing of opium in the Jehol district.

In Shanghai opium transactions are prohibited, but Chu Yu Lung, who is a public security officer, of the Shanghai district is in charge of the liaison office. His principal job is to negotiate with buyers of opium.

The traffic in narcotics is closely related to other organs of the Communist government. For example, there is a close relation with the Peoples' Bank of China and the Bank of China both of which have local branches throughout the country with special counters to handle loans, extend credit, and handle mortgages for opium. The transportation of opium is guarded by the armed forces. These agencies along with the Tobacco Monopoly are also the organs for handling the transactions in opium. The responsible persons of the Tobacco Monopoly in the various districts have close connections with the big opium dealers. They employ the names of recognized firms for their export business and conduct narcotic transactions under the protection and cover of various subterfuges.

In August of 1950, the following kinds of opium, with the morphine content as shown, were held in the various districts:

ITEM	MORPHINE CONTENT IN PERCENT	QUANTITIES (IN TONS)		
		Tientsin	Canton	Hankow
139	12	20	10	10
138	11.36	20	5	20
No. 1 Camel	7.4	40	20	30
Special Camel	9.8	30	10	10
No. 1 Race Horse	6.3	30	30	10
Special Race Horse	8.4	60	20	10
		200	95	90

Since the quality of opium produced in the northwestern and southwestern districts of China is not uniform and the price varies, Lin Siu Hao who has charge of the laboratory attached to the Shanghai Hygienic Department makes the analysis and decides the standard of opium for export purposes.

Opium is a publicly owned property and the people are not officially permitted to produce, transport, smoke, or sell it privately. Accordingly, all the organs for collecting, purchasing, stockpiling and transporting opium are held exclusively in the hands of the Central Opium Prohibition Bureau. The opium which has been obtained for export by traders in Tientsin is conveyed to Taku on boats by the troops stationed there. The opium stored in Canton is delivered to Shun Chan by the army and sold there.

When transportation is by boats, sampans are used for further transportation and the cost is usually two yuan for each liang.

The method of concluding contracts in the Canton district is not uniform so traders sign contracts with the Central Trade Bureau in Sui Chou. Sometimes opium is traded for chemicals at the Trade Bureau in South China. At the time of the transaction the two parties sign a contract at the Shen Chou Warehouse and the Communists take charge of the transportation.

The above organizations and Chinese, Korean, and Japanese Communists are presently operating to smuggle heroin into Japan, from which country a portion is transshipped to the United States, not only to obtain dollars and strategic materials but also to sabotage by creating narcotic addiction.

One of the most important officials in the Communist regime who is responsible for supplying heroin to the illicit traffic in Japan is Cheng Lao San, Director of the Opium Prohibition Bureau for the states of Chiang Su, Che Chiang, and An Hui—three states or districts around Shanghai. Cheng is probably the biggest narcotic dealer in the Communist regime and is known as the King of Opium.

Under Cheng there is the following organization as far as Japan is concerned: Li Chin Sui is Cheng's top man in Kobe and Tokyo. The following known Communists in Japan pooled ¥5,000,000 and bought a ship in which they sailed from Kobe July 4, 1952: Li Tien Cheng, Kuo Chu Hsiu, Lan Kuo Cheng, Pao Wen Han, Pao Jui Sheng, Liu Kan Lung, and Hsieh Chun Mu. All of them are Chinese.

Since that time only Pao Jui Sheng has been known to return to Japan. He came back to Muroran, Hokkaido, on the Dutch ship *Malacca*.

This group of Chinese Communists and Li Tien Cheng negotiate directly with Cheng Lao San for narcotics. Li Chin Sui is a fugitive on a narcotic charge in Japan. He and two other Chinese smuggled approximately four pounds of heroin from China to Japan which was seized on the M.S. *Hermaline* in Kobe in 1951. It is believed 170 pounds were smuggled into Yokohama shortly before the seizure in Kobe, and that this heroin was purchased by Hsieh Chun Mu and Hung En Chu. The latter Chinese and his associate Hsu Yu Fu have been arrested in Japan for trafficking in heroin. Hung and Hsu were both involved in the *Hermaline* investigation and have the same relationship to Li Chin Sui as Li Tien Cheng, who has recently been arrested in Hong Kong and will be deported.

Cheng Lao San supplied heroin to Shibata Tatsuo, a Japanese who was arrested in Tokyo in April, 1952, when he attempted to sell 720 grams of heroin at the rate of ¥290,000 for 110 grams. The heroin was supplied to this Japanese through Lo Chung Chung who trafficks in heroin under the direction of Cheng Lao San. This heroin was the Red Lion brand. In the early part of 1951 this same brand of heroin which had been smuggled into Japan by air from China was seized in the amount of 676 grams. A further seizure of this Red Lion brand of heroin, which is manufactured in quantity in Tientsin, was made in Kobe July 25, 1952, in the amount of 706 grams with a purity of 89.09 percent. Also on October 6, 1952, in Kobe 1,313 grams of the same Red Lion brand of heroin were seized. This heroin had a purity of 84 percent. In all of these seizures the principals were Chinese. The seizures from China in Kobe although several months apart had packages numbered as follows: In July, 00016 and 00019; in October, 00017, 00018 and 00021. These are Chinese factory numbers.

Chen Kun Yuan, a Chinese living in one of the Mitsui mansions in Hongo Meguro, Tokyo, has a close connection with Cheng Lao San. Chen in 1949-50 shipped large quantities of heroin to Tokyo. He became wealthy from this nefarious traffic and in 1951 set himself up in the lacquer business in Tokyo. Just before Chen moved to Tokyo he shipped 40 pounds of heroin to Tokyo by air, and in June 1952 is reported to have shipped 120 pounds of heroin to Tokyo in one-half pound rubberized bags. In each shipment several one-half pound packages were included, and Chen is reported to have paid the pilot of the aircraft ¥200,000 in each case of shipment for taking the heroin in as his own luggage and for making the delivery in Meguro Ward, Tokyo.

This same Chen was a ringleader of narcotic traffickers in Central

China during World War II, and was arrested in Szechwan Province, China, at which time his property was confiscated. Under the Communist regime in China he again trafficked in heroin and amassed millions in two years. Among his followers are a Korean who has charge of transporting raw opium from Korea and Soviet Russia; a Chinese by the name of Chang Liang Tung who is taking care of Chen's illicit narcotic interests in Tientsin and Shanghai; and another Chinese, Tao Tsing Kang, who is engaged in smuggling heroin. After processing the opium, this group smuggled heroin to Singapore, Japan, and parts of China. About one half of their heroin is reported reaching Japan.

Although Li Chin Sui is not known as a Communist, he is boss of the Chinese underground in Japan and has collected large sums of money which he has turned over to the Communist regime of China. In southern China, the exact location is not known, the Ministry of Trade and Commerce has a branch office and Li Chin Sui has a company by the name of Tung Yung Trading Company which really functions as a branch office of this Ministry and handles medical supplies and other strategic materials for the Communist regime of China.

The above-mentioned Liu Kan Lung is closely associated with the sons of the notorious trafficker in narcotics, Li Sui Sen, a Chinese who was arrested on a narcotic charge in Yokohama in October, 1951. One of Li's sons lives in Shanghai, while three more sons live in other parts of Communist China.

Hsieh Chun Mu, the narcotic trafficker mentioned above was closely associated with Kaji Wataru and Mitsuhashi Masao, military spies and Communists about whom there has recently been so much publicity.

In the Atsugi-Gotemba area, Communists, both Korean and Chinese, with the Koreans outnumbering the Chinese, are using street girls to sell heroin to American military personnel. The Koreans and Chinese have taken over the narcotic traffic around the military bases which have been divided as follows: Sasebo, Chinese; Chitose, Koreans; Asaka, Koreans; Kokura, Chinese and Koreans.

Out of a total of 1,494 narcotic violators arrested in Japan from January through November, 1952, 24.6 percent were Chinese and 16.8 percent were Koreans. Thus this element of the population, less than two percent of the total, accounted for more than 41 percent of the narcotic violators. Narcotic agents arrested 52.2 percent of the violators, while the police and customs arrested 39.4 percent. The remaining arrests were made as a result of cooperation between enforcement agencies. A total of 7,843 grams of heroin and 1,827 grams of raw opium were seized during the eleven months period.

In Yokohama is located what is considered the most active group of Chinese narcotic smugglers in Japan since they are reported to be operating regular smuggling ships, complete with false bottoms, for the purpose of carrying heroin and gold from China in exchange for platinum, American dollars, and other strategic materials. In this group of known Communists are: Wu Hua Kuo who has been arrested on charges of smuggling and bribing customs officials; Yang Wen Ting who is connected with a trading company and who was arrested in 1949 on a smuggling charge; Wang Chung I, Wu Kao Ming, and Chen Jen Chi, all so-called traders. Associated with this group was the trafficker, Hsieh Chun Wu, mentioned above who smuggled himself out of Japan and is now living in Peiping. His family followed him on October 11, 1952. Also in this group of Communists are Pi Lei Kuang, Chien Ta Ming, and Liang Pei Hua. The latter is in charge of the Kanto area (Tokyo Plain) for carrying out directives from Red China, and is reported to have received money and heroin from a Lo Chung Chung, mentioned previously as a lieutenant of Cheng Lao San. This Lo used to obtain heroin and entrust it to merchant seamen to bring to Japan. When the ships arrived, Lo would drive to the wharf to receive the heroin.

The information with respect to the previous paragraph came to light when a day laborer in Yokohama was arrested and interrogated. This laborer, a certain Saito, signed on one of the ships of the smuggling group in Yokohama in December, 1950, at Yutsubo and arrived at Reisui, Korea, after three days. The cargo of clothes was discharged and narcotics packed in cartons was taken aboard and later discharged in Shizuoka prefecture, Japan. During this voyage, Saito who was not an addict was tied hand and foot and forcibly given heroin injections until he acquired a craving for the drug.

In January 1951, Saito, who was now an addict, reached one of the smuggling ships lying off the port of Yokohama by small boat. The ship touched at Oita prefecture. After leaving Japan, about 20 boxes of opium, heroin, watches, and revolvers were loaded at another port and the ship sailed for Dairen where she stayed about one week. At Dairen 20 cardboard boxes of heroin were taken aboard. The ship then sailed for Japan and discharged 10 boxes of narcotics and revolvers near Hirado Island, Nagasaki prefecture. These boxes were addressed to the Kyushu and Hiroshima Branches of the Japanese Communist Party. The ship then passed through the Japan Sea to Hakodate, Hokkaido, where 10 boxes were delivered to a Japanese who met the ship by trawler. After this, two boxes were delivered to a

Korean at Matsushima near Sendai, Japan. Late in January the ship returned to Yokohama where the followers of Wu Hua Kuo came out in a small boat and received 10 boxes. The boxes were put in American military vehicles and hidden in wheat in a lumber room in the back yard of Wu.

Saito left Japan again soon afterward on the same ship. The ship carried 500 tires, 100 cases of beer and 100 cases of Suntory whiskey, and arrived in Shanghai in about one week. The cargo was handed over to Red soldiers who provided documents and the ship sailed for a certain destination where provisions, cakes, crude rubber, and narcotics were loaded. The ship then returned to Shanghai where the cakes were discharged, and then to Dairen where 30 cases of narcotics and revolvers were taken aboard. The next port was Vladivostok where nine Japanese left the ship. Later, off the coast of Chiba prefecture, the revolvers and narcotics were delivered to eight or nine Japanese who came out in a small boat, and the ship returned to Yokohama. More than 20 persons, mostly Chinese, listed in the day laborer's statement are known narcotic violators, and Saito was able to identify photographs of these people.

Among the more important cases which can be traced directly to Communist China are the following:

Seizure in Kobe, July 25, 1952—706 grams of heroin

After the arrest of a Japanese pharmacy owner in Kobe and the seizure of 706 grams of heroin, it was established that Chang Shih Ching, a Chinese male aged thirty-nine had brought the heroin to Kobe from Tokyo and had enlisted the help of the Japanese in disposing of the drug. This heroin was 89.09 percent pure, was manufactured in Tientsin, and bore two Red Lion brand labels.

Seizure in Kobe, July 21, 1952—323 grams of heroin

Narcotic agents negotiated for the purchase of a large quantity of heroin from Sai Sei Ichi, a Korean, and later arrested Sai and Yang Yao Mu, a Chinese aged twenty-seven, in possession of 323 grams of heroin. The heroin was 89 percent pure and was contained in the familiar fabric bags in which large seizures of heroin from China have been made.

Seizure in Yokohama, August 5, 1952—83 grams of heroin

Narcotic agents arrested Wu Chun Sheng, a Chinese aged thirty-seven, after they had seized 83 grams of heroin which Wu had left in the home of a Japanese friend for safekeeping. Wu is a close associate of known Communists and narcotic traffickers smuggling from Communist China who were reported in 1951. These traffickers included Jo A Ki, a Chinese who has been charged with narcotic violations on three occasions.

Seizure in Yokohama, September 28, 1952—37 grams of heroin

Narcotic agents arrested Peng Lan Hsi, a Chinese aged thirty, in Kawasaki, which is a suburb of Yokohama. Heroin in the amount of 37 grams and cutting equipment were found in the possession of Peng who is the boss of Communists in Tsurumi Ward, Yokohama. Peng had obtained the heroin from the notorious narcotic trafficker in Kobe, Chang Shiu Shin, a Chinese, who was arrested in December, 1952.

Seizure in Tokyo, October 3, 1952—3,413 grams of heroin

The Narcotic Squad of Tokyo Metropolitan Police on October 3, 1952, seized 2,100 grams of heroin, 97 percent pure, in two biscuit tins at Toyko International Airport where it had just arrived by air. Following the seizure two Chinese, Chu Sun Chong and So Tung Chung, were arrested in Tokyo after which narcotic agents seized 1,313 grams of heroin in Kobe from officials of the Chuang Tai Trading Company, a Chinese concern. This heroin was 84 percent pure and was contained in 50-gram packages. Although the Kobe seizure was made on information obtained from the seizure in Tokyo, it is believed the Kobe seizure originated with Wang Wu Ming, a Chinese trafficker who is reported to have brought the heroin to Japan. The Tokyo seizure was to have been received by the Ento Enterprise Company where two Chinese had made elaborate plans and had made four large shipments of heroin from Communist China to Tokyo. Twenty-one such shipments were traced by officials investigating the narcotic seizure. In addition to the Chinese, ten Japanese were arrested in Japan.

All information obtained from extensive investigations shows the heroin in Japan originated from Communist China. Some amounts arrive from Horai, China, between Tsingtao and Tientsin. The Communists use crews of merchant ships, crews and passengers of aircraft, as carriers, as well as their own Communist couriers and agents, to smuggle narcotics.

KOREA

Opium and heroin reach all parts of South Korea from north of the 38th Parallel. The usual route is via Kangwa Island off the coast near Inchon. Smugglers move down the coast in small boats and deliver the contraband to Communist guerrillas in the central-western part of South Korea in the general area of Kochang. On December 20, 1952, 13.5 pounds of raw opium which had reached South Korea by this route were seized. The opium was being offered at the rate of U.S. $90 per pound.

Heroin which is being seized in Korea is the familiar light tan, coarse, granular heroin which originates in Communist China, being manufactured in Tientsin. The price in South Korea ranges from U.S. $10 to $20 per gram.

Some of this heroin is brought in by political agents who infiltrate across the front lines from North Korea. In other instances the heroin is smuggled in by ship, plane and courier. It is common knowledge in Korea that any trader who cooperates with the Chinese makes tremendous financial gains. One such Korean who was known to have smuggled narcotics with other contraband is reported to have made 10 billion *Won*.

In 1951, in Pusan there was a group of Koreans who were representatives of a North Korean Trading Company with connections in Mukden and Peiping. These men had limited capital, so they trafficked in heroin to recuperate their fortunes. These trading company representatives now have adequate capital and have built their fortunes on narcotic traffic. Money obtained from the sale of heroin in South Korea finally returns to North Korea and Red China either in the form of dollars or of strategic materials.

When the United Nations forces moved through North Korea in October, 1950, a warehouse of the Ministry of Commerce in Pyongyang contained large quantities of opium and morphine. There were at least 300 boxes of opium weighing from 30 to 50 pounds each, while the morphine in one-pound cans was in a quantity sufficient to fill two or three rooms of approximately 10′ x 12′. In Pyongyang it was found the Ministry of Commerce had a factory for processing opium in the same compound in the west part of the city.

All of the non-addict peddlers of heroin in South Korea originally came from North Korea. This is also true of the chemists.

On August 25, 1952, a clandestine laboratory was seized in a room in Pusan. There were 333 grams of heroin of 81.7% purity and smaller amounts of heroin in process. All the persons arrested in this case had permanent addresses in North Korea, and so far as could be determined all the original narcotics came from North Korea.

The ROK Navy seized 500 grams of heroin from a Communist and were able to prove conclusively that the heroin came from North Korea. This heroin was contained in a metal can with a slip-over top. The container closely resembles the cans in which heroin was purchased from Communist Trading Stores in Genzan, North Korea, in 1949.

The small decks or packages of heroin which can be purchased in Seoul, particularly from Chinese, contain the light tan, coarse-textured heroin which is commonly received from Communist China.

HONG KONG

British authorities are making diligent efforts to suppress the traffic from the Chinese mainland.

Li Choy Fat & Company, which includes Li Choy Fat, Li Sui Po, and Kwok Kam Chi, all three of whom are Chinese, were important traffickers in narcotics for several years. Li Choy Fat was formerly of Shanghai and was deported from Hong Kong June 26, 1952.

Li Choy Fat was carrying on his narcotic smuggling full scale. By sea narcotics were moved in vessels ranging from the smallest junk to the biggest commercial liners. Airline and charter planes are also used, and it is reasonably safe to say there is not an airline operating either to or from the colony which has not been used by narcotic smugglers. Late in 1952 it became firmly established that the movement of gold and narcotic smuggling were closely connected and Communist inspired. It was also discovered the same traffickers were shipping strategic war materials to Communist China.

After the deportation of Li Choy Fat, he was sentenced to fifteen years imprisonment in Taipeh for his smuggling activities.

Millard K. Nasholds, a United States citizen, was arrested in Taipeh on a charge of smuggling 26 pounds of heroin which originated in Communist China. He was sentenced to six years' imprisonment and fined U.S. $5,000.

It has been estimated that from 50 to 100 million dollars of gold were smuggled during a two-year period by individual couriers. To estimate the amount of gold and narcotics being smuggled by all means available it is necessary to realize that on occasions the entire crew of certain ships is involved, that the heroin so smuggled supplies a large part of the international illicit traffic, and that anyone having knowledge of these operations including the crews of ships is afraid to divulge the information because of fear of reprisals against members of the family who are in Communist China.

Li Sui Po, the Chinese mentioned above as being part of the Li Choy Fat & Company, was formerly of Shanghai where he was closely associated with Wu Sze Pau, a Chinese who operated from 76 Jessfield Road, Shanghai. This area became known as the Badlands and reeked with narcotics. Wu and Li were the top gangsters of Shanghai and after the death of Wu, Li Sui Po and the wife of Wu Sze Pau teamed up. Sze Oi Chan, (maiden name of the wife of Wu Sze Pau) was reported to have been directly responsible for many shootings in Shanghai, including the shooting of a policeman who stopped her car from crashing a police barricade.

Li Sui Po and Sze Oi Chan late in 1947 began to operate on intimate terms with Li Choy Fat. On September 9, 1952 Sze Oi Chan (aliases Shee So Chun, Yuen Yuk Ying, Mrs. Wu Yen and Yung Mai Kwong) was arrested after she had sold 25 ounces of heroin through a dance girl for H.K. $9,000. This heroin was marked in the same manner as the heroin mentioned above which was seized in Japan. The package bore the Chinese factory number 00040.

Li Sui Po and Sze Oi Chan sold the Red Lion brand of heroin from Communist China and, although practically destitute in 1947, were wealthy when they were deported in 1952. Since that time the wife of Li Sui Po, who operated a retail clothing store as a front, has been arrested for trafficking in heroin and is facing deportation from Hong Kong.

The third Chinese in the Li Choy Fat & Company was Kwok Kam Chi, a Chiu Chow man from Fukien Province. In addition to smuggling of opium and heroin from Communist China, Kwok was using a ten-room isolated house to process heroin from opium until raided by police in December 1952 after which time Kwok was banished from the colony. With reference to Kwok the *Chi Yin Daily News*, Hong Kong, October 18, 1952, carried the following article: "The Chinese Communists have concentrated all the opium from different parts of the mainland at South China for sale abroad so as to obtain foreign exchange. The sale at two certain places has been greatly increased and at the same time organizations have been established in Kwangtung and Kwangsi provinces to undertake the transport of narcotics and work in collusion with traitorous merchants overseas. The details and intrigue were exposed in detail July 7, 1952, and since that time the authorities have paid special attention and for the past three months have exerted great effort in their investigations. It is understood Kwok and a number of other traffickers have left for Japan within the past two months."

In the Transportation Section of the Tin Shing Company the person who was in charge was Chan Shan Yuk, who was the manager of the Chan Brothers Company and of the Sun Hoi Tung Shipping Company. On December 14, 1952, Chan Shan Yuk and nine other Chinese were charged on a piracy count in an attempt to seize the SS *Nidar*, bound for Japan, and deliver it to the Communists at Canton. Chan Shan Yuk had successfully pirated a ship and delivered it to the Communists some six months previous to the above incident.

Associated with Chan Shan Yuk in the Chan Brothers Company was Judah I. Ezra who was deported from the United States after serving a term of imprisonment after a conviction for narcotic smuggling.

The China Syndicate and Company, late in 1952, offered to deliver 200 tons of opium from Communist China to a broker, L. Y. Goh and Sons, Bangkok, Thailand, on behalf of what was found to be a nonexistent Swiss firm. When approached with reference to large quantities of opium, officials of the China Syndicate and Company stated they could furnish "tons and tons" of opium from stockpiles in Canton. They also stated the opium would be available at Shum Chan, a town in Communist China just across the line from the Hong Kong colony, from which place they would move the opium and deliver it to a ship. The price quoted was U.S. $12.50 per pound. Before opium or heroin will be delivered in quantity the buyer must put his money in escrow in a bank and the seller is likewise represented by a bank. When the purchase is to be consummated the buyer and seller arrange for the delivery of the narcotics after which the money is collected from the bank by the seller. China Syndicate officials also offered 200 *taels* of smoking opium and produced samples. They also stated they would sell any amount of heroin and suggested materials rather than money be provided for payment.

Late in 1952, British authorities in Hong Kong seized 231 ounces of crude morphine which arrived from Bangkok aboard a surface vessel. Shortly before the seizure the narcotics were transferred to a sampan. The morphine originated in Yunnan Province.

The latest seizure in Hong Kong was on February 7, 1953, at which time 26 ounces of heroin were seized from Li Wan, a Chinese, and his two Chinese associates.

Related News Dispatches

The following dispatch appeared in *Hsing Tao Jih Pao,* independent newspaper, Hong Kong, December 28, 1952:

"(Dispatch from Canton) In order to earn more foreign exchange the Chinese Communists are continuing to export opium and other native produce to foreign countries. It was mainly for this purpose that the Chinese Peoples Aviation Company inaugurated a regular passenger-freight service from Chungking to Kunming to Canton via Nanning. A plane brought 25 cases (of about 62 catties each) of raw opium from Kunming to Canton on the afternoon of December 20. It is said that the opium will be exported to a nearby foreign area." [Note: 1 cattie equals 1 1/3 pounds.]

The following item taken from the *Hua Chiao Jih Pao,* conservative newspaper, Hong Kong, February 19, 1953, further substantiates the position of Macao in the traffic of narcotics with Communist China:

"(Dispatch from Swatow) Since the fall of the Teochew-Swatow area into Communist hands over three years ago, peasants living in Kityang and Puning *hsien* in the area, encouraged by the Communist authorities, have planted opium poppies extensively every year in October, providing the biggest source of revenue for the Communists. Last year poppy planters in Kityang and Puning alone sold a total of over 210,000 taels of raw opium to the Communist Teochew-Swatow Trading Company which made big profits by smuggling the drug to Hong Kong and Macao for sale. According to an unconfirmed report, about 80,000 *mow* of opium poppies were planted in October last year in the two *hsien* of Kityang and Puning alone. No wonder the Communist authorities here are paying a great deal of attention to taxing the poppy planters. K'ang Tzu-wen, formerly Vice-Administrative Commissioner for the Teochew-Swatow area, has recently got himself appointed to the post of Chairman of the Board of Directors of the Teochew-Swatow Trading Company so that he may have a finger in the pie.

"Before the planting season for opium poppies began last year, Communist Peoples Bank and Trading Company officials in various *hsien* in the Teochew-Swatow area had already advanced huge sums of money to the planters, most of whom agreed to sell their produce to the Communists in advance at a price determined by the latter."

Another dispatch concerning Hong Kong and Macao's relation to Communist China in the narcotic traffic is that found in the *Kung Shang Jih Pao,* Hong Kong, October 16, 1952:

"(Dispatch from Canton, October 15) Four hundred and fifty cases of raw opium arrived in Canton from Yunnan Province on October 4, 1952. The cases of opium, all of which were sealed by the Provincial Peoples Government of Yunnan, were consigned to a certain firm in Yat Tak Chung Lu, Canton. It was learned that this firm is owned by Ch'en Keng and a certain Yang who is Ch'en Keng's personal representative in Canton. It is also learned the opium was intended for Hong Kong and Macao."

That opium continues to be available for the international traffic is due to the encouragement offered growers by the Chinese Communists as shown by the following dispatch:

"The 8th moon of the lunar calendar is the time for the planting of the poppy, and the Chinese Communist authorities are taking into consideration conditions in various areas in fixing tax tariffs on poppies cultivated. The Kwangtung Communist leader, Yeh Chien-ying, on September 3 issued secret instructions to authorities in the various *hsien* and municipalities in the province to the effect that since the prohibition of poppy cultivation could not be fully enforced in the remote and hilly areas, they might as well enforce the policy of seeking prohibition through taxation so that the people would be made to abandon poppy cultivation voluntarily.

"The taxation rate of 280 catties of grain for every 100 poppy plants cultivated was fixed, and tax evasions would be severely punished. The news amounted to the lifting of the ban on poppy cultivation, and peasants in various parts of Kwangtung were elated.

"In the scores of *hsiang* in the suburbs of Canton, it was stated that all the dry fields would be devoted to poppy cultivation since it brought a greater yield than rice cultivation." (This dispatch is from the *Hsing Tao Jih Pao,* Hong Kong, September 10, 1952.)

Yunnanese opium smugglers into Thailand are often better armed than the police themselves. On one occasion there was a group of one hundred of these smugglers that attacked the police in September, 1952, about 100 miles north of Chiengmai. On another occasion about the same time the smugglers and police fought it out at a point only fifteen miles north of Chiengmai. Prior to this incident on August 28, 1952, a band of the Yunnanese opium smugglers stopped a Chiengmai-bound bus and forced it to wait almost an hour while a caravan of approximately 200 opium carriers crossed the road.

An Associated Press dispatch from Taipeh January 26, 1953 suggests the magnitude of the narcotic smuggling operation by the Chinese Communists:

"The *Tatao News Agency,* recognized publicity medium for the Chinese Nationalist Ministry of the Interior, today alleged that the Chinese Reds were selling huge amounts of narcotics to Southeast Asia and used the proceeds to initiate communist activities. The Agency, which claims to get its information from underground sources on the mainland, said that 1,500,000 ounces of opium and other narcotics had been shipped to the countries of Southeast Asia from the South China province of Kwangse since it was overrun by the Reds in 1949."

PHILIPPINES

Illicit opium and heroin in the Philippines come from Communist China. These narcotics arrive by surface ships and by air. The heroin has the same physical characteristics as the heroin which has been proved to originate in Communist China.

Large scale smuggling into the Philippines from Communist China was disclosed on October 21, 1952, in Manila following the arrest of two Chinese by the police. Arrested and charged with violation of the opium law and facing possible deportation, if found guilty, were Joso Lao Ko Kua, thirty, and Tio Eng Tiong, fifty-four.

SOUTHEASTERN ASIA

That opium from Communist China reaches Malaya in large quantities is shown by the seizure on the Burmese vessel *Hswe Hla Min* at Pulau Paya June 8, 1952. The vessel carried 5,789 pounds of opium, 353 pounds of grey drugs containing morphine, and 25 pounds of brown powder containing morphine. The opium was traced to Communist China and had passed through the Shan States of northern Burma. The group conducting the bartering, buying and selling of the narcotics with Communist China had its headquarters in Rangoon, and the operation was financed from Penang and Singapore. These smugglers had been operating for a considerable period of time and the seizure was the ninth or tenth of a regular series of shipments of opium and other narcotics. It is estimated this group had been responsible for at least 30 tons of opium being smuggled from Communist China in a year.

SMUGGLING TO THE UNITED STATES

As already stated, large quantities of heroin have reached the United States from Communist China. Emissaries have been sent to the United States to arrange for the details of the smuggling transaction. One of the principals in a case in which at least 200 ounces of heroin were smuggled in from Communist China is now serving a ten-year imprisonment sentence. In another case which is still under investigation and in which at least 260 ounces of heroin were smuggled in from Communist China, a defendant has been sentenced to fifteen years imprisonment. In still another case in which an estimated 40 ounces were involved the two defendants were sentenced to five years and to seven years imprisonment. The latest seizure of a comparatively large amount, 36 ounces, was made November 9, 1952 in San Francisco on the S.S. *President Wilson*. A Chinese had brought the heroin from Hong Kong. It was manufactured in Communist China.

INSIDE COMMUNIST CHINA

Large quantities of heroin are manufactured in Communist China all the way from Tsingtao and Tientsin down to Canton. This heroin is of approximately the same percentage of purity, unusually high, and has the same physical characteristics as the heroin from this region over a period of years. In one factory alone in Western China the capacity is 300 pounds per day and all of this is for export.

That the United States is a target of Communist China to be regularly supplied with dollar-earning, health and morale-devastating heroin is shown by the information contained in the following dispatch, the truth of which is borne out by facts previously related in this report:

"(*Toa News Service,* Hong Kong) In order to cover the expenses required for its fundamental construction for fiscal 1953, Communist China is recently using various means to develop the sources of its central and local revenues. According to reliable information gained from the continent, financial and economic organs of Red China's Central Regime met behind closed doors in Peiping in early December and decided to expand sales activities abroad this year, primarily in Japan, Southeast Asian countries and the United States.

"According to information reaching from Peiping, financial and economic leaders of the Foreign Trade, Commercial and Financial Divisions of the Chinese Communist Regime as well as of the Southwest, South China and North China Districts held a secret meeting in Peiping on December 5. The meeting it says was presided over by Po I Po, Chief of the Finance Division; and attended by Yeh Li Chuang, Chief of the Foreign Trade Division; Yao I Lin, Vice-Chief of the Commercial Department; Chen Hsi Shih, Vice-Chairman of the

Southwest Military Political Committee; Liu Hsiu Feng, Chairman of the North China Financial and Economic Committee; Hsiu Hsian, Vice-Chairman of the South China Financial and Economic Committee; and others.

"Information which leaked out of the conference indicates that the revenue obtained from its sales of narcotics abroad for fiscal 1952 reached approximately 70,000,000 American dollars, out of which 30,000,000 dollars were sent to the Chinese Communist Regime and the rest was spent for party activities as well as information collection; that the largest outlet was Southeast Asia countries, followed by Japan and the United States.

"The drugs when shipped directly from the continent are sent via Tientsin and Tangku in the north and Kwangchow Bay and Nampo Island southeast of Yangchiang, Kwangtung Province, in the south. The same report says that crude opium of over 1,000 tons was sent abroad through Kwangchow during the one-year period from June 1951 to June 1952.

"Heretofore the sales abroad of opium and other narcotics were handled directly by the Finance Division of the Chinese Communist Regime. However, it is reported, it was decided at the conference that the sales method would be changed, and that the business would be conducted exclusively by the Overseas Trade Division. Further, the following important decisions were made at the conference:

1. Qualities and grades of narcotics gathered from various districts will be standardized and definite marks will be established. Crude opium, for example, was divided into several grades in the past and this was a factor in the sales thereof. However, under the new system the various sorts of opium will be standardized.

2. Export promotion regulations are established, and private concerns are permitted to participate in the transportation and sale. Moreover discriminatory prices are established so that merchants may be encouraged to sell narcotics abroad more aggressively.

3. Powerful leaders are sent secretly to various places to encourage sales activities, especially in Tokyo, Singapore, Bombay, and other places. For this purpose, the Social Division and the South China Bureau of the Chinese Communist Regime have decided to select and send those most experienced in selling narcotics and to place them in charge of promoting sales.

4. Each local organ of the Communist China Regime is prohibited from wantonly sending large quantities of narcotics overseas for sale for fear it may affect the overseas market. However, each such local organ is permitted to derive 20% of its income from the sales of narcotics.

"According to the Peiping information, Communist China's activities to smuggle narcotics into the Japan area are conducted under the Tientsin Office of the Overseas Trade Division. There are at present approximately forty smugglers in the Tientsin area who sail from Tangku to the vicinity of Kyushu and return carrying cargoes of gasoline, steel ingots, automobile parts, medical instruments, and other material. It is clear that non-Chinese are also participating in the smuggling organization."

(The preceding was published in the Tokyo *Shimbun*, January 8, 1953.)

The smuggling of gold from Saigon and Bangkok, which is obtained from Europe on letters of credit which are paid in foreign exchange within one week after receipt of the gold, the exchange of the gold with Communist China for narcotics and other high-value exports which in turn are sold to obtain foreign exchange to pay for the original letters of credit, is the explanation which most nearly fits the actual conditions prevailing in the Far East. The foreign exchange is supplied from all countries to which the narcotics are destined.

Seizures

Seizures during 1952 which may be attributed to Communist China are as follows:

Hong Kong	Raw opium	935	kgs.	
	Morphine hydro-chloride	5	kgs.	via Bangkok
Singapore	Raw opium	950	kgs.	
	Morphine hydro-chloride	4	kgs.	via Bangkok
Malaya	Raw opium	3879	kgs.	
	Morphine alkaloids	180	kgs.	
Marseilles	Heroin	1	kg.	
Taiwan	Raw opium	2	kgs.	
	Heroin	11.8	kgs.	

Honolulu	Prepared opium	.224 kgs.	via Hong Kong
United States	Heroin	1.7 kgs.	In magazines from Hong Kong
	Heroin	.096 kgs.	At Wilmington from crew member of S.S. *President Jefferson,* from Hong Kong
Japan	Heroin	7.843 kgs.	
	Raw opium	1.827 kgs.	

(NOTE: *In addition to the above a considerable amount of heroin has been seized by Hong Kong authorities in 25-ounce lots. These seizures would total at least three kilograms)*

CONCLUSION

While Communist China has denied the allegation that she is supplying a large part of the narcotics in the international illicit traffic, and has stated that in fact a strict control has been placed on narcotics, the above portion of this report and the following extracts and dispatches from newspapers and documents show: that traffic in narcotics has been encouraged for monetary reasons and sabotage; that cultivation of the poppy plant has not been prohibited; and that efforts to control addiction within Communist China have been feeble and ineffectual since the authorities, realizing the terrible and lasting scars on any civilization which widespread addiction guarantees, have relied on fanning the fanaticism of communism to encourage abstention from narcotics, have taken at face value declarations from addicts that they were "cured" even while unofficially these addicts were still receiving narcotics, and have from all indications created a staggering incidence of addiction within Communist China. There can be little doubt of the true purposes of Communist China in the organized sale of narcotics. These purposes include monetary gain, financing political activities in various countries, and sabotage. The Communists have planned well and know a well-trained soldier becomes a liability and a security risk from the moment he first takes a shot of heroin.

The following throw considerable light on the true situation in Communist China:

An editorial in the *South China Morning Post,* Hong Kong, July 7, 1952, remarks as follows:

"Peking declared these stories were fabrications and insisted that it has 'consistently and determinedly adopted as well as enforced the policy of strict prohibition.' The pro-Nationalist newspapers here recently asserted that poppies were planted in many parts of Kwangtung and that the new authorities like the old were content to tax it heavily rather than enforce the ban. On the other hand the pro-Communist papers say the Regime has made 'definite progress in suppression' since the Suppression Commission was formed in Canton in 1950. It added however that though the peasants had agreed not to plant the poppy, it was necessary that 'the suppression movement must be continued and made into a mass movement for thorough realization.' This indicates that the ban is not effective. But it is significant that when the authorities seized off Penang a single consignment of 6,000 pounds of opium—half the total world seizures last year—it was described as 'Burmese opium.' "

Another dispatch from the *Hua Chio Jih Pao,* Hong Kong, October 22, 1952, is as follows:

"The Chinese Communist authorities appear to be pushing with great vigor the campaign for the suppression of opium in the various *hsien* on Hainan Island and in southern Kwangtung. Actually the addicts are required to be cured in stages and meantime opium is sold by the authorities to smokers who have been duly registered."

All available reports from the mainland press clearly indicate continued use of and traffic in narcotic drugs within Communist China. The Communists have carefully avoided mention of traffic out of Communist China, but the *Nan Fang Jih Pao,* Canton, editorial of June 3, 1952, stressed the fact that Canton's proximity to Hong Kong, Macao, and Indo-China facilitated drug smuggling, and added that Canton continued to be the principal center of narcotic traffic in Asia.

On May 19, 1952, the Hankow *Ch'ang Chiang Jih Pao* carried an article covering a meeting of the Opium and Narcotics Suppression Committee on May 13-16. The chairman of the Committee, Chang Nan Hsien, stressed the need of a mass movement for the suppression of opium and narcotics. The vice chairman followed by analyzing the causes leading to the situation being still serious. He pointed out the failure of the full mobilization of the masses and reliance on them for wiping out the evil. He said the mass movement to be launched beginning with the prohibition of transportation, the prohibition of preparation, and the prohibition of marketing, after which the prohibition of poppy cultivation and smoking and use of narcotics would be easy of accomplishment. Cheng Shao Wen was the official who made this statement.

On June 4, 1952 the same newspaper carried a report by this same vice chairman of the Committee, Cheng Shao Wen. After stating that the prohibition of poppy cultivation had been "basically accomplished in the Central-South region," he gave a resumé which indicates the extent of narcotic traffic within Communist China. In the districts of Honan, Changsha, Liuchow, Nanning, Kwelin, Wuchow, Ichang, Shasih and Yuanling, Cheng Shao Wen stated that more than 18,000 cases of opium trafficking had been disposed of, 2 million tacls of opium had been seized and several thousand taels of heroin had also been seized.

In Canton, Cheng continued, from the time the Communists took over until March, 1952, there were 271 cases of opium traffic and manufacture disposed of, 3,943 opium dens were discovered, 7,267 addicts were arrested, and 2,000 taels of opium, 200 taels of morphine, and 300 taels of heroin were seized. He added that of the 5,723 addicts registered in Canton 90 percent had been cured and in a part of Hunan province where 90 percent of the households were opium smoking and 80-90 percent were addicts, in two years the number of addicts was reduced to 3.5 percent and the number of opium smoking households to about 11 percent.

In suggesting that the opium evil is still rampant and suppression must be resolutely carried out Cheng stated "opium and narcotics have been chiefly imported from abroad to the Central-South region." He made this further statement: "When nobody engages himself in opium traffic, poppy growers will not be able to sell their products and will cease to grow poppies. When no opium can be bought, the addicts will certainly cease to smoke opium."

In the *Nan Fang Jih Pao*, Canton, June 3, 1952, Ku Kuan Hsien, vice chairman, Canton Municipal Committee for Suppression of Opium and Narcotics, stated: "The suppression of opium and narcotic trafficking and manufacturing was carried out together with the suppression of poppy cultivation and the smoking of opium, but this had not been carried out on an organized basis and achievements have not been marked."

Here we have the words of Chinese Communist newspapers in

contrast to their Foreign Minister's statement that our report is fabrication.

Further statements made by Cheng Shao Wen as published in the June 4, 1952, issue of the Hankow *Ch'ang Chiang Pao,* are:

"The opium evil is still rampant, especially opium trafficking. A number of unscrupulous merchants such as Ho Hung Fu have smuggled opium to poison the people and destroy the fatherland with a view to profiteering. Since the liberation, narcotic smugglers have smuggled narcotics through the various railways of the Hengyang Railway Administration amounting to 804,879 taels of opium, 109,414 taels of morphine, and 35,297 taels of heroin which have been distributed to 297 merchants in the cities along the railway lines of the Chengchow Railway Administration. In the past three years a total of 38,028 taels of opium and 13,475 taels of heroin have been smuggled and transported through railway lines.

"During the 5-anti movement in Hankow, according to data and materials from denunciation and frank exposures by the merchants, there were 451 traffickers and smugglers who had smuggled and transported 559,421 taels of opium, 278,731 taels of morphia, and 302,540 taels of heroin. During the 5-anti movement in Nanning, according to data and materials from denunciations and frank exposures, of the 32 categories of trade, 459 firms smuggled and transported a total of more than 800,000 taels of narcotics. As the quantity of narcotics smuggled was so great there must be a large number of addicts. According to estimates of the Department of Public Security of the Central-South MAC there are 81,300 addicts in Honan Province, constituting approximately 27 percent of the population.

In the Canton *Nan Fang Jih Pao,* June 3, 1952, it was stated:

"The organizations and machineries for the suppression of opium and narcotics have not been established, or are not developed in a wholesale manner. Too great leniency has been adopted in the disposal of drug cases." The following statement is also made: "The traffickers used Canton as the center to distribute the drugs to leading cities in the Southwest, Central-South, East China and North-West regions. Many of the unscrupulous merchants have colluded with corrupt elements in shipping, railway and highway organs to carry out the evil traffic. They have even bribed some of the retained personnel in the organs of public security, tax revenue and maritime customs to harbor them. The data and materials exposed through the 3-anti and 5-anti movements have evidently shown that this situation is prevalent in large cities, as well as in medium and small cities. The amount of narcotics smuggled each time has been estimated at more than 1,000 taels, and even as much as from 40,000-100,000 taels. The narcotic 'king' even dared to sneak into Canton to make arrangements for his narcotic traffic. The use of opium and narcotics is still being constantly discovered in cities."

These lesser officials must indeed be naive to make such statements when the Communist Government of China is doing everything possible to cultivate and encourage traffic in narcotics, at least outside China, with China.

Against all the evidence contained herein the statements of the Ministry of Foreign Affairs of the Chinese Communist Regime, as published in United Nations Document E/2233, May 27, 1952, that "the sale of opium and other narcotics is thus completely illegal in Communist China" and "the Chinese Communist Regime, together with the whole Chinese people, protests in the strongest terms against the lying report directed against Communist China by the representative of the United States Government" have little weight indeed.

The evidence for 1952 is in and, added to that of 1951 and prior years, is irrefutable.

UN COMMISSION ON NARCOTIC DRUGS

EXCERPTS FROM THE SUMMARY RECORD OF THE TWO HUNDRED AND TENTH MEETING, HEADQUARTERS, NEW YORK, APRIL 14 AND 15, 1953

MR. ZONOV *(Union of Soviet Socialist Republics)* said that his statement at the previous meeting had evidently been misunderstood by the French representative. He wished to make it clear that, in referring to accusations brought against the People's Republic of China, he had had in mind political accusations against a specific country and government and not individual violations of narcotics regulations.

He failed to understand the assertion which the United States representative had made at the same meeting that the USSR had not submitted a report for the year 1952. The USSR invariably submitted an Annual Report, which always included information relating to chapter V. [Here and elsewhere reference to the chapter is to the Annual Report of the individual country wherein the same subject matter is treated in the same chapter as a uniform pattern for all Reports.]

At the invitation of the Chairman, Mr. Devakul (Observer for Thailand) took a seat at the Commission table.

The CHAIRMAN welcomed the observer for Thailand and recalled the invitation the Commission had extended to the Government of Thailand at the beginning of the session to be represented at the conference table during the discussion of item 8 of its agenda—abolition of opium smoking in the Far East.

In reply to MR. VAILLE *(France)* and MR. OR *(Turkey)*, MR. DEVA-KUL *(Thailand)* said that opium was not cultivated in Thailand except in the north of the country where, as in neighboring countries, control was difficult.

MR. ANSLINGER *(United States of America)* pointed out that Thailand was the only country which still permitted opium smoking and enquired how supplies of opium were obtained for smoking dens, if neither the cultivation nor the importation of opium was authorized.

MR. DEVAKUL *(Observer for Thailand)* replied that, while raw opium was occasionally imported into Thailand, the supplies for smoking dens were mainly derived from seizures.

Since many factors which were not purely technical were involved in the situation in Thailand, he felt that a public statement on the matter would be somewhat embarrassing and that it would be more appropriate for the information requested by the United States representative to be obtained through diplomatic channels. As the United States representative was aware, the Government of Thailand was attempting gradually to suppress the traffic in opium. Legislation would not be effective for the purpose and might in fact make the situation worse. The traffic in opium did not originate in Thailand and had increased substantially since the war, a state of affairs to which political conditions in northern Burma and Indochina had contributed.

MR. ANSLINGER *(United States of America)* proposed that further discussion of the matter should be postponed until the Commission was dealing with item 8 of its agenda relating to the abolition of opium smoking.

It was so decided.

Mr. Devakul (Thailand) withdrew.

The CHAIRMAN commented on the small number of countries which had responded to Economic and Social Council resolution 436 (XIV) C and said that any further replies received by the Secretariat would be submitted to the Commission at its next session.

MR. KRUYSSE *(Netherlands)* suggested that, in circulating replies from governments, it would be useful if the Secretariat in future reproduced the resolution to which the replies related.

MR. CELINSKI *(Secretary of the Commission)* said that the Netherlands representative's suggestion would be noted.

MR. NIKOLIC *(Yugoslavia)* enquired why there was no reference to Yugoslavia in chapter II of the document, since to his certain knowledge Yugoslavia had submitted an annual report for 1952.

MR. HUANG *(Secretariat)* replied that the report for Yugoslavia had been received by the Secretariat on 3 March 1953. It had not been included in chapter II of the document because it had provided no information on chapter V.

MR. ANSLINGER *(United States of America)* pointed out with reference to chapter III of the document that by far the largest seizure of prepared opium had been reported by Iran. He wondered what the reason for that was.

MR. KRISHNAMOORTHY *(India)* and MR. ANSLINGER *(United States of America)* noted that in three of the cases of the smuggling of raw opium and morphine by air mentioned in chapter V of the document, the aircraft had come from Bangkok. In view of the fact that Thailand neither cultivated nor imported opium, some explanation seemed indicated.

MR. EZZAT *(Egypt)* drew attention to the statement in paragraph 42 (1) in chapter V that raw opium had, as usual, been smuggled into Egypt from the East. The phrase "as usual" was particularly appropriate, since 95 per cent of the narcotic drugs entering Egypt did so across its eastern borders.

MR. ANSLINGER *(United States of America)* said with reference to chapter VII clandestine manufacture was extremely important. He congratulated the French Government on its reports on clandestine laboratories which contained all the needed information and hoped that other governments would emulate the French example.

MR. SHARMAN *(Canada)* endorsed the United States representative's remarks, adding that under the International Conventions governments had agreed to report on important cases of illicit traffic. He thought that any case involving a discovery of a clandestine laboratory should be deemed important and reported automatically.

MR. NIKOLIC *(Yugoslavia)* pointed out that at the previous session the Economic and Social Council, at the recommendation of the Commission had adopted largely at the insistence of the United States representative, a resolution on illicit trafficking by the crews of merchant ships and civil aircraft (436 (XIV)). He wondered, therefore, how to interpret the fact that, according to chapter VIII of document E/CN.7/252, over half of the ships reportedly implicated in seizures during 1952 were of United States registry. Even more disquieting was the fact that certain ships of United States registry had been mentioned over and over again in the reports. He thought the intention in adopting the resolution (436 (XIV)) had been to ensure that such persons lost their seamen's licenses.

The CHAIRMAN pointed out that under the resolution governments were required to report only on crewmen convicted on or after 1 January 1953.

MR. ANSLINGER (*United States of America*) said that the United States had enacted legislation providing penalties of $50 per ounce for the master of any ship involved in the smuggling of narcotic drugs. He pointed out that seizures were often made in ports outside the United States. It would greatly help the fight against the illicit traffic if other countries would adopt penalties as heavy as those imposed in the United States. Before the Second World War certain captains had been fined as much as $750,000 and the shipping companies had cooperated very effectively in eliminating smuggling. Legislation which provided penalties only for drugs found aboard without imposing a fine on the master of the ship was inadequate.

There was no doubt that smuggling by seamen constituted the largest source of drugs for the illicit traffic and in compliance with the Council resolution the United States would submit by 1 July 1953 a lengthy list of seamen convicted on charges of smuggling whose licenses had been revoked. He hoped that other governments would act promptly under the resolution and submit similar lists to the Secretariat as soon as possible for immediate circulation to governments. That was essential to prevent persons convicted in one country from seeking berths on ships of other nationalities.

MR. SHARMAN (*Canada*) pointed out that the nationality of a ship was not always indicative. For example, the ship of Canadian registry mentioned in chapter VIII was beyond the control of the Canadian Government. It was not manned by Canadians and had not approached Canadian waters for many years but operated in the vicinity of Macao far beyond the limits of Canadian jurisdiction. He assured the Commission that the Canadian Government would very much like to get control of the ship.

MR. NIKOLIC (*Yugoslavia*) observed that under maritime law a ship was subject to the laws of its country of registry.

The CHAIRMAN said that the Secretary-General had communicated Economic and Social Council resolution (436 (XIV)) to governments and was awaiting their replies.

MR. ANSLINGER *(United States of America)* suggested that the memorandum on the illicit traffic prepared by the Secretary-General for the Commission's next session should contain a special chapter on smuggling by seamen.

It was so agreed.

The CHAIRMAN proposed that the foregoing discussion should be considered as disposing of item 7 (d) of the agenda.

It was so agreed.

MR. KRUYSSE *(Netherlands)* said with reference to chapter IX that he had noted with interest that prices for illicit drugs had been quoted per unit of weight which made it possible to make certain comparisons. Of course, as prices were affected by rates of exchange, the figures would have to be interpreted with that in mind. The chapter showed a distinct improvement over the former method of presentation.

MR. EZZAT *(Egypt)* drew attention to the great difference in the prices of opium and Indian hemp in Israel and in Egypt. In Israel, opium was quoted at approximately $200 to $250 per kilogram and Indian hemp ranged between $330 and $400 whereas in Egypt the price of opium per kilogram ranged from $13,000 to $15,000 while Indian hemp fetched from $900 to $12,000. That reflected the excellent work being accomplished by the Egyptian anti-narcotics administration and the Narcotics Bureau of the Arab League.

MR. SHARMAN *(Canada)* referring to chapter X said that the Canadian report had mentioned the effectiveness of whippings in deterring certain criminals who had been inducing young people to take drugs and he asked that the paragraph on Canada should be amended to refer to the penalty.

MR. HUANG *(Secretariat)* said the necessary corrigendum would be issued.

MR. NIKOLIC *(Yugoslavia)* said it would seem from the report on Hong Kong either that narcotics offenders were subject only to fines or that there had been no offenses in 1952 serious enough to be punished by imprisonment.

MR. HUANG *(Secretariat)* said that chapter X did not refer to legislation in general but was merely a compilation of the penalties mentioned specifically in the seizure report.

MR. ANSLINGER *(United States of America)* said he was not satisfied with the penalties imposed in the United States on narcotic drug traffickers although they were usually heavier than those imposed elsewhere. He suggested that the Commission might consider that question when it took up the problem of laws and regulations. It was encouraging to note the United Kingdom report that a sentence of three years had been imposed for the unlawful possession of Indian hemp.

MR. WALKER (United Kingdom) said that that was the highest sentence yet recorded in the United Kingdom for that offense. The court had taken into account the fact that the person concerned was of bad character and had been previously convicted for the same offense. It had also been aware of the social menace of Indian hemp.

MR. EZZAT (Egypt) said that the penalties reported in the paragraph on Egypt had been imposed under the old, comparatively lenient legislation. Decree Law No. 351 promulgated on 25 December 1952 imposed much higher penalties including a maximum sentence of life imprisonment and fines ranging from £E 3,000 to 10,000.

MR. SHARMAN (Canada) thought the reports on Hong Kong should be reviewed as it was his impression that prison terms had also been imposed in 1952.

MR. WALKER (United Kingdom) pointed out in connection with Hong Kong that the summary of annual reports of governments for 1951 referred on page 49 to penalties including fines up to $HK 10,000 ($1,750) or imprisonment for terms up to two years, or both, and in many cases banishment had been imposed.

MR. HUANG (Secretariat) said that prison terms had been mentioned in the Annual Report for 1951 in conjunction with penalties imposed in Hong Kong.

The CHAIRMAN suggested that the Commission should note the various documents it had considered on the illicit traffic with appreciation, subject to the comments made by the various members during the debate. The question of the illicit traffic in Italy and the Far East was still pending.

MR. ZONOV (Union of Soviet Socialist Republics) pointed out that the Commission had not yet finished with chapters V of Annual Reports for the year 1952 or with the summary of Annual Reports of governments for 1951. He had said at the very outset of the debate that he had a few comments to make on the summary and he wondered when he would be given an opportunity to speak.

MR. WALKER (United Kingdom) suggested that the Commission should postpone taking note of the summary of Annual Reports of governments for 1951 until it had finished its consideration of the item on illicit traffic.

The CHAIRMAN pointed out that at the previous meeting he had specifically called for comments on the summary of Annual Reports of governments but as no one had asked for the floor he had assumed that the debate was concluded. The Commission could, however, postpone its final action on the various documents until the debate on the illicit traffic had been concluded.

MR. ZONOV *(Union of Soviet Socialist Republics)* suggested that the Commission should follow its customary procedure of putting the question to the vote after the debate had been concluded.

MR. ANSLINGER *(United States of America)* suggested that the most convenient procedure in the circumstances might be to take up the item concerning illicit traffic in Italy at the present meeting, reserving the item on illicit traffic in the Far East for the following one, at which there would be opportunity for the USSR representative to bring up the points he had in mind.

MR. VAILLE *(France)* supported the United States proposal.

The United States proposal was adopted unanimously.

* * *

MR. VAILLE *(France)* said that the French newspaper *France-Soir* of 18 March 1953 contained reports concerning attempts to cover up illicit traffic in heroin in Italy, the drug being put on the market, at a low price, as codeine. He doubted the veracity of the reports, which he had compared with those submitted by the Italian Government to the Secretariat, but hoped that the Observer for Italy would have an opportunity of clarifying the situation.

MR. CANAPERIA *(Observer for Italy)* was glad of the opportunity accorded him to make a statement to the Commission on behalf of the Italian Government. His presence indicated his Government's respect for the Commission and its desire to cooperate in the suppression of illicit traffic.

His Government's main work in that connection was recorded in the various reports which the Commission had recently examined. He thanked the United States representative for his words of appreciation regarding that work. During the last twelve months twenty-nine police operations concerned with illicit traffic had been carried out, leading to the seizure of 22 kilograms of heroin, 1 kg. 650 gr. of opium, 627 grams of cocaine, and some smaller quantities of other drugs. All those responsible were prosecuted in the courts. He felt that those activities were proof of his Government's increased efforts and a successful contribution to the campaign against the international drug traffic.

Concerning the Schiapparelli case, he stated that the Schiapparelli firm, an old-established Turin firm of pharmaceutical and chemical products, had been granted the authorization to extract and transform alkaloids from opium in 1942. Like all such firms, it was under strict periodical inspection and nothing irregular had been found during the inspections carried out in 1952 and in previous years. Investigations carried out towards the end of 1952 following the discovery of a case of illicit traffic by a wholesaler had disclosed a connection between the proprietor of the firm concerned and Professor Migliardi, technical director and general manager of the Schiapparelli company. A further inspection of the Schiapparelli company at the beginning of 1953 had revealed that a quantity of heroin, estimated by the Financial Police at 350-400 kg., had been manufactured and illegally disposed of by Professor Migliardi since 1948, who, taking advantage of his position, had been able to divert from normal production a quantity of morphine to be transformed illicitly into heroin. Although the initial inquiries had indicated that Professor Migliardi was solely responsible, the operations of the firm had been suspended by the competent authorities; further inquiries had confirmed the exclusive responsibility of Professor Migliardi, who had been prosecuted for the clandestine production of and illegal trafficking in narcotics, and the suspension had therefore been of limited duration. The exact quantity of heroin illegally manufactured was being determined by a commission of technical experts at the request of the judicial authorities. Since the Financial Police's estimate, which had been based on indirect calculations, might have been exaggerated, it was probable that the episode, which had been exploited internationally by rival national firms, would be reduced to more modest proportions. In any event, the Italian Government would take any further action required.

Concerning the Commission's recommendation that the Italian Government should completely prohibit the manufacture of heroin in Italy, he recalled that production had been suspended since July 1951. Stocks at that time had been 78 kilograms, representing approximately a one and a half year's supply for normal consumption, but of that total, 28 kilograms still remained at the present date. Seventeen kilograms of that were held by the military medical authorities and the remaining 11 kilograms were divided in small quantities among narcotics manufacturers, pharmaceutical firms (for use in the production of medicines), and registered wholesalers. The heroin held by narcotics manufacturers was used exclusively by the National Public Health Department for the direct replenishment of the stocks of hospitals and sanatoria on the basis of periodical and appropriately certified requests. The question of complete prohibition was still under consideration by the Italian Government. As objections had been raised by the medical authorities on the grounds that it was not possible to replace heroin for therapeutical purposes by synthetic products, the question had been placed before the National Council of Health which had then requested further information on the subject. He was confident that at the next WHO Assembly, in May, the Italian Government would be able to give a favorable answer on the subject, but at present it was awaiting the advice of the National Council of Health, which would hold its session on 21 April.

MR. ANSLINGER *(United States of America)* thanked the Observer for Italy for his information. In view of the large diversion of heroin into the illicit traffic he would like to know what the position of the Schiapparelli firm would be in the future. He understood that another firm had been involved in a drug contravention two years ago but that the court had not yet reached a decision in the case. He was particularly interested in those matters because much of the heroin which entered the illicit market in Italy was later smuggled into the United States. He hoped the Italian Government would give favorable consideration to the complete prohibition of the manufacture of heroin.

MR. CANAPERIA *(Observer for Italy)* explained that after the second police investigation in the Schiapparelli case, as a result of which Professor Migliardi was found to be the only member of the firm involved, it was not possible, under the law, to maintain the suspension of the firm's activities. He was fully aware of that deficiency in the Italian legislation and said that new legislation was being prepared which would provide for such cases. Concerning the second query, the facts were that court proceedings had been taken against Mr. Calascibetta, a director of the S.A.C.E. firm of wholesalers, for illicit traffic in narcotics and the license of the firm had been revoked.

MR. KRISHNAMOORTHY *(India)*, answering a question raised by the Canadian representative at a previous meeting concerning the seizure of a quantity of opium at Simla, said that the latest information from his Government was that the case was still under trial. If he received further information before leaving New York he would report it to the Commission.

*   *   *

MR. ANSLINGER *(United States of America)* referred to a case of substantial diversions of narcotic drugs imported into Ecuador on certificates issued by the United States, the United Kingdom, and Switzerland and asked the Secretariat to request the Ecuadorean Government for a seizure report concerning them.

MR. WALKER *(United Kingdom)* supported the United States representative's request.

The CHAIRMAN said that the Secretariat would take note of the request.

*   *   *

MR. VAILLE *(France)*, continuing the previous day's discussion [situation in Italy], asked the Italian Observer for additional information on the Schiapparelli case. He wished to know what quantities of heroin had been diverted, whether Professor Migliardi had been arrested, and whether he had been convicted, and if so, what penalties had been imposed. Furthermore, he was surprised that the firm in question, which had failed to exercise effective control over its staff and the outgo of narcotic drugs, had not been prosecuted. If it was not possible under Italian law to revoke the firm's license, he wondered what methods were followed in Italy with regard to licenses and whether the number of manufacturers in that country would not increase unduly, contrary to the spirit of the conventions.

MR. CANAPERIA *(Italy)* stated that it was difficult to estimate exactly the quantities of heroin diverted, for they could be established only on the basis of the quantities of reagent used. That was a complicated procedure and the Italian authorities had had to appoint a committee of experts to look into the matter. The first investigation had been made by the fiscal squad of the police who specialized in the field. The members of that squad had some knowledge of the methods of production and extraction but they were not technicians. Consequently, the quantities of heroin diverted could not be definitely established until the results of the inquiry of the committee of experts were available.

In reply to the French representative's second question, he said that Professor Migliardi had not been arrested. He was at present under police surveillance and his passport had been withdrawn.

Under Italian law, a person could not be arrested unless he had been caught in the act. Professor Migliardi would be brought to trial shortly, as soon as the judges were in possession of all the complex facts of the case.

With regard to the granting of licenses, five firms had been authorized to manufacture opium alkaloids, the number having been determined with due regard to the volume of production and consumption of those products in Italy. Licenses were granted in accordance with the provisions of the 1925 Act. The Italian Government had been concerned with the lacunae in that Act and had prepared a new bill which, taking into account the recommendations of the Commission on Narcotic Drugs, provided for more severe penalties and would give the High Commissioner for Hygiene and Public Health the power to withdraw a manufacturing permit if any irregularities were suspected.

MR. ANSLINGER (United States of America) observed that, according to the investigation that had been carried out, Calascibetta had received from Migliardi the large quantity of 875 kg. of heroin, which he had then resold to various traffickers, many of whom had been convicted. It was now two years since Calascibetta had been denounced and the Italian Government had been in possession of evidence against him. He wondered why the trial had been so long delayed. He also wished to know whether the firm of Schiapparelli still held a license for the manufacture of heroin.

MR. CANAPERIA (Italy) explained that the first investigation had established that only 350-400 kg. of heroin had been clandestinely manufactured. The figure cited by the United States representative was that appearing in the report on the Calascibetta case, which included quantities of heroin that the accused had procured from other sources. The case had been handed over to the court the previous year. His trial would not take place until the results of the investigation of Migliardi were available, for the authorities intended to have both tried at the same time, as the two cases were connected.

Schiapparelli's authorization to manufacture heroin had been suspended. There had been no authorized manufacture of heroin in Italy since July 1951. He assured the Commission that the Italian Government exercised strict control over the production of the five firms in question. Two specialist inspectors had been detailed to supervise all operations with regard to drugs, from the stage of manufacture to that of distribution. It had not yet been possible to forbid the consumption of heroin because of the opposition of the medical profession but the remaining stocks were distributed only in hospitals and sanatoria and it was almost unobtainable in pharmacies.

MR. ANSLINGER *(United States of America)* said that the heroin estimates submitted by the Italian Government to the Supervisory Body and to the Permanent Central Opium Board from 1946 to 1950 had been 200 kg. per year. That production had probably been divided among different firms. He wondered how Migliardi had been able to divert such large quantities.

Furthermore, the figure of 200 kg. per year was very high compared with the corresponding figures for Switzerland and France. He had the impression that the diversion had been possible because the estimates had been too high.

MR. SHARMAN *(Canada)* shared the United States representative's view of the Italian estimates. As a member of the Supervisory Body, he was in a position to say that both the Supervisory Body and the Permanent Central Opium Board had been disturbed by that figure, which appeared to be excessive. Annual world consumption being about 400 kg., Italy's estimated consumption had for several years been about half that of the whole world.

Generally speaking, he was concerned about the situation in Italy, where there seemed to be very peculiar ideas with regard to the granting of licenses. The firm of Schiapparelli had not been closed. Its managing director and its technical director seemed to have some share of responsibility for the diversion; in any case, there were certainly others guilty beside Migliardi, since it was unlikely if not impossible that he could operate all by himself. Yet the two directors of the firm had not been indicted.

MR. VAILLE *(France)* stated that the annual consumption of heroin in France and the French Union was 13 kg. and was tending to decrease. France felt, however, that it was premature to prohibit the use of heroin for medical purposes.

He was surprised at the laxity of Italian courts, which permitted a man like Migliardi, who had put millions of ampoules of heroin into circulation and who was obviously more guilty than a petty trafficker or an addict, to remain at large. The reports submitted by Italy for 1952 showed that there was apparently no question of convictions.

He wished to know whether the firm of Schiapparelli, which no longer manufactured heroin, was manufacturing other drugs, such as codeine or dionine, since in that case further diversions were to be feared.

MR. MAY (*Permanent Central Opium Board*) shared the views of the preceding speakers. The Italian Government should respect public opinion, which could ill conceive that a man who was responsible for the misfortune of thousands of persons should remain at large and should not yet have been tried.

MR. CANAPERIA (*Italy*), in reply to the United States representative, stated that although Italy had indeed consumed 200 kg. of heroin in 1946, the annual consumption had since then been reduced to 50 kg. The allocation of raw materials was effected by dividing the quantities of raw opium imported among the five firms, each of which was authorized to manufacture a certain quantity of the various narcotic drugs for therapeutic purposes. The quantities were fixed by the High Commission for Hygiene and Public Health.

Some representatives felt that Italy's production was too high in relation to its population. In that connection, he drew the Commission's attention to document E/OB/8 (page 9), which gave figures showing the consumption of diacetylmorphine per million inhabitants. Italy appeared among the countries with a high consumption, although lower in recent years than that of Finland, Sweden, Australia, and the United Kingdom. The important thing, however, was that since 1951 Italy had reduced its consumption of diacetylmorphine to 50 kg.

In reply to the French representative's remarks, he repeated that under Italian law only those persons could be arrested who had been caught in the act, i.e., who had been found to be in possession of narcotic drugs or against whom there was conclusive proof that they engaged in illicit traffic. That was not the case with Migliardi; in that case there was only circumstantial evidence, based on the difference of the reagents used; but many points remained to be cleared up. That was why the Italian Government had transmitted only a preliminary report to the Secretariat, hoping to be in a position later to transmit a final report.

In his opinion, the aim of the Commission and of the other international organs engaged in combatting illicit traffic was to ensure effective international cooperation in preventing and hindering illicit traffic, since prevention was preferable to suppression. If that were so, it mattered little whether a firm continued to manufacture while the inquiry was in progress. The main thing was to make sure that no quantity of the narcotic drugs produced could be diverted from its proper destination. On behalf of his Government, he formally assured the Commission that the firms were subject to such strict control that it was no longer possible for a single milligram of narcotic drugs to be diverted. In addition, he emphasized that his country would always be ready to cooperate with the Commission in its work and to follow any suggestions the Commission might wish to make.

MR. ANSLINGER *(United States of America)* was not satisfied with the explanations of the Italian observer and regretted that Italy's conception of the control of manufacture of narcotic drugs was different from that of other countries.

MR. VAILLE *(France)* shared the United States representative's view. There could be no permanent control over a firm if the honesty of its directors could not be relied on. A firm holding a license must be above suspicion, for, even when it was, offenses were sometimes committed. In a large enterprise it might well happen that a worker stole a few grams or even kilograms of narcotic drugs, but the diversion of the entire production of a firm by its managers could not be treated lightly. He cited, in that connection, a case which had occurred in France. It had been found that a firm had not furnished accurate accounts of its stocks and, although an investigation had shown that there had been no diversion, the firm's license had been revoked and its directors had been indicted and convicted. He drew attention to the danger of countries not complying strictly with the conventions and not imposing the necessary penalties, for that would encourage the manufacturers and traffickers to move to those countries where they could be assured of impunity.

MR. CANAPERIA *(Italy)* said that he would certainly transmit the views expressed by the Commission to his Government. The investigation of the case in question was not yet completed and he assured the Commission that his Government would make it its business to send a final report which would undoubtedly satisfy the Commission.

* * *

The CHAIRMAN pointed out that the Commission had not finished the consideration of the above chapter [on illicit traffic of document E/NR.1951/Summary]. At the 203rd meeting the USSR representative had submitted a proposal on which the Commission had yet to take a decision. The USSR representative had asked for the deletion of various passages which he felt contained a number of false and slanderous allegations against the People's Republic of China.

At the CHAIRMAN's request, MR. CELINSKI *(Secretary of the Com-*

mission) read out the relevant passage of the provisional summary record of the two hundred and third meeting, which ran:

It (the USSR delegation) therefore proposed that all such references should be deleted from E/NR.1951/Summary now before the Commission and that document E/CN.1951/101 should be removed from the records. The same should apply to the references to the smuggling into Japan of heroin alleged to have come from China (page 46 of E/NR.1951/Summary) and to other false statements contained in the sections of the document which summarized the reports on the United States and Hong Kong.

MR. LIANG *(China)* opposed the USSR representative's proposal for the following five reasons.

The data given in the Chinese Government's Annual Report for 1951 were for the most part based on confidential information collected on the mainland by secret agents of the Chinese Government; the remaining information came from Hong Kong. While he could say no more about how the information was obtained, its authenticity was beyond doubt.

Furthermore, the information furnished by the Chinese Government for 1951 tallied with that provided the preceding year.

Thirdly, it was corroborated by certain facts cited in the reports of other Governments for 1951. In that connection he quoted the sixth paragraph of the summary concerning the United States, which reported the seizure of 627 grams of diacetylmorphine; the bags in which the drug had been concealed had borne the stamp of the Red Lion Company, which showed that the drug had been manufactured on the Chinese mainland. Likewise, in the summary of the Japanese Government's report it was stated that almost all the diacetylmorphine confiscated in Japanese territory had been of Chinese origin. Lastly, he cited a passage concerning Hong Kong, which referred to smuggling from China.

In the fourth place he noted that no one, not even the USSR representative, had been able to prove that the Chinese Government's statements were inaccurate on a single point.

Lastly, he recalled that, as the Canadian representative had acknowledged on several occasions, his Government had been fighting against the illicit traffic in narcotic drugs and the clandestine cultivation of the opium poppy for twenty-five years. To withdraw its report from the files and to give no credence to the information it supplied would be a totally undeserved act of censure.

With regard to that part of the Chinese territory which was under his Government's control, namely Formosa, neither the opium poppy nor Indian hemp were cultivated there. The use of heroin had been prohibited for a long time and traffickers were severely punished.

MR. VAILLE (France) said that he would vote against the USSR proposal because it would imply that the Commission had the right to change at will the texts of reports submitted by governments to the Secretariat. His vote had no political implications whatever.

MR. WALKER (United Kingdom) associated himself with those observations. The Commission was not competent of its own will to change official reports from governments. Anyone who felt that a report contained false allegations was free to prepare another document refuting those accusations and to ask that it should be circulated as an addendum to the report which had been questioned. Needless to say, governments must in turn be careful not to make charges, even by implication, against other countries or territories unless they could substantiate them by solid proof.

He regretted that the USSR representative had described certain information contained in the summary of the report for Hong Kong as false and slanderous without trying to prove those affirmations. The report spoke of the illicit traffic in opium along the Hong Kong land frontier. The Government of the Colony had simply described an actual situation, which was in no way surprising. It was a known fact that opium smuggling was rife along many frontiers in the Far East. The Government of the Colony had not made the slightest accusation against the Central People's Government of the People's Republic of China. The report did not even say, as it might have said, that more cooperation from the Central People's Government would greatly assist in suppressing illicit traffic in that region.

In conclusion, he said that his Government rejected certain allegations regarding Hong Kong and Singapore contained in the Chinese Nationalist Government's report for 1951. He himself had had inquiry made into some of the facts mentioned in the report and had found numerous inaccuracies. It would take too long to refute point by point the Formosa Government's assertions and to save time he would deal with a few of them only. On pages 4 and 5 of the report much emphasis was placed on labels which supposedly proved that the opium was of Chinese origin. While those labels bore the well-known marking 1—3—8, that was no guarantee of the contents of the packages. Other opiums were in fact sold under the same label.

The prices referred to in the same part of the report did not correspond to the usual Hong Kong prices, which were $HK55 per tael (37.8 grams) of opium and $HK8,000 per tael of morphine. The prices quoted in the report were much lower.

Other inaccuracies were to be found in paragraph 4 of page 6 of the report. The remarks about illicit traffic in the Shum-Chun area were not correct. The Ta-ch'ang Company had been dissolved in November 1951 and there had never been any evidence that it had engaged in traffic in narcotic drugs. Most of the persons mentioned in that passage were unknown to the Hong Kong authorities. One of them was known to reside at Macao and not at Hong Kong.

The information given in the Chinese Government's report concerning Singapore also called for the most formal reservations.

By virtue of its situation, Hong Kong was inevitably one of the centers of illicit traffic not only from China but also from Thailand. The authorities of the Colony were among the first to deplore that state of affairs. In cooperation with Japan and the United States, they had made tremendous efforts to suppress the traffic. In any case, the Chinese Nationalist Government had no right to make inaccurate and irresponsible statements which implied criticism of the authorities of certain British territories.

Mr. Anslinger (United States of America) regretted that the USSR representative was again trying to expurgate reports transmitted by other governments in order to delete any passages which displeased him.

Mrs. Kowalczyk (Poland) recalled that at the 203rd meeting she had given the reasons for her support of the USSR proposal. Nothing had occurred since then to make her change her view; the Kuomintang representative had added nothing new to the discussion. It was clear, therefore, that before it could approve the reports in question the Commission must decide to suppress the slanderous passages.

Mr. Zonov (Union of Soviet Socialist Republics) noted the United Kingdom representative's statement to the effect that the Hong Kong authorities had not intended in their report for 1951 to make any accusations against the Central People's Government of the People's Republic of China. He had also rightly stressed the need for governments to exercise great caution in drafting their reports. Each year the Kuomintang representatives repeated the same slanderous accusations, which, they claimed, were based on secret information. The Commission could not regard reports which rested on such a shaky foundation as reliable. The United Kingdom representative had just shown how little credence could be placed in document E/NR.1951/ 101. After that statement, there was nothing left of the report.

No one would dream of denying that there was illicit traffic in the Far East. It was scandalous, however, that the Kuomintang clique, which had no right to speak on behalf of the Chinese people, should, in cooperation with the United States and Japan, make accusations against the Government of the People's Republic of China, which was not represented on the Commission and was therefore unable to defend itself.

Mr. ANSLINGER *(United States of America)* pointed out that it had originally been the USSR representative who had introduced a political aspect into the debate. The Commission had heard from the USSR representative propaganda concerning the illicit traffic rather than statements of fact.

With regard to the question of hearing a representative of the Communist Government of China, if all that representative could contribute to the debate was the statement issued by the Ministry of Foreign Affairs (E/2233) which contained little but abuse and vilification, he thought the hearing would not lead to any constructive action. He wondered in fact why that regime had not submitted a factual report to the Commission on the subject if it sincerely wished to contribute to the elimination of the illicit traffic.

The USSR delegation had raised the political issue many years earlier. In fact at the previous session he had been attacked by Communists because of the statement he had then made concerning the illicit traffic in the Far East. All kinds of denunciations and insolent distortions had been made indirectly. They were obviously traceable to the fact that he personally had submitted a factual statement on the subject. He suggested that if the Chinese Communist regime wished to reply to his report, it might take up his statements paragraph by paragraph. That was the usual method of procedure. Charges of slander were not sufficient answer to the facts he had cited.

The CHAIRMAN put to the vote the USSR proposal that the Annual Report of the Chinese Government for 1951 should be removed from the records and that certain passages concerning China in the summary of Annual Reports should be deleted.

The proposal was rejected by 10 votes to 2, with 2 abstentions.

V

FEDERAL JURISDICTION

THE BUREAU OF NARCOTICS, ESTABLISHED IN THE UNITED STATES Treasury Department in 1930, is the Federal agency charged with the duty of regulating, supervising, and controlling the trade in narcotic drugs and marihuana, under the several applicable Federal laws. It serves as the special administration which the United States was obligated to create for this purpose under Article 15 of the Narcotics Limitation Convention of 1931.

Narcotic drugs include opium and the various derivatives thereof, such as morphine, heroin and codeine; coca leaves, and their derivatives, such as cocaine; isonipecaine (Demerol); and any other drug found by the Secretary of the Treasury to have addiction qualities similar to those of morphine or cocaine and so proclaimed by the President.

The term *marihuana* means all parts of the plant *Cannabis sativa L.*, whether growing or not; the seeds thereof; the resin extracted from any part of the plant; and every compound, manufacture, salt, derivative, mixture, or preparation of such plant, its seeds, or resin; but shall not include the mature stalks of such plant, fiber produced from such stalks, oil or cake made from the seeds of such plant, any other compound, manufacture, salt, derivative, mixture, or preparation of such mature stalks (except the resin extracted therefrom), fiber, oil, or cake, or the sterilized seed of such plant which is incapable of germination.

It will be noted that the barbiturates (principal component of the well-known sleeping pills), or other drugs of somnifacient nature such as chloral and paraldehyde, are not included. While

117

it is recognized that the barbiturates are subject to much abusive use, there are different aspects to the problem of control which should be met by legislation of a nature and scope different from and independent of the legislation controlling narcotic drugs and marihuana. It must be borne in mind that narcotic drugs and marihuana are subject not only to national control measures but also to an interrelative system of international control under the various conventions and protocols.

The three principal Federal statutes controlling the substances under discussion are the Harrison Narcotic Law, as amended, now incorporated in the Internal Revenue Code, the Marihuana Tax Act, as amended, also incorporated in the Internal Revenue Code, and the Act of May 26th 1922, as amended, known as the Narcotic Drugs Import and Export Act.

HARRISON NARCOTIC ACT

This Act as re-enacted in the Internal Revenue Code requires registration with the Director of Internal Revenue and the payment of a graduated occupational tax by all persons who import, manufacture, produce, compound, sell, deal in, dispense, or give away, narcotic drugs. The special tax for importers, manufacturers, producers or compounders is $24 per annum; for wholesale dealers $12 per annum; for retail dealers $3 per annum; and physicians, dentists, veterinary surgeons and other practitioners, as well as persons engaged in research, instruction or analysis are required to pay $1 per annum.

A commodity tax at the rate of 1¢ per ounce or fraction thereof is imposed upon narcotic drugs produced in or imported into the United States and sold, or removed for consumption or sale. This tax, it might be added, is in addition to any import duty imposed on the drugs. Exempted from certain restrictions of this Act is the manufacture, sale, distribution, giving away, dispensing or possession of preparations and remedies not containing more than 2 grains of opium, more than ¼ of a grain of morphine, or more than ⅛ of a grain of heroin, or more than 1 grain of codeine or any salt or derivative of any of them in 1 fluid ounce or, if a solid or semi-solid preparation, in 1 avoirdupois ounce, or to liniments, ointments or other preparations which are prepared for external use only, provided however that there is no intent to use these remedies for the purposes of evading the Act and provided further that a record of their use is kept for two years and is readily accessible to inspection by an officer, agent or an employee of the Treasury Department.

Sales or transfers of narcotic drugs are limited generally to those made pursuant to official order forms obtainable, in blank, by registrants, from the Director of Internal Revenue. Exception from the order form requirement is made in favor of dispensing to a patient by a qualified practitioner in the course of his professional practice only, provided however, that such physician, dentist, or veterinary surgeon shall keep a record of all such drugs dispensed or distributed. The record must include the amount dispensed, the date, the name and address of the patient to whom the drugs are dispensed except in cases where the drugs are dispensed by the physician in the course of personal attendance. Another important exception from the requirement of the Act is found in the case of a sale by a druggist to or for a patient, pursuant to a lawful written prescription issued by a qualified physician, dentist, or veterinary surgeon. Penalties are provided for violation of the Act and the Secretary of the Treasury is given the power to make, prescribe, and publish all the needed rules and regulations for carrying the provisions of this Act into effect. This Act is designed to direct the manufacture and distribution of narcotic drugs through medical channels to consumption use for medical or scientific purposes only.

MARIHUANA TAX ACT

In enacting this Act Congress had definite goals in mind; first of all, to make it extremely difficult for marihuana to be acquired by persons who might desire to use it illicitly, and secondly, to develop an adequate means of publicizing dealings in marihuana in order to tax and control the traffic effectively. In accordance with these avowed purposes the Act requires registration with the Director of Internal Revenue in the district wherein the business is situated and the payment of a graduated occupational tax up to $24 upon all persons who import, manufacture, produce, compound, sell, deal in, dispense, prescribe, administer or give away marihuana. No commodity tax is imposed on this drug. A tax is imposed, however, upon all transfers of this drug at the rate of $1 per ounce or fraction thereof, if the transfer is made to a tax-payer who has previously paid the special tax and is registered under the Act, or, at the rate of $100 per ounce if the transfer is made to a person who has not paid the special tax and registered under the Act. Transfers also are limited generally to those made pursuant to official order forms obtainable from the Director of Internal Revenue. Furthermore, if a transfer is made without an official order form and without payment of the tax by the transferee, the transferor is liable for such tax as may be due. Exception from the order form and transfer tax requirement is made in favor of dispensing to a patient by a qualified practitioner in the course of his professional practice only, and in favor of a sale by a druggist to or for a patient, pursuant to a lawful written prescription issued by a qualified practitioner. In view of the fact that marihuana has been deleted from most pharmacopoeias the last exception is today academic.

In upholding the constitutionality of the Act the United States Supreme Court, in the case of *U.S.* v. *Sanchez* [340 U.S. 42] pointed out that its regulatory effect and its close resemblance to a penalty were not sufficient to invalidate the Act; that a tax is not invalid because it regulates, discourages, or even definitely deters the activities taxed, even though the revenue obtained is obviously negligible, or the revenue purpose of the tax is secondary, since an Act purporting to be an exercise of tax power is not any the less so because it tends to restrict or suppress the thing taxed. Additionally, said the court, it is not invalid because it touches on activities on which Congress might not otherwise legislate.

NARCOTIC DRUGS IMPORT AND EXPORT ACT

This Act authorizes the importation only of such quantities of opium and coca leaves as the Commissioner of Narcotics shall find to be necessary to provide for medical and scientific needs under such regulations as the Commissioner shall prescribe. Importation of any form of narcotic drugs except such limited quantities of crude opium and coca leaves for medical and scientific uses is prohibited. The importation of smoking opium or of opium prepared for smoking is specifically prohibited, and possession of such opium is made prima facie evidence of an offense. The aim of this latter section is to stamp out the use of narcotics in this country except for legitimate medical purposes. While numerous attacks have been made on the validity of this section, the courts have held that under the power accorded it by the Constitution Congress had the power to regulate foreign commerce to create the presumption contained therein. The act also permits exportation of manufactured drugs and preparations under a rigid system of control, designed to assure their use for medical needs only in the country of destination.

The three principal Federal statutes controlling these dangerous substances have been supplemented by other legislative measures designed to control further possible sources of supply and to facilitate the task of enforcement.

OTHER LEGISLATION

By an Act of Congress approved January 17, 1914, a tax of $300.00 per pound was levied upon all opium manufactured in the United States for smoking purposes, and certain stringent conditions were imposed with respect to such manufacture. The purpose, of course, was to make such manufacture prohibitive, and the Act was held constitutional though the tax was so high as to be prohibitive of the traffic. Since, as previously indicated, no opium can lawfully be imported for the purpose of manufacturing smoking opium, and the product can not be lawfully sold, it is legally impracticable for one to seek to operate as a manufacturer under this Act, even if undeterred by the prohibitive conditions explained. The Act affords an additional prosecutive basis, however, where clandestine manufacture of smoking opium can be established by evidence.

Under an Act of Congress approved August 9, 1939, as amended August 9, 1950, it was made unlawful to transport, carry, or convey any contraband narcotic drug in, upon or by means of any vessel, vehicle or aircraft; to conceal or possess any such drug in or upon such vessel, vehicle or aircraft or upon the person of any one in or upon such vessel, vehicle or aircraft to facilitate the transportation, carriage, conveyance, concealment, receipt, possession, purchase, sale, barter, exchange or giving away of any contraband narcotic drug. The definition of the term contraband article as it relates to narcotic drugs (including for the purposes of this Act marihuana) is extensively stated in the statutes, but it may be briefly, if necessarily not wholly accurately, summarized as any narcotic drug which has been or is possessed with intent to sell in violation of law or which has been acquired or is possessed, sold, transferred or transported in violation of law. Any vessel, vehicle or aircraft so unlawfully used may be seized and forfeited. An appreciable number of vehicles are seized under the Act by the Bureau of Narcotics, and forfeited to the United States. After forfeiture some of these vehicles, as authorized by law, are used in enforcement work in the investigation, detection and arrest of other violators. Thus an important facility for illicit narcotic peddling is taken from the violator and becomes a facility on the side of law enforcement for detecting and eliminating other violators.

By a special Statute approved July 3, 1930, the Commissioner of Narcotics is authorized and empowered to pay to any person from funds appropriated for the enforcement of the Federal narcotic laws of the United States, for information concerning a violation of any narcotic law resulting in a seizure of contraband narcotics, such sum as he may deem appropriate.

PUBLIC HEALTH SERVICE HOSPITALS

The Act of Congress approved January 19, 1929, provided for the establishment of two Public Health Service hospitals, later erected at Lexington, Kentucky, and Fort Worth, Texas, respectively. These hospitals, under the administration of the U. S. Public Health Service, were dedicated to the treatment and cure of narcotic drug addicts convicted of offenses against the United States, and narcotic drug addicts who voluntarily submit themselves for treatment. The original Act provided, and a superseding Statute still provides, that the Surgeon General (of the Public Health Service) shall cooperate with the States for the purpose of aiding them to solve their narcotic drug problems and shall give authorized representatives of the States the benefit of his experience in the care, treatment and rehabilitation of narcotic addicts to the end that each State may be encouraged to provide adequate facilities and methods for the care and treatment of its narcotic addicts. It is important to note that any of those men or women who have become addicted to narcotic drugs as defined by Federal law are eligible for admission. According to the Federal statute an addict is a person who uses narcotic habit-forming drugs to the point that he has become dependent upon them. This dependence may jeopardize his general health and welfare, and the individual has lost his self control as far as the drug is concerned. The habit-forming narcotic drugs are opium and its derivatives; isonipecaine and its derivatives, compounds, and preparations; the opiates; cocaine; and marihuana. It is important to note that persons addicted to the barbiturates or alcohol are not eligible for treatment at the hospital unless they are also habitual users of one of the drugs cited above.

REGISTRATION OF PHYSICIANS AND DRUGGISTS

A physician who intends to practice medicine and to administer or dispense narcotic drugs in the course of such practice must apply for registration under the Harrison Law with the Director of Internal Revenue of the district in which he proposes to practice, and must pay the appropriate occupational tax for the fiscal year applicable. Before being entitled to such registration, however, he must be lawfully entitled under the laws of the State or Territory or district wherein he intends to practice, to distribute, dispense, give away, or administer narcotic drugs to patients upon whom he, in the course of his professional practice is in attendance [26 U.S.C. 3220]. In the case of a medical practitioner, this requirement usually means that the applicant is a physician who holds an unrevoked and unrestricted license to practice medicine in the particular State, Territory, or district.

To be entitled to registration, however, in the case of any type of practitioner of the healing art, it must appear that he is entitled under the State laws to distribute, administer, or dispense narcotic drugs to patients whom he is professionally attending.

*The right to register and pay tax under the Federal statute depends on the right to dispense under the State laws.**

The provisions of the law are substantially the same for a druggist. A druggist who intends to sell and deal in narcotic drugs must apply for registration under the Harrison Act with the Director of Internal Revenue of the district wherein his business is located, and must pay the required occupational tax. Furthermore, he must be licensed under the State laws in order to register and pay tax under the Federal statute.

INVENTORY

Every person making application for registry or re-registry as a physician or druggist shall, as of December 31 preceding the date of his application, or any date between December 31 and the date of applying for such registry or re-registry, prepare in duplicate an inventory of all narcotic drugs and preparations on hand at the time of making such inventory. The inventory shall be prepared on the reverse side of Form 678, copies of which may be obtained from Directors of Internal Revenue upon request. The original inventory shall be forwarded to the Director with the application for registration, and the duplicate shall be kept on file by the maker for a period of two years.

REGISTRY NUMBER

Upon approval of the application for registration the Director of Internal Revenue will assign a registry number to the applicant and will issue him a special tax stamp in Class IV as a practitioner, or in Class III as a druggist. This special tax stamp must be kept posted conspicuously on the premises covered by the registration, i.e. the physician's office or the drug store.

---

* Perry v. Larson, 104 F. (2d) 728; Waldo v. Poe, 14 F. (2d) 749; Bruer v. Woodworth, 22 F. (2d) 577; Burke v. Kansas State Osteopathic Assn., 111 F. (2d) 250; Georgia Assn. of Osteopathic Physicians and Surgeons v. Allen, 112 F. (2d) 52; Cavanagh v. Fowler, 146 F. (2d) 961.

CHANGE OF ADDRESS

A physician registrant who changes the location of his office shall, within 30 days, execute a new return on Form 678, marking it "Revised Registry." The return shall set forth the date of change and the new address. The return shall be forwarded with the special tax stamp to the Director who issued the stamp for recording the change. If the removal is to another State, Territory or district, the physician must, of course, be qualified in the new location to administer, dispense or distribute narcotic drugs to patients, which usually means that he must also be licensed to practice medicine in the new location.

ORDER FORMS AND INSPECTION

A physician may obtain narcotic drugs for direct dispensing or administration to patients only on official order forms. He may not obtain narcotic drugs on a prescription for general office use. Official order forms in triplicate are obtainable from the Director of Internal Revenue in a book of ten for ten cents. The form is to be prepared in triplicate and signed by the physician, the original and triplicate copy being forwarded to a qualified manufacturer or wholesaler, and the duplicate retained by the physician for a period of two years subject to inspection by a duly authorized Federal or State narcotic officer. The order form may be prepared in typewriting, ink or indelible pencil, but not by the use of an ordinary lead pencil.

PRESCRIPTIONS

A prescription for narcotic drugs may be issued only by a duly registered physician for a bona-fide patient for medical purposes only, which prescription may be filled by a qualified druggist.

LEGALITY

A prescription, in order to be effective in legalizing the possession of unstamped narcotic drugs and eliminating the necessity for use of order forms, must be issued for legitimate medical purposes. The responsibility for the proper prescribing and dispensing of narcotic drugs is upon the practitioner, but a corresponding liability rests with the druggist who fills the prescription. An order purporting to be a prescription issued to an addict or habitual user of narcotics, not in the course of professional treatment but for the purpose of providing the user with narcotics sufficient to keep him comfortable by maintaining his customary use, is not a prescription within the meaning and intent of the act; *and the person filling such an order, as well as the person issuing it, may be charged with violation of the law.*

FILLING PRESCRIPTIONS

A prescription for narcotic drugs shall be dated as of and signed on the date when issued and shall bear the full name and address of the patient and the name, address and registry number of the practitioner. A physician may sign a prescription in the same manner as he would sign a check or legal document, as, for instance, John H. Smith, J. H. Smith, or John Henry Smith. Prescriptions should be written with ink or indelible pencil or typewriter; if typewritten, they shall be signed by the practitioner. The refilling of a prescription for taxable narcotic drugs is prohibited. The practitioner is responsible in case the prescription does not conform in all essential respects to the law, and regulations. However, a corresponding liability rests upon the druggist who fills a prescription not prepared in the form required by law.

When the names of fictitious patients are discovered on narcotic drug prescriptions filed with a druggist it is usually a clear indication of wilful catering to drug addiction, whether or not the so-called prescriptions are also discovered to be forged. Sometimes the physician will insert a fictitious patient's name, however, because he wishes to conceal from the druggist the fact that the real patient is consuming drugs, notwithstanding that the real patient is claimed to have a bona fide medical need therefor. The law does not permit the use of a fictitious name upon a prescription.

The furnishing of narcotic drugs pursuant to telephone advice of practitioners is prohibited, whether prescriptions covering such orders are subsequently received or not, except that in an emergency a druggist may deliver narcotic drugs through his employee or responsible agent pursuant to a telephone order, provided the employee or agent is supplied with a properly prepared prescription before delivery is made, which prescription shall be turned over to the druggist and filed by him as required by law.

A physician's prescription blanks should be most carefully safeguarded and never left where persons who may be drug addicts will have opportunity to take them, and to prepare and have filled forged narcotic prescriptions. A physician's official order forms should be likewise safeguarded, and great care should be exercised by the physician in keeping his stock of narcotic drugs secure from robbery or pilfering. The medicine case containing narcotic drugs should never be left in an unattended automobile.

STATE CONTROLS

The Uniform State Narcotic Law differs from the Federal Law in some respects—for instance, it requires manufacturers of and wholesale dealers in narcotic drugs to obtain a license from the appropriate State agencies and prescribes certain qualifications for these licensees and it directly and specifically penalizes the forgery or alteration of a narcotic prescription. In so far as the professional use of narcotic drugs is concerned, however, the statutory standard is practically the same as that provided by the Federal Narcotic Law. Whereas Section 2554 of the Internal Revenue Code requires no record to be kept where the doctor is in personal attendance, Section 9 of the Uniform Narcotic Drug Act requires no record where the narcotic drugs are administered, dispensed or professionally used in the treatment of any one patient when the amount administered does not exceed in forty-eight consecutive hours 4 grains of opium or ½ of a grain of morphine, or any of its salts, or 2 grains of codeine, or any of its salts, or a quantity of any other narcotic drug, or any combination of narcotic drugs that does not exceed in pharmacologic potency any one of the drugs named in the quantity stated.

It is important to note, however, that some States, such as New Jersey, North Carolina, Iowa, and the District of Columbia, and others require a record to be kept of all drugs administered and dispensed, regardless of amount. Thus under the Uniform Act a physician in good faith and in the course of his professional practice only is permitted to prescribe and administer narcotic drugs, or may cause the same to be administered by a nurse or interne under his direction and supervision. Under the same Act a druggist in good faith may sell and dispense narcotic drugs to any person upon a written prescription of a physician.

It is also important to note that under the Harrison Act preparations containing not more than 2 grains of opium, or more than ¼ of a grain of morphine, or more than ⅙ of a grain of heroin, or more than 1 grain of codeine, or any salt or derivative of any of them in 1 fluid ounce, or if a solid or semi-solid preparation in 1 avoirdupois ounce, are exempt preparations. The original Uniform Narcotic Drug Act made these same preparations exempt, but the States of Colorado, Vermont, Wisconsin, Kentucky, Louisiana, New Jersey, North Dakota, Oregon, Montana, Iowa, South Dakota, Minnesota, and the Territory of Alaska have changed these exemptions to apply only to preparations that contain in 1 fluid ounce, or if a solid or semi-solid preparation in 1 avoirdupois ounce, not more than 1 grain of codeine or any of its salts. The main effect of this change in the law was to put paregoric under prescription.

There is no limitation on the quantity of narcotics externally used preparations may contain, provided such preparations contain other ingredients rendering them unfit for internal use. Preparations containing cocaine or pantopon in any quantity, whether for internal or external administration, are never exempt, nor are preparations containing any of the synthetic narcotic drugs.

PROFESSIONAL LIABILITY

A recent State civil suit in Massachusetts * against a physician for malpractice arising out of the improper prescribing of narcotic drugs disclosed that the plaintiff was suffering from nausea, but without pain, and that the defendant doctor without any physical examination or without any complaint of pain by her or questions as to her medical history, gave her increasing hypodermic injections of morphine. These injections continued with

* King v. Solomon 81 N.E. 2d 838.

increasing frequency until ultimately she was receiving them three or more times a day. The doctor was discharged from the case and the plaintiff experienced a complete black-out and was admitted to the hospital suffering from morphine addiction "one-quarter of the way along to confirmed addiction." Subsequently plaintiff was found to be suffering from gall bladder trouble and had her gall bladder removed and after the operation the nausea ceased. Medical testimony at the trial disclosed that the nausea was caused by the gall bladder trouble; that it was possible to have gall bladder trouble with nausea and without pain; that gall stones do not arrive suddenly; that it was improper medical practice to administer morphine to a patient who complained of nausea but not of pain, or over a period of time where there was no pain involved; and that it was not proper to continue giving morphine in the absence of a diagnosis of a condition that could not be cured. The jury found in favor of the plaintiff. One of the defenses by the defendant physician was the section of the Massachusetts law which says

A physician may personally administer any narcotic drug at such time and under such circumstances as he, in good faith and in the legitimate practice of medicine, believes to be necessary for the alleviation of pain and suffering and for the treatment and relief of pain.

The Court, however, held that this section was intended, when complied with by the physician, to exempt him from the penal provisions pertaining to the sale and distribution of narcotic drugs and that it was not intended to relieve him from civil liabilities applicable generally to physicians. Said the Court,

The decision rests upon evidence of improper and non-professional conduct on the parts of the defendant leading to addiction in the plaintiff, Eva King. Nothing contained herein need cause anxiety to an honest physician who administers narcotics to a patient in accordance with the prevailing standards of practice.

It is important to note in the facts that the defendant physician prescribed narcotics without any physical examination or questions as to medical history. Recent investigations have disclosed that many physicians have prescribed narcotics to patients without any physical examination and mainly on the representations of the patient. It would thus unquestionably follow that the lack of a physical examination would have a strong bearing on the question of the good faith of the physician.

There has not been too extensive litigation on this question of a physician's civil liability with regard to the administration of narcotic drugs. However, one thing does seem clear and that is that a physician who prescribes narcotics solely on a representation of a patient and without any attempt to secure the facts of the past history or examine the patient is certainly exposing himself within the scope of the aforementioned decision, depending, of course, on the facts of the case. From an evidential angle, unless a serious illness requiring narcotic drugs could be proven, prescriptions issued with increasing frequency by a doctor might certainly tend to inculpate the doctor in a violation of the penal provisions of the law or a possible civil liability, based on malpractice, or both. At any rate, it would certainly be wise for all physicians to treat this subject of administering or prescribing narcotic drugs with unusual care. As an example of the types of violations which have been found and which are fairly common are the following:

1. Prescribing without seeing the patient.
2. Administering to a known addict.
3. Administering and prescribing to a known addict and giving prescriptions in advance.
4. Prescribing solely on the unsubstantiated history of an illness given by the patient.
5. Prescribing without a physical examination.

INDISPENSABLE USE—CHECK POINTS

In the instruction * to a series of articles printed in *The Journal* of the American Medical Association in 1931 on the Indispensable Use of Narcotic Drugs, Dr. Morris Fishbein has presented to the medical profession some excellent suggestions dealing with the general professional use of narcotic drugs. If all physicians would accept and conscientiously follow these sug-

* Various authors; "The Indispensable Use of Narcotic Drugs," 96:856, 1931.

gestions, which are quoted below, irregularities in prescribing and dispensing of narcotic drugs by physicians would be reduced to a minimum.

The problem of narcotic addiction merits the attention of physicians for many reasons. . . . the medical profession must do everything possible to minimize the prescribing of narcotics in order to make unnecessary further restrictive measures. Physicians should give more serious consideration to the materia medica, pharmacology, and therapeutics of narcotics.

Physicians may, by the exercise of more thought in practicing, do much to avoid censure in relation to narcotic addiction. They may substitute, whenever possible, non-habit-forming drugs in the place of morphine or other opium alkaloids. When narcotics are indispensable, however, as shown in this series of articles, no more should be administered than is necessary to achieve the desired end. Patients requiring daily administration should be seen often by the doctor and the amount of drugs ordered or supplied should not exceed that required by the patient until seen again. Independence of administration on the part of nurses should be strictly limited to prescription and any change in treatment should be in writing.

In conclusion, a physician could avoid the pitfalls attendant to criminal and civil liability if the following fundamental rules were observed:

1. Secure a complete history of the ailment.
2. Make a complete and thorough physical examination in every case.
3. Ascertain whether the illness requires narcotics and good medical practice demands their prescription.
4. Use non-habit-forming drugs instead of opiates wherever possible.
5. Beware of strangers and itinerant patients who suggest their need for drugs.
6. Remember always that improper and prolonged dosages can cause an individual to become an addict.
7. Don't write a prescription for office use. That supply should be secured on a drug order form.

RESPONSIBILITY OF THE DRUGGIST

As has been said many times, narcotics can be either a blessing or a curse. In order to prevent indiscriminate trafficking and other abuses, the prescribing, selling, and dispensing of these drugs to the consumer have been vested, by law, in doctors and druggists. They, therefore, have the obligation to discharge this public trust in a manner which is above reproach and the only way that can be done is by observing a high moral standard and by obeying the letter of the law to its fullest extent.

Druggists should consider the following suggestions:

1. Refuse to compound an improperly prepared prescription.
2. Make no delivery of a telephone prescription without receiving a properly prepared prescription before delivery of the narcotic is made.
3. Never sell a narcotic drug except upon prescription.
4. Remember that narcotic prescriptions may not be refilled.
5. Be familiar with the quantities a customer is using; exorbitant quantities over a long period should warrant close scrutiny.

A druggist cannot lawfully fill a prescription for narcotics if he knows or has reason to know that it was not issued in good faith. However, a druggist is under no affirmative duty to inquire into the lawfulness of a prescription for a narcotic drug before filling it if he has no knowledge of its illegality.* Without knowledge there can be no guilt and knowledge consists of either direct proof or what may be inferred from the circumstances. It should be noted, however, that a negligent failure to inquire is no substitute for knowledge.

As in the case of doctors, quantities of narcotics sold also bear on the good faith of the pharmacist. Evidence that a store dispensed six hundred times as much morphine annually as an average store, much of it to addicts, has been held sufficient to be a jury question on the issue of making sales on prescriptions which the druggist should have known were not issued in good faith.**

* Doremus v. U.S. 262 Fed. 849.
** Montgomery v. U.S. 290 Fed. 961.

CONSTITUTIONALITY OF THE HARRISON NARCOTIC ACT

The constitutional validity of the Harrison Narcotic Act was challenged in the courts not long after its enactment. A physician in Texas had been indicted for violating the law in that he made sales of 500 one-sixth grain tablets of heroin to a person described as a drug addict, not in the course of professional practice. The claim was made that the statute was unconstitutional because it was not actually a revenue measure and was an invasion of the police power reserved to the states. The United States Supreme Court, in 1919, rejected this claim and held that the statute was constitutional as a revenue measure, and that it could not be declared unconstitutional because its effect might be to accomplish another purpose as well as the raising of revenue. In the same year, the Supreme Court held in another case that an order for morphine issued by a physician to an habitual user merely to keep him comfortable by maintaining his customary use was not a physician's "prescription" as that term was used in the Harrison Act. In a third case, decided in 1920, the Supreme Court very clearly stated the nature of the responsibility of the physician and the druggist under the applicable section of this law, as follows:

Manifestly the phrases "to a patient" and " in the course of his professional practice only" are intended to confine the immunity of a registered physician, in dispensing the narcotic drugs mentioned in the Act, strictly within the appropriate bounds of a physician's professional practice, and not to extend it to include a sale to a dealer or a distribution intended to cater to the appetite or satisfy the craving of one addicted to the use of the drug. A "prescription" issued for either of the latter purposes protects neither the physician who issues it nor the dealer who knowingly accepts and fills it.

In the meantime, non-registered drug peddlers whose principal source of supply was smuggled and therefore contraband narcotics, were being prosecuted and convicted principally under two sections of the law which prohibited respectively the purchase or sale of narcotics except in or from the original tax-stamped package and the sale of narcotics except pursuant to an official order form. In 1927 a convicted unregistered purchaser of narcotics challenged the constitutionality of the tax-stamped package provision and in 1928 a convicted peddler challenged the constitutionality of the official order form provision of the Act. The Supreme Court upheld the constitutional validity of both sections and affirmed the judgments of conviction.

By 1928, therefore, it was authoritatively settled that under the Harrison Act, narcotics could not be sold or transferred for the purpose of gratification and spread of drug addiction, whether the sale or transfer was made by a drug peddler, or by a physician or druggist under color of professional practice. In 1943, however, the Supreme Court had occasion to pass upon the question of the responsibility of a manufacturer and wholesale dealer who sold narcotics to a registered physician on official order forms, but with knowledge that the physician was distributing narcotics illegally. A drug manufacturer in Buffalo, New York, had been convicted of conspiracy with a South Carolina physician and three other persons, to violate the Harrison Act, in that the manufacturer sold quantities of narcotics to the physician on the latter's official order forms knowing of illegal narcotic sales by the physician. The manufacturer's argument to secure reversal of the judgment of conviction was, in substance, that the sales made by him were legal because made pursuant only to official order forms, even though accompanied by knowledge that the physician was distributing narcotics illegally. The Supreme Court rejected this contention and sustained the judgment of conviction, pointing out that there was a significant difference between sales of articles of free commerce and articles necessarily restricted, like narcotics, because of inherent susceptibility to harmful and illegal use.

CONTROL AT SOURCE OF SUPPLY

It is important to note that the Federal Bureau of Narcotics has no authority to revoke a physician's license since that power is solely vested in the Licensing Boards of the various States and as long as the physician is licensed he may continue to purchase narcotics. However, the Bureau is not completely powerless to prevent a physician who is misusing narcotic drugs from obtaining them even though they may not revoke his license. The case of *Ratigan* vs. *Commissioner of Narcotics* is authority for the proposition that the Bureau of Narcotics may properly request registered drug manufacturers and dealers to refrain from filling narcotic orders for a particular physician.

In January, 1932, Dr. Thomas P. Ratigan, Jr., of Seattle, Washington, was reported by agents of the Bureau of Narcotics for serious violations of the Federal narcotic law. The report was based on sales of morphine by means of hypodermic injection to numbers of drug addicts merely to gratify the habit. He was indicted for these offenses on May 4, 1934, but after a trial before a jury, was found not guilty on October 13, 1934.

After his acquittal, Dr. Ratigan not only continued but increased his sales of morphine by hypodermic injection to drug addicts. Investigating officers observed, on one day, that some seventy-five drug addicts visited Dr. Ratigan's office to purchase injections of morphine. For the period of time from January 1, 1932 to September 19, 1936, Dr. Ratigan purchased from drug firms the enormous total of 445,980 one-half grain morphine tablets to supply his illicit trade. By actual computation, Dr. Ratigan purchased and sold, during a period of one and one-half years, about four and one-half times the total amount of morphine purchased by all the other 172 physicians and the 23 hospitals in Seattle.

A continued careful investigation by narcotic officers resulted in the collection of evidence upon which he was again indicted on November 15, 1935, and after a lengthy trial before a jury he was found guilty on August 19, 1936, and on August 28, 1936, he was sentenced to serve a term of imprisonment of seven years and to pay a fine of $10,000. He appealed to the U.S. Circuit Court of Appeals which affirmed the judgment of conviction, and then petitioned the United States Supreme Court for writ of certiorari, which was denied. He was committed to the United States penitentiary at McNeil Island, Washington, on June 17, 1937 to serve his term of imprisonment. His State medical license was revoked on May 16, 1938, by the Department of Licenses of the State of Washington for unprofessional conduct.

Even after his conviction, Dr. Ratigan was unregenerate and indicated his intention to continue supplying addicts with morphine. Registered drug manufacturers and dealers were requested by the

Bureau of Narcotics to refrain from filling any orders for narcotics submitted by Dr. Ratigan without first notifying the Bureau. While released on bond pending the result of his appeal, Dr. Ratigan made every effort to continue his illicit narcotic traffic but experienced difficulty in purchasing supplies of morphine from registered dealers. In December, 1936, he filed a bill of complaint in the District Court of the United States for the District of Columbia, praying for a temporary and permanent restraining order against the Commissioner of Narcotics, alleging that the Commissioner was preventing him from obtaining narcotics for use in the course of his practice as a physician. The court issued a rule to show cause upon the Commissioner, and a return to the rule was filed setting forth the justification for the Commissioner's action. Upon a hearing on December 23, 1936, the court ordered that the rule to show cause be discharged and that Dr. Ratigan's application for a temporary injunction be denied. Dr. Ratigan did not proceed further with this litigation, and the decision became final.

CIVIL LIABILITY

Emphasis thus far has been placed on the criminal side of the problem, but the question of civil liability can neither be underestimated nor forgotten. Without doubt, one malpractice suit involving misuse of narcotics could destroy an unblemished professional career, and it is imperative for a doctor and druggist to be familiar with this phase of the law.

The litigated civil actions to date have been predicated on loss of consortium, society, companionship, or services, and in cases where death has resulted, have been coupled with an action for wrongful death.* The underlying factor for suits of this type was first established when the existence of substances—which, through constant use, would effectively destroy the power of the consumer to cease the use thereof and also would injure or destroy normal physical and mental health—was first recognized. In this case it was held that an unknowing husband, whose wife had become addicted, had had a legally protected marital right invaded by reason of such addiction.** This theory has so evolved that today the rule is that an action will lie by either spouse

* Moberg v. Scott 161 N.W. 998.
** Houd v. Peck, 56 N.Y. 202.

against one knowingly selling a habit-forming drug to the other spouse, except for a lawful medical purpose, if the sale causes or aggravates the habitual use of narcotics. Since there is a loss of volition to act, the defense of contributory negligence is not available to the seller.

Briefly, therefore, where a husband or wife is concerned, it is an established rule of law today that improper sales of habit-forming drugs can cause harm to legally protected marital interests and liability will attach to the vendor unless the other spouse consents or a physician prescribes the narcotics.* Furthermore, in some cases liability has been found even though no law was violated, and in extreme cases, both compensatory and punitive damages have been awarded. It is noteworthy that while the violation of a statute is negligence per se, no recovery can be secured unless the wrongful act is shown to be the proximate cause.** It should be noted that this same doctrine has been applied in a suit by a parent against a pharmacist for repeated and wilful sale of a narcotic to a minor.***

OPIUM POPPY CONTROL ACT OF 1942

Due to the shortage of supplies of imported poppy seed after the beginning of World War II, certain persons in the United States commenced to grow the opium poppy, ostensibly for seed yield, ignoring friendly warnings communicated by the Commissioner of Narcotics that the seed pods contained morphine which could and would be readily extracted, even in impure form, by peddlers with the inevitable result of spreading drug addiction. The Commissioner sought and obtained the enactment of special legislation—the Opium Poppy Control Act of 1942—which prohibited the growth of the opium poppy in the United States except under a special license issuable only upon a demonstrated need for domestic production of the opium poppy to supply opium derivatives for medical and scientific uses. No such need has arisen nor is it likely under modern developments that such

* Restatement of Torts, Volume 3, p. 497.
** Scott v. Greenville Pharmacy, Inc., 45 S.E. 2d, 324.
*** Tidd v. Skinner, 225 N.Y. 422.

need will ever arise, and no licenses have been issued. The few crops of opium poppies that were growing were seized, and those, who had planted them in defiance of the statute, sought an injunction against the seizure on the ground that the statute was unconstitutional. After a thorough hearing, a three-judge Federal Court in California held the statute constitutionally valid as the execution of an international obligation under the 1912 Convention, and the crops were destroyed.

FEDERAL LEGISLATION IMPLEMENTING THE CONVENTIONS

At the time the 1912 Convention was signed, the first narcotic regulatory statute of the United States, the Act approved February 9, 1909, had been in effect for over three years. This statute prohibited importation of opium and its preparations and derivatives except for medicinal purposes and absolutely prohibited the importation of smoking opium or of opium prepared for smoking. After the Convention was signed but before it was ratified, an Act approved January 17, 1914, added to the 1909 statute a prohibition against the exportation of any opium or cocaine or of any salt, derivative or preparation thereof except to a country which regulated the entry of such drugs, and in accordance with such regulations. The exportation of smoking opium or of opium prepared for smoking was absolutely prohibited. Another statute, approved on the same date, January 17, 1914, placed a prohibitive tax upon opium manufactured in the United States for smoking purposes and placed certain other conditions upon such manufacture. These statutes implemented some of the obligations assumed by the United States under the 1912 Convention, particularly with reference to control of imports and exports.

A further important step was taken towards implementation of the obligations assumed under the 1912 Convention by the enactment of the Act of December 17, 1914, popularly known as the Harrison Narcotic Law. This statute was enacted in the form of a revenue measure and required registration and the payment of an occupational tax by all persons who produced, imported, manufactured, dispensed or otherwise dealt in opium or coca leaves or any compound, manufacture, salt, derivative, or preparation thereof. All sales or transfers of these drugs were required to be made on official order forms, but an exception from the order form requirement was made in favor of a registered practitioner dispensing to or prescribing for a patient in the course of professional practice only, and in favor of the registered druggist who filled the narcotic prescription. About four years later, the Act was amended by adding a commodity tax stamp provision (1¢ per ounce or fraction thereof), by imposing graduated rates of occupational tax, and by certain other provisions designed to prevent evasion of these taxes. The duty of enforcing the statute was assumed by the Bureau of Internal Revenue through its field officers engaged in enforcement of all internal revenue laws. Originally, there was no separate specialized group of officers assigned exclusively to the duty of enforcing this statute.

Although enacted as an internal revenue measure, the Harrison Narcotic Law, as amended, has the effect of limiting the availability of narcotic drugs to medical and scientific uses only. It regulates production and manufacture, and distribution through channels of medical supply to the dispensing registrants, the qualified practitioner and druggist. Except for scientific use, the purpose of the law is to restrict ultimate consumption of these drugs to patients who have a bona fide medical need therefor, the drugs being prescribed or dispensed by a qualified practitioner in the course of his professional practice only.

Early in the history of enforcement of the Harrison Narcotic Law as a measure controlling the domestic narcotic traffic, it became evident that there was need for a more comprehensive measure of control over imports and exports of these potentially dangerous drugs than was provided by the Act of February 9, 1909, as amended January 17, 1914. This older statute was extensively revised and in the revised form was reenacted by Congress, becoming the Narcotic Drugs Import and Export Act, approved May 26, 1922. By this statute there was instituted, so far as the United States was concerned, a strict system of import and export control which antedated by six years the obligation of the parties under the 1925 Convention to establish definite controls over imports and exports. The statute authorized the importation of such quantities only of opium and coca leaves as the then Federal Narcotics Control Board (now, the Commissioner of Narcotics) found to be necessary to provide for medical and legitimate needs. Importation of any form of narcotic drug, except such limited quantities of crude opium and coca leaves, was prohibited. Thus, all derivatives of these crude drugs, such as morphine, heroin, codeine, cocaine, etc., were excluded from lawful importation, and the importation and exportation of smoking opium continued to be prohibited. Exportation of manufactured narcotic drugs and preparations was permitted under a system of control designed to assure their use for medical needs only in the country of destination. A special amendment to this statute, approved June 7, 1924, prohibited the importation of opium for the purpose of manufacturing heroin, and the legal manufacture of heroin in the United States promptly ceased.

The 1931 Convention required the parties to establish (unless it was already established) a special administration for applying the provisions of the Convention; for regulating, supervising and controlling the trade in the drugs; and for organizing the campaign against drug addiction, by taking all useful steps to prevent its development and to suppress the illicit traffic. In the United States this special administration, the Bureau of Narcotics, had already been established in 1930.

In the United States, the limitation of manufacture of opium and coca leaf derivatives required by the 1931 Convention had already been applied for nine years, or since the effective date of the Act of May 26, 1922, because the restriction on imports of crude opium and coca leaves—the only source of supply of our manufacture—automatically limited the total quantity of derivative drugs, producible from such crude material, to medical and scientific needs.

In the United States, national legislation controlling synthetic drugs preceded by two years similar international control under the Protocol of 1948.

Thus it will be seen that the application in the United States of national control over dangerous drugs has generally preceded the application of measures of international control over the same drugs.

NARCOTICS IN RELATION TO SHIPPING

The principal supply of narcotics for the illicit market in this country is represented by the quantities smuggled or unlawfully introduced into the United States from abroad and for this reason the problem is very closely allied with shipping.

In certain foreign countries where preventive organizations are not adequate to combat the illicit narcotic traffic within their territories, and in others which do not live up to their international obligations to confine the use of and trade in drugs to medical and scientific purposes only, narcotics are readily procurable for smuggling. As the dragnet tightens around them, the drug traffickers move from one country to another where control is still weak or non-existent, and contrive more and more clever ways of getting their poisons to their customers.

Drug trafficking is a very ingenious and resourceful business. All the tricks and ruses of the professional magician, all the devices and inventions of Houdini himself seem tame and unimaginative beside the innumerable dodges and disguises thought up by the tribe of international drug traffickers. The big smuggler spares no expense to get his contraband to his eager customer.

PREWAR METHODS

In one case a smuggler even built a sea-going yacht at tremendous expense just to carry his wares. In 1931 the auxiliary schooner *Marabella*, flying the flag of Panama, left Hong Kong clandestinely and without official clearance for Kwang-chow-wan enroute to the United States. Built in a small shipyard at Hong Kong, she had been especially designed to carry Chinese emigrants and opium to be smuggled into the United States.

At some point on the Coast of China, the *Marabella* embarked some 123 Chinese emigrants and a cargo of from one to four tons of opium, after which she set sail for the Pacific Coast of North America. Careful watch was kept for the ship on the Pacific

Coast of the United States and of Canada, but fog and weather conditions prevented its seizure. On one occasion, when hard-pressed by American Coast Guard vessels, it was said that some fifteen Chinese were thrown overboard from the *Marabella* with weights attached to their feet. Eventually she reached port in Mexico and when boarded and searched by Mexican authorities, neither aliens nor contraband could be found. The ship was later confiscated by the Chinese maritime customs and put in pursuit service where her business was to chase smugglers rather than to conceal them—a true case of poetic justice! Her master was banished from Hong Kong.

While this enterprise constituted one of the largest smuggling operations ever attempted on the shores of the United States, nevertheless "cargo" smuggling was the custom around 1930, and seizures were aggregating as much as 3½ tons (mostly morphine) in a single year.

Prior to 1936, when its anti-smuggling vessels were eliminated, the United States Coast Guard performed an important part in the prevention of smuggling of narcotics into the United States. Maintaining a patrol of United States coastal waters, Coast Guard vessels often went well out to sea to meet and keep under observation vessels which were suspected of having aboard narcotic drugs intended for unlawful traffic. In those days it was a general practice of smugglers to drop overboard before docking sausage-shaped packages of narcotics to be picked up by accomplices in small speed boats. Certain vessels were for this reason escorted into and out of port under observation, and every vessel that had touched a port where narcotics were obtainable was regarded as a potential smuggler. While the Coast Guard seldom participated in large seizures of narcotics, its activity was such that much smuggling was prevented, and many seizures were made ashore as a result of the cumulative effect of its valuable cooperation.

In some cases, the narcotic drugs were lowered into the water from ships, heavy tackles being used to assist in sinking the contraband. In a case involving the arrest of a smuggling organization in Seattle, Washington, in 1934, a search of the residence disclosed a complete light-weight diving suit, together with oxygen bottles and other paraphernalia. The diving outfit was used by a Chinese in recovering from the harbor narcotic drugs which had been thrown overboard from vessels arriving at Seattle from the Far East. In another instance at Seattle, when the anchor of a vessel was lifted, it came up with a large package of opium.

In other cases, narcotics were first placed in cellophane wrappers and then placed in rubber, waterproof bags, the bags then being partially inflated (to keep them afloat) and thrown into the water from Japanese vessels to be picked up by fishing boats. In the case of one Chinese who smuggled drugs into Honolulu in quantities of from 100 to 600 tins of smoking opium, as well as large quantities of morphine, a code system was used between the smugglers and operators of the kind of small boats known as sampans, whereby the smugglers would throw the drugs overboard to be picked up by the sampans and taken ashore.

It was also the common custom in those days to ship large quantities of narcotics falsely manifested as legitimate merchandise, such as lighting apparatus, furs, corn on the cob, spaghetti, coffee, rags, cottons, olive oil, toys, brushes, bowling pins and balls, ladies slippers, black olives, antique furniture, Turkish wool, spare machine parts, and also in oil drums. Even coffins have been used to conceal smuggled drugs! Seizures involving 2,000 pounds of opium, and 6,000 ounces of heroin were not uncommon. The steamship *Alesia* in 1930 arrived at a pier at Brooklyn, New York, with a shipment from Istanbul, consisting of 25 cases, listed as furs. When examined, the cases were found to contain a total of 17,500 cans, each containing one ounce of morphine, there being no furs whatever in the shipment. During the same year the S.S. *Innoko* arrived at Hoboken, New Jersey, containing a shipment billed at lighting apparatus which upon examination was found to be 214 pounds of morphine.

As a result of the 1925 and 1931 international conventions, the amount of morphine produced in licensed factories abroad was cut in half between 1929 and 1932, and the manufacture of heroin was curtailed even more.

The policy of the Bureau of Narcotics was directed primarily to eliminate smuggling and large-scale trafficking, and to secure more effective international agreements and cooperation.

During the first year of the operation of this policy, seizures increased eight-fold. The amount of morphine alone seized in the illicit traffic mounted from 3,400 ounces in 1929 to 26,500 ounces in 1930.

Through these combined efforts, the smuggling picture was soon changed. Cargo lots and large lots concealed in merchandise dwindled to lots of the suitcase variety, and later to cases involving a few ounces at a time smuggled on the persons of seamen.

Under statutes placing a liability upon the master or owner of a vessel in the amount of $25 per ounce for each ounce of smoking opium discovered on board the vessel, and a penalty of $50 for each ounce of heroin, morphine, or cocaine, and $10 for each ounce of crude opium, fines totaling thousands of dollars were assessed, particularly against Japanese vessels then engaged in the Far Eastern trade. In 1931, for instance, total fines assessed under these statutes amounted to almost $400,000.00 These fines which are very high constitute the only measure which has effectively brought home to the steamship companies the necessity of maintaining measures to prevent narcotic drugs from being placed on board ships enroute to the United States.

The Canadian Pacific Steamship Company maintained the best system of preventive measures known. The Bureau of Narcotics has repeatedly urged that all companies take similar steps. The company spent a great deal of money yearly to prevent smuggling of narcotics by its ships. All of its vessels were free from contact by unauthorized craft in the Far East, and the company employed on each ship three trained masters at arms to prevent narcotic drugs from entering or leaving vessels. They were supplied with and made a careful study of all seizure reports showing places in which narcotic drugs had been found on board vessels. The Canadian company found this to be of great advantage, and it minimized the risk of the Canadian Pacific Railroad (its owners) having to pay heavy fines for carrying contraband. No seizure of importance was made on the C.P.R. vessels after the adoption of these measures.

When smuggling was rampant on Japanese vessels, the N.Y.K. (Japanese) Steamship Company adopted measures which included daily and general inspections on board vessels during the voyage. The Japanese officials claimed this expense was justfied because they no longer had to pay heavy fines.

POSTWAR METHODS

Notwithstanding the degree of control achieved during the past two decades over the international narcotic drug traffic, smuggling continues to present a serious problem.

The fact that more effective national control makes very difficult the diversion of supplies from the regular medical channels causes a sharp rise in prices in the domestic illicit market, and the consequent large profits form a constant temptation and incentive to the smugglers who are still able to obtain the drug abroad at comparatively modest prices.

Facts and figures presented to the Seventh Session of the United Nations Commission on Narcotic Drugs by the United States Representative, indicated that the postwar international illicit traffic in narcotic drugs has increased dangerously, and it was recognized that strong efforts will have to be made immediately to cope with the problem.

The illicit traffic in the United States is now supplied chiefly by seamen acting on their own account, but sometimes there is a tie-up with waterfront racketeers in these smuggling ventures. Members of the crews of merchant vessels are tempted by the opportunity to obtain abroad a supply of heroin, for instance, for a small sum because they know that a few ounces, representing a sale value in the United States of hundreds of dollars, may be concealed on the person and the smuggler may thus elude detection at the port of entry and reap the large profits incident to the illicit sale in the United States.

Particularly in the Orient, traffickers in narcotics approach crew members in an endeavor to have them act as carriers when returning to the United States. This opportunity, and the temptation of large profits to the seaman as long as he can escape Customs detection, continues by reason of the nature of his employment. While a number of such cases are detected, it is evident that many such efforts are successful in introducing quantities of contraband narcotics into the illicit traffic of the United States and other victim countries.

Increased surveillance of ships in foreign ports, as well as daily inspections on board vessels during the voyage, deserve careful attention by all Governments and by all ship operators. The policing of vessels while in port should be under the direct charge of a port captain or of the office of the resident agent of the steamship company, and they should be held responsible for the proper policing of the vessel. The master and officers and owners must exercise the highest degree of care and diligence in order that narcotic drugs are not on board.

In 1945, a bill in which much interest was expressed and one which would go far to prevent the smuggling of opium and other narcotic drugs into the United States was introduced by the late Congressman Wilbur D. Mills, in the United States House of Representatives.

The bill provided that all shipments to the United States from any country where opium or other narcotic drugs are permitted to be sold to consumers for nonmedical purposes shall be marked with large, conspicuous letters with the name of such country; that on arrival at any United States port of entry all shipments from such countries shall be set aside for special inspection and examination, consisting of opening each and every package to ascertain if the shipment contains opium or other narcotic drugs; that the American consular officer stationed in a country which permits sale of opium for smoking or eating shall certify that said country permits such sale of opium to the public on each consular invoice and on each bill of health issued to any vessel clearing from such country for any port in the United States; and that, on arrival in any American port of any such vessel, clearance shall not be given until a complete inspection is made of said vessel, its hold, cabins, crew quarters, and of each and every person, whether passenger or crew, on said vessel to determine if any opium or other narcotic drug is being unlawfully imported into the United States.

This bill died with the adjournment of Congress. Mr. Mills introduced a similar bill in the House of Representatives in 1951.

On February 11, 1952, a bill was introduced by the late Congressman Sabath in the United States House of Representatives, which proposed a radically different approach in placing the responsibility for illicit importation of narcotics. This bill would require banks, ship owners and operators, air transport owners and operators, and insurance companies insuring cargoes coming to United States shores, to take effective steps to cut off at its source the supply of narcotic drugs which feeds the drug traffic in the United States and its possessions. It also provides for full cooperation by those countries producing and manufacturing narcotics. Mr. Sabath stressed that "direct, forceful and stringent legislation is absolutely necessary to eliminate, as fully as possible, the importation of illicit drugs."

At the 1952 meeting of the Commission on Narcotic Drugs, emphasis was placed on the fact that various governments should take strong measures to put an end to the smuggling of narcotics by seamen, and the following resolution relating to the illicit trafficking in narcotics by the crews of merchant ships and civil aircraft, was adopted:

THE ECONOMIC AND SOCIAL COUNCIL,

Having been informed by the Commission on Narcotic Drugs that there has been an increase in the illicit traffic in narcotics on merchant ships and civil aircraft during the past five years and that this increase is principally owing to smuggling by merchant seafarers and crews of civil aircraft,

Desiring to take all measures possible to combat this illicit traffic,

1. Requests the Secretary-General to compile as soon as may be convenient and thereafter to bring up to date at convenient regular intervals a list of merchant seafarers and members of civil air crews who have been convicted of offences against narcotic laws on or after 1 January 1953 setting out so far as possible the following information:

   a. Name (including aliases where appropriate);
   b. Nationality;
   c. Date of birth;
   d. Nature of offence and disposition of the case.

2. Instructs the Secretary-General to send the list to the governments of all States with the recommendation of the Council;
   a. That they take appropriate measures
      i. to revoke certificates and licenses currently held by merchant seafarers or members of civil air crews so convicted and
      ii. to withhold the issue to such persons of such licenses and certificates, such revocation or withholding of such licenses or certificates to be either temporary or permanent as may be appropriate in the circumstances of any particular case, provided that if either course does not accord with national law or usage the government concerned shall send a copy of the list to the competent authorities for such action as the latter may decide to take under their own domestic laws, or shall have recourse to such other legal measures as may be open to this government to prevent merchant seafarers or members of civil air crews from carrying out their profession;
   b. That they send a copy of the list to the maritime and aeronautical unions and companies in their territories for their consideration in connexion with the exercise of their disciplinary functions and any functions which they may exercise in connexion with the engagement of crews.

At the 1950 session of the Commission, the United States representative had introduced a resolution concerning illicit trafficking by the crews of merchant ships containing these and other provisions.

Thus in both the United Nations action and in the repeated demands of the United States Congress, there is an urgent and insistent pressure for greater cooperation of enforcement officers in overseas smuggling ports, and particularly for greater vigilance on the part of steamship companies and officers, to prevent the introduction of narcotics into vessels bound directly or indirectly to the United States.

BUREAU OF NARCOTICS

The Commissioner of Narcotics, under the direction and supervision of the Secretary of the Treasury, has general supervision of the enforcement of the narcotic and marihuana tax provisions of the Internal Revenue Code, the Opium Poppy Control Act of 1942, and related statutes, including the administration of the permissive features of the Narcotic Drugs Import and Export Act. It cooperates with the Customs Bureau in the enforcement of the prohibitive features of the latter act. The Commissioner also cooperates (1) with the State Department in the discharge of the international obligations of the United States concerning the traffic in narcotic drugs and (2) with the several States in the suppression of the abuse of narcotic drugs in their respective jurisdictions. The Commissioner represents the United States on the United Nations Commission on Narcotic Drugs.

The duties of the Bureau include the investigation, detection, and prevention of violations of the Federal narcotic laws (including the Federal marihuana law and the Opium Poppy Control Act of 1942), the determination of quantities of crude opium and coca leaves to be imported into the United States for medical and legitimate uses, and the issuance of permits to import the crude narcotic drugs and to export drugs and preparations manufactured therefrom under the law and regulations. An annual report is made to Congress which also serves the purpose of the report on behalf of the Government for transmittal through the State Department to the nations signatory to the International Drug Conventions of 1912 and 1931.

An example follows of the Bureau's thorough investigational methods as set forth in its Annual Report.

TRAFFIC IN OPIUM AND OTHER DANGEROUS DRUGS
SMUGGLING FROM MEXICO

Cross-country drug distributors and members of international smuggling organization convicted

Members of notorious gangster 107th Street Mob of New York, and their California-Mexico suppliers apprehended

A most important case illustrating the cunning which must be met in matching wits against the complicated operations of drug distributors, was climaxed in California, when Salvatore (Sam) Maugeri, (Italian-born) drug dealer and smuggler, was sentenced to twenty years' imprisonment and fined $10,000 for selling 630 ounces of prepared opium and 8 ounces of morphine, for the sum of $22,000 in cash. (These quantities would sell for more than five times this amount in the illicit market by the time they reached the consumer.) Joseph Tocco (The Eye), representative of the group of persons operating in New York City and California, known to the underworld as the "107th Street Mob," who was transporting these drugs across country, was apprehended by narcotic agents as he was changing trains in Chicago. He was later sentenced to ten years' imprisonment and fined $5,000.

Previously, one of the California members of the gang apparently had been "taken for a ride" under bizarre circumstances. The West coast "boss" of the Mob known as Big Nosed Charlie LaGaipa, had been under day and night surveillance by narcotic and customs officers. However, during an interval of a few hours when this surveillance was incomplete due to the manpower shortage handicapping the agencies, LaGaipa disappeared. He was known in the underworld as a double-crosser. A customs agent subsequently discovered his automobile in Oakland, California, and on its instrument panel traces of human brain tissue were found. No further trace of him has been reported. LaGaipa, a well-known New York racketeer, had removed from there to California, from which place he engaged in the smuggling and distribution of drugs on a large scale. After LaGaipa's disappearance, his principal lieutenant, Salvatore (Sam) Maugeri, took over his drug business.

During this investigation another major violator was murdered by rival gangsters, one disappeared, and two fled to Mexico.

LaGaipa, Maugeri and Tocco were members of an international organization engaged in smuggling large quantities of morphine and opium from Mexico for distribution in various sections of the United States, particularly in the vicinities of Los Angeles, San Francisco, Boston, and New York City. Maugeri intimated he would consider no transactions involving less than $10,000 to be paid in advance.

The case had its origin in New York when narcotic agents started looking into the activities of the so-called 107th Street Mob, composed of Charles (Bullets) Albero and some of the most notorious gangsters in New York. They had been sending their trusted men to California, where they would obtain Mexican opium from the Charles LaGaipa organization. This would then be transported to New York, where it would be converted into heroin for distribution in New York and other large cities throughout the United States. As a result of this phase of the investigation, thirty-one persons were indicted, but the narcotic violations were continued by the mob.

The trail led to Boston, where several distributors of narcotics in New England were arrested.

Purchases had been made from some of the principals of the 107th Street Mob, and seventeen members were indicted, including Charles Albero, alias Charlie Bullets, Eugene Tramaglino, Steve Armone, and Joseph Tocco, of New York; Ralph C. Carbone, of Newark, N. J.; and Basil Herbert McKinney, Huckart W. Bethel, and Burton F. Rowe, of Nassau, Bahamas.

A collateral development in the case was an attempt by two of these men to influence a Government witness by offering a bribe. This resulted in the re-arrest of Tramaglino and Carbone shortly after their indictment.

The mob had attempted to exploit a source of supply in the Bahamas. It had raised funds for the purchase of small boats, and obtained small consignments of drugs from Nassau, and was endeavoring to establish a steady source of supply from the Bahamas and from Haiti via the Bahamas to Florida and New York City. In these negotiations the mob had used some of the same personnel who had stolen a quantity of drugs from a drug manufacturer in Brooklyn, N. Y.

Since it appeared that the major source of supply was Mexican opium and the New Yorkers were dealing with members of the old Black Tony Parmagini * gang in California, the emphasis was shifted to the West Coast, where narcotic and customs agents conducted a joint investigation. At great personal danger because of the gang's connection with a number of murders, a narcotic agent who spoke Italian infiltrated himself into a remnant of the Parmagini gang, gained the confidence of the leader Maugeri sufficiently that he, the agent, was actually chosen by the gangster—who feared a double-cross from fellow conspirators on the distribution end—as over-night custodian of a fortune in drugs. Unable to act lest he expose the Government's hand and enable the mob leaders to escape, the officer ruefully saw the drugs turned over to the buyers the next morning. The agents followed through, however, and arrested the runner, Joe Tocco (The Eye), in Chicago, in possession of the drugs. Joseph Dentico, alias Bari, member of the 107th Street Mob, went to California to deliver

* Antone Parmagini, alias Black Tony, who had been "king" of the racketeers on the Pacific coast, was convicted of narcotic law violations and sentenced to serve seventeen years in the penitentiary and fined $17,000.

the $22,000 in cash for the drugs. He was indicted, disappeared, and later apprehended.

The New Yorkers were also dealing with one William Levin, former partner of Parmagini, and just released from a seventeen-year-prison sentence on drug charges. Levin, along with his wife, Elizabeth Levin was arrested, following the seizure of 10 pounds, 1 ounce, 219 grains of prepared opium, and subsequently was sentenced to serve ten years' imprisonment and fined $2,500. Elizabeth Levin was sentenced to one year's imprisonment.

It was discovered that Levin was dealing with Jack Sieman in Vancouver, Canada, also of the old Parmagini gang. Sieman sent a confederate, Morris Irwin, a Canadian customs inspector, from Vancouver to Los Angeles, California, with approximately $8,000, which was delivered to William Levin for 140 ounces of prepared opium. Irwin was arrested as he was about to board a train for Canada, and was later sentenced to twelve years' imprisonment (five years to be served and seven suspended on condition that he leave the United States). Sieman was convicted and sentenced in Canadian courts to seven years' imprisonment and fined $1,000.

The investigation of Levin indicated that he was securing drugs from one Jack W. Morse and his wife, Sally Elsie Morse, of Santa Monica, Calif., and in April and again in July Morse was arrested in possession of opium. The Morses had both been arrested in Norfolk, Va., many times. They went to California in 1942 when Morse was given a conditional release from a Federal institution on a ten-years' sentence for a narcotic law violation. It was reported that during his incarceration Mrs. Morse had, through antisocial activities in Norfolk, accumulated approximately $40,000 which served as capital for them in California to purchase large quantities of opium from Mexico for sale. Lenneth F. Williams was used by the Morses to deliver drugs. After extensive investigation these three persons were arrested in an automobile on the highway en route from Santa Monica to San Francisco in possession of approximately 70 ounces of opium, which they had obtained from a well-known Mexican smuggler, Enrique Diarte. Diarte was also the source of supply in Tiajuana, Mexico, from whom William Levin obtained his opium. Morse was sentenced in California to serve five years' imprisonment; Mrs. Morse to serve three years' imprisonment, but she was released on an appeal bond of $7,500; and Lenneth F. Williams to five years' imprisonment and fined $1,000.

It was ascertained that Enrique Diarte, one of the most flagrant smugglers of narcotic drugs operating out of Mexicali and Tiajuana, Mexico, was expecting to deliver a large quantity of opium to Morse at San Diego, California. His confederates, Jesus Velasquez and Consuelo Landeros de Vasquez, his wife, were arrested by customs and narcotic officers in San Diego, in possession of 175 ounces of prepared opium, and 20 ounces of pure heroin. Diarte avoided arrest by escaping to Mexico, and his confederates captured at the time of the seizure, subsequently forfeited $5,000 and $500 cash bonds, and returned to Mexico.

Diarte's body was found on a Mexican roadside. He had been murdered, having been shot through the heart, his throat cut, and his skull crushed with a heavy instrument. Frank Orbe, onetime drug-smuggling associate of Diarte and later a competitor, was arrested in connection with the slaying. Max Webber, known as Step and a Half, of San Diego, California, was subsequently arrested in Mexico and was also charged with the murder of Diarte. The latter was allegedly killed at a Tiajuana hide-out when he argued with Webber over the price of opium. Webber was asserted to be the brains of the Diarte ring. In connection with this case, 106 persons were arrested in Mexico in what was described by Mexico's Inspector General of Police as "one of the biggest arrests made in the history of Mexico." The traffic was largely in opium grown in Sonora, Mexico.

Previous Criminal Records of Violators in Foregoing Case

Albero had a long criminal record including convictions for possession of concealed weapons, robbery, burglary, and violations of the narcotic laws. Tramaglino had previous convictions for grand larceny and for counterfeiting. Steve Armone had previous convictions for violations of the narcotic laws and a conviction for assault with intent to kill. Carbone had previous convictions on charges of highway robbery, attempted extortion and counterfeiting. In addition to narcotic law violations, Morse had a long record including convictions for attempted robbery, carrying concealed weapons, and assault. When Morse and Mrs. Morse were sentenced previously on narcotic charges newspapers published the fact that Morse had been arrested 43 times in thirteen years, fined 23 times, and ordered to be imprisoned 12 times. Lenneth F. Williams had previous convictions for housebreaking, grand larceny and robbery. Dentico had a previous conviction for robbery, and Maugeri for counterfeiting and violation of the narcotic laws.

The criminal records cited are forceful illustrations of the fact that most narcotic law violators are dangerous criminals and travel in a vicious circle from violation to violation.

In sentencing Salvator Maugeri and Joseph Tocco, Louis E. Goodman, Judge of the United States District Court for the Northern Division of California, made the following comments:

"This nation has agreed with other nations to combat to the utmost the narcotics-selling evil. I don't think there is any statute in existence, the violation of which causes more misery, deprivation, or degradation than that covering narcotics. In this case, the amount and value of the contraband were so great that I can see no other course open but to impose this very severe penalty."

VI

THE STATES AND THEIR RESPONSIBILITY

AT A MEETING OF THE NATIONAL CONFERENCE OF COMMISSIONERS on Uniform State Laws, held in Washington, D. C., in 1932, the fifth tentative draft submitted by the subcommittee on Uniform State Laws was approved and adopted by the Conference as a model Uniform State Narcotic Act. This Act has been enacted into law, substantially as drafted, by forty-three States and the territories of Alaska, Hawaii, and Puerto Rico, and the District of Columbia. Of the five States which have not adopted the Uniform Narcotic Law, two—Pennsylvania and California—have in effect, State narcotic laws which are considered to be of comparable efficacy.

THE ARGUMENT FOR UNIFORM LEGISLATION

Before launching into any discussion of the Act itself it is important that we understand the reasons for uniform legislation. Unfortunately, in the twenty years which have passed since this Act was drafted, the reasons for its enactment have become obscured. As a result, despite the fact that most of the States have enacted it, the obligations of the various States under the terms of the Act have not always been fulfilled as the legal authorities who framed this Act had intended.

Prior to the enactment of any Federal statute the States which legislated against the use of narcotic drugs were impelled to do so in order to secure their citizens against injury to their health, morals, and general welfare. The very early laws were designed

155

to eradicate the evils of opium smoking and the maintenance of opium dens. Later, however, some of the States enacted laws covering other narcotic drugs and providing various penalties for their violation, but so little knowledge of the traffic was possessed by the framers of the various acts that an examination of them revealed such a varied expression of ideas on a single subject that it could only be classed as chaotic and absurd.

When the Harrison Act was enacted by the Federal Government, it was contemplated that the authorities of the several States would accept and discharge the responsibility of investigating, detecting, and preventing the local illicit traffic conducted by the retail peddler, together with the institutional care and treatment of drug addicts within their respective jurisdictions. The expectation, however, proved to be totally unfounded. Instead, notwithstanding the limited power of the Federal Government, State officers became imbued with the erroneous impression that the problem of preventing the abuse of narcotic drugs was one exclusively cognizable by the United States Government and that the Federal law, alone, should represent all the control necessary over the illicit narcotic drug traffic. During the years from 1914 to 1932 the situation was such that very few States made any attempt to accept a just part of the burden of enacting and enforcing adequate laws to control the traffic.

This attitude on the part of the States resulted in an anomalous situation. The public press each day brought news of banks being robbed by organized gangs, details of kidnappings, of burglaries and of gambling rackets, and other articles concerning the operations of bandits who held up stores and citizens. Newspaper editorials criticized the police, and clamorous demands were made upon them to eliminate these menaces to the community well-being. No authoritative source then suggested, or has since suggested, that these matters were anything but State problems. As a matter of fact the person who would suggest that the Federal authorities be called upon to come into the State and catch a hold-up man would be castigated. Furthermore, the local police would be outraged. Yet, in the same community, the insidious drug peddler, carrying on his nefarious work of unlawfully taking away not only the property but also the peace of mind and the morals and health of the citizens and of undermining the general welfare of the community, was considered an exception to the general rule. In spite of the fact that the right to punish such criminals under certain circumstances lay only within the police power of the State, and despite the fact that the founders of our country never contemplated that such activities should be dealt with by the Federal Government, enforcement officers, as well as legislators and administrators in a number of States, conveniently decided that the United States had exclusively assumed the burden of coping with this particular problem of the local community.

This illogical, indifferent attitude not only prevented the passage of adequate laws of inestimable benefit to the State's own citizens, but it resulted in a number of the States in an almost complete failure to enforce the laws already on the statute books, even in those aspects of the crime with which only the State itself could deal. Federal courts became flooded with cases of a minor character which should have been handled in the State courts but which were not thus handled, either from lack of adequate laws or because the duties and responsibilities appeared burdensome, expensive, or distasteful. This in turn caused a slowing up of the prompt and orderly process of justice in major cases, and in many instances cases were continued from term to term because of congestion in the courts and were finally dismissed on account of the unavailability of witnesses or the unknown whereabouts of the defendants. Moreover, if the defendant pleaded guilty he was often accorded so much consideration that a fine or a short sentence was imposed and he immediately resumed his illegal activity.

Some of the reasons advanced by many State and municipal prosecutors for their reluctance or open refusal to prosecute narcotic cases were as follows:

FIRST, that sentences imposed in Federal courts were more severe than those imposed in the State courts. Such sentences were, of course, those meted out to major violators; however, it was obvious that it did not lie within the power of State and municipal courts, where the State law was either inadequate or non-existent, to impose a sentence equal to those which were imposed in Federal courts in cases of greater magnitude and where the offense was a felony.

SECOND, that it was difficult to find a jury which would convict because in the smaller communities the menace of narcotic drugs was not understood. This argument was as incorrect then as it is now. The general public was, and is, fully aware of the destructive menace of drugs, and in smaller communities it has generally been found that the violation of such laws was regarded as an extremely grave, criminal offense.

THIRD, that, when the accused was a woman, the State often had no suitable institution in which to care for her. This only served to point up the need for the enactment of State legislation providing for the care and treatment of all addicts, both men and women. An argument such as this arose only from the desire to place the burden of the necessary financial outlay upon the shoulders of the Federal Government.

FOURTH, that voluntary applicants for treatment strenuously objected to incarceration in a State prison. This only reinforced the necessity for the enactment of legislation by the States for the purpose.

In addition to the reasons heretofore set forth many others were given. There is no need to recount them all. They served as excuses and pretexts to avoid responsibility. They did, however, serve to point up the need for a Uniform State Narcotic Drug Act.

Furthermore, the States, having supreme police power within their own boundaries to enact and enforce all laws necessary to the peace, health, morals, and general welfare of their citizens, are not hampered by the narrow limitations that restrict the Federal Government in its fight to control the illicit narcotic drug traffic. In other words, there were gaps in the Federal law which the States could and should plug. For example, the Federal law did not directly prohibit self-administration by a physician, and the Federal Government could not deprive him of his right to purchase narcotic drugs until the State had first deprived him of his license to practice his profession.

Another example would be the case of a drugstore robbery where the culprit was apprehended by Federal officers while in possession of tax-paid narcotic drugs. This, of course, did not constitute a Federal offense and here again a State law was necessary. Such a situation could be covered in every State law by making mere possession of narcotic drugs a felony and only making it necessary for the State to show that the defendant was within the jurisdiction of the court when apprehended.

In brief, it can readily be seen that the reasons for and the need for a Uniform State Narcotic Act were both cogent and obvious. In recognition of this fact, work was started by a committee of experts in 1927 and after prolonged discussions, much study, and thorough debate, the fifth tentative draft of a uniform act was finally accepted by the Conference of 1932. This law was not perfect, nor did it present a complete solution of the narcotic problem, but it did represent a very important step toward uniformity in the laws as well as in the cooperation between the States and the Federal Government. In drafting the Uniform Act the committee had to take into consideration two Federal laws —the Harrison Act and the Narcotic Drugs Import and Export Act. While it was a fact that without these Federal laws on the subject, the individual States would have been greatly handicapped in combating the distribution of narcotic drugs within their borders, it is important to remember that these acts were not for the purpose of exercising any police power, which is a prerogative of the State. Their validity was predicated on the power of the Federal Government to tax, to regulate interstate and foreign commerce, and to make treaties.

Two other considerations were important; (1) that the State laws did not contravene Federal law; and (2) that there would be no provisions requiring records that would require the citizens in the various States to duplicate their efforts in complying with both laws.

Inherent in the drafting of the Act was the necessity of providing for the protection of those who would use the drugs legitimately, and at the same time establishing penalties for those who might use them illegally, since the architects of this Act did not lose sight of the dual fact that those who were protected by its various provisions might under certain circumstances seek to use the drugs illegally.

THE UNIFORM NARCOTIC DRUG ACT

The Act contains twenty-six sections. In discussing the various sections of the Act it might be well to point out some of its salient provisions. First of all, it prohibits any person from manufacturing, possessing, having under his control, selling, prescribing, administering, dispensing or compounding any narcotic except as authorized in the Act. It provides for the licensing of manufacturers and wholesalers and for the qualifications thereof, as well as setting forth the classes to whom and the manner in which drugs may be sold or dispensed.

One of the sections of the Act deals with sales by apothecaries and provides that an apothecary, in good faith, may sell and dispense narcotic drugs to any person upon a written prescription of a physician, dentist, or veterinarian. A companion section deals with the professional use of narcotic drugs and provides that a physician or a dentist, in good faith and in the course of his professional practice only, may prescribe, administer, and dispense narcotic drugs. It goes without saying that the members of the professions should be thoroughly familiar with these sections of the Act and that they should observe them implicitly.

Further sections set forth the exempt preparations of which more will be said later, prescribe the records to be kept, set up the requirements concerning labeling, and provide for the authorized possession of narcotic drugs by certain individuals.

Section 15 of the Act provides that upon the conviction of any person of the violation of any provision of the Act, a copy of the judgment and sentence and of the opinion of the court, shall be sent by the clerk of the court to the board or officer by whom the convicted defendant has been licensed or registered to practice his profession or to carry on his business, and further provides that upon the conviction of such person the court may, in its discretion, suspend or revoke the license or registration of the convicted defendant to practice his profession or to carry on his business, with the additional provision that upon the application of any person whose license or registration has been suspended or revoked, said board or officer may reinstate such license or registration. The section is both important and necessary; but despite that fact many States have either omitted it entirely or have inserted a watered-down provision in its place. Effective narcotic control in any State would demand its inclusion.

Obtaining or attempting to obtain a narcotic drug or procuring or attempting to procure the administration of a narcotic drug by fraud, deceit, misrepresentation, or subterfuge or by the forgery or alteration of a prescription or of any written order, or by the concealment of a material fact, or by the use of a false name or the giving of a false address is prohibited. Further sections allocate the responsibilities for the enforcement of the Act as well as the penalties for violations.

Provisions with regard to care and treatment of addicts, and search and seizure were omitted from the Act. Since it was felt that each State could better legislate on those subjects individually, and recognizing that the question of care and treatment was of vital and paramount importance and that the cure of addicts was as much a duty of the State as was the care of its insane, the committee recommended that no State delay in making an immediate and complete study of this problem. In connection therewith, the experts were in almost unanimous agreement on two points; (1) that the treatment of drug addiction was a medical and not a penal problem, and (2) that treatment looking toward the cure of addiction, without confinement in a drug-free atmosphere, was uniformly unsuccessful.

From the practical standpoint it is fundamental that a business, legal or illegal, would be bound to fail if deprived of customers, and the peddler of narcotic drugs is no exception. If the peddler were deprived of a market for his illegal wares, he would cease to exist. As long as the addict is at liberty to come and go, the peddler has a steady customer. When the addict is institutionalized he not only loses his value to the peddler but he is also thereby prevented from contaminating others.

Any one reading the draft of the Uniform Act as reprinted in the Appendix will be impressed that so complex a subject could be handled so clearly and briefly by its framers. With the exception of Sections 1, 5, 8, 9, and 20, the law remains as it was originally drafted in October, 1932. Sections 1 and 9 were amended in August, 1942, only because in 1932 it had been assumed that the dangerous drug principle of the *Cannabis* plant was limited to the flowering tops of the female plant. When it was subsequently determined that this dangerous drug principle was contained in the leaves and foliage of both the male and female plants, it became obvious that the Uniform Law should be made to apply to all of the potentially dangerous parts of the plant. Accordingly changes were made in both Sections 1 and 9. The 1942 amendment of sub-paragraph 5 of Section 5 of the Uniform Act was a technical amendment which authorized the sale of narcotic drugs by a licensed manufacturer or wholesaler to certain specified persons employed on ships or aircraft.

The August 1942 amendment of Section 8 of the Act was an excellent and much needed amendment. Section 8 of the original Act exempted from its general requirements medicinal preparations that *contained* in one fluid ounce or, if a solid or semi-solid preparation, one avoirdupois ounce: (1) not more than two grains of opium; (2) not more than one quarter grain of morphine or of any of its salts; (3) not more than one grain of codeine or any of its salts; (4) not more than one eighth of a grain of heroin or of any of its salts; (5) not more than one half of a grain of extract of *Cannabis* nor more than one half of a grain of any more potent derivative or preparation of *Cannabis*. The effect of the 1942 amendment to Section 8 was to limit the exemption to medicinal preparations that contained in one fluid ounce or, if a solid or semi-solid preparation, in one avoirdupois ounce, not more than one grain of codeine or of any of its salts. The reason for the change was the fact that world conditions indicated that the original provisions were too liberal, and the change had the effect of conserving the supply of opium and its derivatives as well as reducing the possibility of sale of narcotics for abusive use since persons who were unable to obtain their supply of narcotics from illicit sources were turning to druggists and other legal sources and purchasing drugs exempted under Section 8 of the original Act.

Experts in the field of narcotic control were in complete agreement that the 1942 amendment of Section 8 of the Act was necessary and in the public interest, and despite the fact that the proposal was fought in several States, forward-looking States such as Colorado, Kentucky, Louisiana, Iowa, North Dakota, Wisconsin, Minnesota, Montana, Oregon, New Jersey, South Dakota, Vermont, and the Territory of Alaska adopted this amendment. In relation to this section, it is noteworthy that heroin is neither lawfully manufactured in, nor imported into, the United States.

Some States have inserted in the Uniform State Narcotic Law sections providing for confinement and treatment in State hospitals for persons convicted under the Act, while other States have made drug addiction an offense under the Disorderly Persons Act. Practically every State has provided a section in their Act relative to search and seizure. Some States, such as Delaware, North Carolina, New Jersey, Maryland, and New York have added sections regulating the possession of hypodermic syringes and needles.

Section 21 of the Act, which provides that no person shall be prosecuted for a violation of any provision of the Act if such person has been convicted or acquitted under the Federal narcotic laws for the same act, or omission which it is alleged constitutes a violation of the Act, has been deleted by New Jersey and Maine. The courts have held that a single offense which violates both Federal and State criminal laws results in distinct offenses against two separate governments. In view of the viciousness of the illicit narcotic traffic, who would not want to see the offenders subject to two long prison terms?

New Jersey, considered by experts to have the strongest and finest laws in the United States pertaining to narcotics, has recently adopted as a type of offense what is known as proselytism in regard to narcotic drugs. New Jersey law, which can be particularly effective where juveniles are involved, provides that any person who induces or persuades any other person to use any narcotic drug unlawfully, or aids or contributes to such use of any narcotic drug by any other person, is guilty of a high misdemeanor, and subject to a penalty of up to seven years imprisonment, together with a fine. This broad enactment should prove a powerful weapon for prosecutors.

Section 7 of the Uniform Act, which deals with the professional use of narcotic drugs, is extremely important. It provides that a physician in good faith and in the course of his professional practice only, may prescribe, administer, and dispense narcotic drugs. This same provision is also contained in the Federal law. Most States have required the prescription to be in writing. Federal regulations require that the prescription be in writing, except in the case of exempt preparations or where the drugs are dispensed to bona-fide patients directly. Thus, the physician's privilege is predicated on two elements—the patient, and the dispensation in the course of professional practice only. It follows, of course, that if that important second element is not present, the physician's privilege is nullified.

The Act is silent with relation to the specific diseases for which a narcotic drug may be supplied, and the question of what constitutes bona-fide medical practice is determined by a consideration of the evidence and the circumstances. The answer resolves itself on whether the prescription was real and genuine and was predicated on bad faith rather than bad judgment. A physician may prescribe narcotic drugs for a disease or injury in the treatment of which narcotic drugs are medically indicated; however, dispensing the drug for the purpose of satisfying the craving of an addict for the drug is not dispensing or distributing it in the course of professional practice and is therefore illegal.

VII

CONTROL AND ENFORCEMENT

NARCOTIC ADDICTION IS NOTHING NEW IN THE UNITED STATES.
Thirty-five years ago it was two or three times more prevalent
on a per capita basis than it was at the outbreak of World War
II. Toward the war's end narcotic addiction was still further
greatly reduced; and when that war ended, addiction in this
country was at the irreducible minimum.

NARCOTIC LAW ENFORCEMENT

The Federal narcotic laws and the State narcotic laws have
been in force for only a long generation. Throughout that period
and until just recently there had been a steady, substantial decline in addiction. It coincided with the enforcement of penal
narcotic laws. There was a deviation from a straight decline in
a rather sharp upsurge after World War I, but that soon subsided.
In the early 1920's, heroin and morphine were available at
$25.00 to $50.00 an ounce. A few unscrupulous doctors were
writing prescriptions for narcotics in large amounts. Drugs were
smuggled into the country in trunk lots. It was common for
addicts to have tremendous habits: 5, 10, 20, or even 50 grains
of morphine a day! Today, the unscrupulous doctor has almost
disappeared. The occasional cheater dares to prescribe a few
grains only instead of ounces. Wholesale diversions are non-
existent except for an occasional bona-fide robbery or burglary.
Smuggling is in small amounts that can be concealed on the
person.

The addiction of persons in their *late teens,* loosely referred to as teen-age addiction, is not novel in this country. Heroin was used by this age group in the early 1900's. It was one of the developments which brought about the enactment of the Harrison Narcotic Law in 1914 and later on, other Federal and State laws outlawing the narcotic traffic. The following is cited from a report of a special committee appointed by the Secretary of the Treasury in 1919: "Most of the heroin addicts are comparatively young, a portion of them being boys and girls under the age of twenty. This is also true of cocaine addicts." But after the post-World-War-I outbreak, the tendency was for fewer young people to become addicted. The new addicts were in a slightly older category, and the youthful addict became an exception and a curiosity.

On the basis of World War I experience, the Bureau of Narcotics feared and predicted some rise in addiction after World War II, and these forebodings proved to be well justified. An increase in addiction was noted around 1948, first as a trickle and then as a small stream. By 1952, admissions to Federal narcotic hospitals and other factors showed that the crest of that increase had been passed. However, the situation remains a dangerous one, the correction of which is a challenge to the best efforts of everyone concerned.

It is the considered judgment of officials in the Bureau of Narcotics that this epidemic of narcotic addiction among younger people is primarily an extension of a wide-spread surge of juvenile delinquency. While it can not be completely dismissed or completely described as a big city problem, that, practically speaking, is the situation. Also, it is a problem confined for the most part to those areas where many factors contribute to delinquency and lawlessness among the affected youth.

The new addiction is a contagious manifestation which endangers fringe groups with whom the hoodlum comes in contact.

Not the least consideration in the revival of narcotic addiction in this country was the fact that the field force of the Bureau of Narcotics had been reduced approximately 25 percent from the pre-World-War-II roster. This was a logical development during the World-War-II years when the narcotic traffic subsided to practically an irreducible minimum. When efforts were made to get the force back to something like reasonable numerical strength, difficulties were encountered because of competition with military preparedness and other high priority programs. The 82nd Congress, however, restored the force of narcotic agents to prewar strength.

Again, in many cities the relatively good situation had brought about the disbanding of or a great reduction in the specialized local forces needed for narcotic policing. While in some places these men were retained as a nominal narcotic squad they were assigned other duties.

PROSECUTION AND THE COURTS

Also, the narcotic traffic had an incentive for revival in an atmosphere where the courts had veered from a course of dealing vigorously and rigorously with these racketeers to a practice where relatively short sentences and general leniency were the rule. This was perhaps a not too surprising development. As the traffic was lessened, some of the cases brought before the courts seemed to be of a less consequential nature. However, this atmosphere was simply an open invitation to professional racketeers. To it attaches some of the responsibility for the revival of the traffic and for the inability of the Bureau of Narcotics to deal summarily with it when it reappeared.

Likewise, the prosecuting arm must take some of the blame, since in many jurisdictions there was great delay and dilatoriness in bringing cases to justice. In many instances the Bureau of Narcotics would arrest a trafficker three or four times before his first case was brought up for trial.

Beginning in 1943, certain United States Supreme Court decisions put brakes on the whole Federal law enforcement machinery in the areas of arrests, searches and seizures, and confessions. These decisions work a special hardship in the investigation of rackets so covert, so elusive and so transitory as narcotic violations. Hope for relief in one direction is indicated by a more recent decision, but the disabilities are still very real.

There has also been a climate of public opinion which has favored the spread of narcotic addiction. Contributing to this was a very unfortunate report released some years ago by the so-called LaGuardia committee on marihuana. The Bureau immediately detected the superficiality and hollowness of its findings and denounced it. However, it gave wide circulation to the idea that this drug is relatively innocuous. Now marihuana is found to be the introductory drug to much of the heroinism in young people in the United States. The LaGuardia report is the favorite reference of the proselytor for narcotic-drugs use.

The general public does strange things which often bring about undesirable situations; then it looks to the schools or the police or somebody else to correct the mistakes. Few will dispute that entertainment-world headliners make a terrific impression on youth. But, consider how the public reacts respecting glamorous entertainment characters who have been involved in the sordid details of a narcotic case. Is there a spontaneous reaction which drives them out of show business as might have been done a generation ago? Not at all. There seems to be some sort of public approval of these degenerate practices. The character is not ostracized. Instead he or she immediately becomes a box-office headliner.

RESPONSIBILITY FOR ENFORCEMENT

In a recent report the Senate Committee on Organized Crime in Interstate Commerce said "the most effective means of combating the narcotic problem is through effective enforcement facilities." That means enforcement at every possible level and by every possible means. In the policing phases of enforcement there is of course a tremendous Federal responsibility. This crime is certainly characteristically an interstate one. As a matter of fact, it is international. Therefore, the Federal Government has a burden of trying to eliminate sources abroad, of attempting to shut off the introduction of the drug at ports and borders, and of combating the interstate traffic within the country.

There is also a heavy responsibility on the local police because of their general concern with law and order. Most of the States have the Uniform State Narcotic Law. All of them have some sort of narcotic laws. Many communities have special narcotic ordinances. The great interest and wide support given by local police in campaigns to stamp out the narcotic evil has contributed much to the Federal control pattern. Cooperation between Federal narcotic officers and the local police in the enforcement of the narcotic laws has been about as close to perfection as human frailty will permit. Every day from St. Paul to New Orleans, from Los Angeles to New York, narcotic agents are engaged in cooperative ventures with one police agency or another. It is a fine testimonial to the feeling of mutual confidence which exists with other law enforcement officers and prosecutors that few narcotic cases of consequence are developed in the United States without the active participation of the Bureau of Narcotics.

When increases in Bureau law-enforcement personnel were requested, the legislators were insistent on knowing whether or not the local communities had been shouldering their proper share of the burden in narcotic law enforcement. Fortunately, in many localities there had been a quick response by the police departments to the emergency. This included the specialized training in narcotic information of the police departments, the creation or augmentation of specialized narcotic squads, and similar programs. Narcotic enforcement is a unique operation. It cannot be effectively handled by officers who do not have particular training. These officers should not be given other duties. The hours and the difficult working conditions are such that narcotic duties are likely to suffer if the officer can properly divert any of his attention to other work. Because of the interstate and source-of-supply features, there should be the closest liaison with Federal narcotic officers. Every bit of information which might run back to original sources should be exploited.

However, there are many types of cases which can and should be handled independently. Simple possession type cases, the usual forgery cases, those arising from the robbery or burglary or larceny of narcotic drugs where no interstate organized ring is indicated, all could best be handled on the initiative of local police. In the interest of conserving manpower, it is important that cooperation between various services does not result merely in a doubling up of officers on an operation which could be performed just as well or better singly.

In addition to suppressing the traffic in narcotics, police activity against drug addicts is a very essential part of general police operations. The great majority of addicts are parasitic. This parasitic drug addict is a tremendous burden on the community. He represents a continuing problem to the police through his depredations against society. He is a thief, a burglar, a robber; if a woman, a prostitute or a shoplifter. The person is generally a criminal or on the road to criminality before he becomes addicted. Once addicted he has the greatest reason in the world for continuing his life of crime. Most policemen recognize that one of the best ways to break up waves of pocket-picking, petty thievery and burglary in a community is by making a round-up of the narcotic addicts. Often, a long term of imprisonment for a narcotic addict on narcotic charges will rid the community of a burglar or thief for that period.

Still to be attained in most States is proper control over the addict. It is the young addict who contaminates other youth with his dreadful vice. He should be plucked out of the community and quarantined, forced to undergo a cure. He will not do it voluntarily. People who argue against this on the basis of cost of hospitalization forget that $50.00 a day or more may be the cost of the addict's criminal depredations.

Public concern about the narcotic problem has brought an increase in the force of the Federal Bureau of Narcotics. It has enabled some police departments to augment or create specialized squads to deal with the criminal narcotic traffic. It has brought about more prompt and vigorous prosecution in many places. Courts are imposing more severe sentences under the Boggs Act which was passed by Congress and approved by the President on November 2, 1951. Legislation similar to the Boggs Act has been enacted by several of the States as an amendment to their Uniform State Narcotic Law.

During the early part of 1952, there were definite indications that the increase in teen-age drug addiction had been halted and that a downward trend in drug addiction again existed. This does not mean, however, that there can be any dimunition of efforts against the narcotic traffic.

ADDICTION AND THE CRIMINAL

It is well established that a large proportion of the pickpocket artists, the shoplifters, the professional gamblers and card sharks, the confidence men operating fake horse race or fake stock sale schemes, the "short con" men such as the "short change artist" or the coin matchers, are addicted to the use of narcotic drugs. By the very nature of their criminal activities, they are required to be migratory and could be classed as roving criminals. No community seems to be entirely free of their depredations and activities. Particularly is this true of tourist centers and other places where large crowds congregate.

A skilled gang of pickpockets can steal and will steal an average of sixty pocketbooks a day, and a good day's work will net them $1,500 or more. The elite among the confidence men, preying on the gullible, may have incomes that reach really impressive figures.

The records of criminals, of the type referred to, usually disclose numerous arrests; but it is interesting to note that in the majority of cases the charges were merely vagrancy or suspicion. This no doubt was due to the very nature of their criminal activities, which makes it difficult to apprehend them in the commission of the crimes in which they specialize, and still more difficult to obtain sufficient evidence to secure a successful prosecution. The criminal is released from custody by the posting of a small cash bond and as a rule fails to appear to answer the charges.

PLACES OF CONCEALMENT

In view of the high percentage of addiction among these criminals, it is suggested that a thorough and systematic search for narcotic drugs be made of their persons, effects, baggage, rooms, and automobiles. The search should be conducted by at least two officers, not only for completeness but to assure corroboration in case of prosecution. It should be thoroughly systematic from the head to the feet. The suspect should be disrobed and his wearing apparel minutely examined. (The disrobing is important because narcotic drugs have frequently been found attached to intimate and other parts of a prisoner's anatomy.) They also have been found concealed in hat-bands, neckties, seams of clothing, hidden small pockets in coats, vests, trousers, and also in the cuffs of the trousers, in fountain pens and watches, as well as in the heels and inner soles of shoes. These suggestions apply to female as well as to male suspects.

Instances have occurred where pockets of trousers, handkerchiefs, and sheets of paper have been saturated with a concentrated solution of a narcotic, thus assuring a supply in case of arrest and detention. These devices are known in the vernacular as sachets.

The search of rooms and living quarters presents a more difficult problem due to the ease with which narcotic drugs can be concealed. Here a thorough and systematic search should be conducted, starting with some focal point. Narcotics have been found hidden in the bottoms of talcum-powder cans and other cosmetic containers, fixtures, bedsteads, window-sills, chandeliers, door knobs, backs of dresser drawers, secret places in the woodwork, and many other ingeniously devised places of concealment.

Baggage and trunks should be searched for secret compartments.

Narcotics have been found concealed in hub-caps, in back of headlights, in spare tires and tubes, and other secret places in automobiles. Under certain circumstances, vehicles used for the transportation and concealment of narcotic drugs can be seized and forfeited to the United States Government.

Often local officers can be of considerable assistance if, when arresting dealers in narcotics, they will look particularly for indications of the source of supply of the drugs. Most drugs in the illicit traffic must be smuggled into the country originally and, therefore, it follows that dealers and users of drugs inland must be supplied from coastal or border points. Sometimes deliveries are made by dealers in person, but often drugs may be shipped by mail, express, or as baggage. Often upon the persons or premises of an arrested dealer will be found communications, usually written in a guarded manner, as well as telephone numbers and addresses. Since wholesale dealers in illicit narcotics, in distributing centers, often play a comparatively safe game by shipping their wares to distant points only, without catering to any local trade, information of the sort indicated, if conveyed to the proper authorities may prove to be particularly helpful in locating, and eventually apprehending distant wholesalers. In this connection, it should be borne in mind that ordinary trade or geographical considerations do not always govern the distribution of illicit narcotic drugs. Someone on the Pacific Coast, close to a seaport where, ordinarily, it would be thought that narcotics would be available, may nevertheless send to New York for his illicit drugs because of price or personal considerations. Relevant documentary evidence, as well as narcotic drugs found, should be duly identified by all the seizing or searching officers, in order to ensure its acceptance as evidence in court.

In carrying out enforcement activities against those who are both criminals and addicts, the utmost caution should be exercised, and the officer should never relax his guard for a moment, otherwise tragedy may ensue from the viciousness and recklessness of this type of criminal.

On Sunday morning, September 24, 1950, Narcotic District Supervisor Anker M. Bangs was shot to death by a narcotic addict while search was being made of the addict's living quarters. This is merely one example from hundreds of cases in which law-enforcement officers have been killed or grievously wounded by drug addicts.

VIII

NARCOTICS AND MODERN MEDICAL SCIENCE

NO OTHER DRUG IS SO UNIVERSALLY USEFUL IN THE PRACTICE OF
medicine as opium, either as such or in the form of morphine.
It is unexcelled as a pain reliever, and is widely used in disorders
of the intestinal tract, in pulmonary diseases, and in certain
cardiac disorders.

Unfortunately morphine induces in persons who employ it for
any considerable time a condition of dependence upon it which
leads to serious physical and mental disorders. Morphine produces a condition of euphoria in the individual and gives release
from mental worries and from bodily discomforts with a resulting
feeling of well-being. When the euphoria passes off the old worries and discomforts return, perhaps with increased mental depression. These symptoms can be relieved by another dose of
morphine and thus the addiction is established. In addition tolerance to the drug is established in the individual so that larger
and larger doses are required to produce the same results.

Because of the dangers resulting from the addicting properties
of morphine and opium, most governments have enacted legislation in an endeavor to confine its use to medical and scientific
purposes. In the United States, passage of the Harrison Act in
1914, together with the ceaseless efforts of enforcement officers
of the Government, has resulted in a very considerable decrease
in the number of narcotic addicts.

RESEARCH

In 1929 the National Research Council appointed a Committee on Drug Addiction and undertook a definite program of study.* In 1939 the work was taken over by the National Institute of Health and all the experimental work was transferred to Washington. From 1929 to 1939, the program consisted of two divisions—experimental, including laboratory and clinical studies, and a review of the literature of the subject in both its chemical and pharmacological aspects.

The chemical portion of the experimental work was carried out at the University of Virginia under Dr. Lyndon F. Small and Dr. Erich Mosettig, together with a staff of chemists and graduate students. This portion of the work embraced a study of the chemistry of the morphine molecule with the synthesis of allied compounds, and also of compounds based upon the phenanthrene nucleus which is contained in morphine. In all, more than four hundred compounds were prepared during the ten years of work.

The pharmacological study of these compounds was carried on at the University of Michigan by Dr. Nathan B. Eddy. From the large group of substances received from Dr. Small a small number were selected for clinical trial and these were studied in various hospitals especially as to their effect upon pain and cough. Only those compounds were subjected to clinical trial which showed in the pharmacological study that they possessed strongly some of the desired characteristics of morphine without being too toxic or exhibiting undesirable side actions. The addicting property was studied principally upon man.

The clinical investigation was largely carried out under the United States Public Health Service. Studies were made upon addicts confined in the Federal Prison at Leavenworth, Kansas, and later at the U. S. Public Health Service Hospital at Lexington, Kentucky. The hospitals of the Health Department of Massachusetts at Waltham and at Pondville, the Walter Reed Hospital at Washington, the Marine Hospital at Baltimore, and the Uni-

* See Appendix II for a summary of the accomplishments of this committee.

versity of Michigan Hospital at Ann Arbor, were all used in the various clinical studies.

The study of the literature naturally divided itself into two portions, chemical and pharmacological.

CHEMISTRY OF THE OPIUM ALKALOIDS

Chemistry of the Opium Alkaloids prepared by Dr. Small, Consultant in Alkaloid Chemistry, United States Public Health Service, was published by the United States Public Health Service in 1932 (Supplement No. 103 to the Public Health Reports).

The material in this volume was assembled in the course of a systematic study of the literature of the opium alkaloids undertaken in a research project established at the University of Virginia by the Committee on Drug Addiction of the National Research Council. It makes accessible what is known of the chemistry of these alkaloids and their derivatives. The literature to January 1, 1932 was covered, and every reaction and every compound described in the literature is mentioned. The volume extends far beyond the scope of a systematic collection of facts, however, in describing historically the discovery and investigation of each opium alkaloid, and in discussing critically and exhaustively the structural question. The author has himself made valuable experimental contributions to the chemistry of the opium alkaloids.

In Part I the benzylisoquinoline and minor alkaloids are considered in separate chapters, each having a bibliography.

The phenanthrene alkaloids are treated in Part II, with bibliography arranged to facilitate specialized study.

Practically all data have been taken from the original literature, which is widely scattered in the journals of all lands. Copious literature references are supplied, and the source of every statement made is shown.

Dr. Small has used painstaking effort and care in organizing the extensive material on the opium alkaloids into this excellent monograph. It is of vast assistance to those interested in the subject.

THE PHARMACOLOGY OF THE OPIUM ALKALOIDS

A review of the biological work on opium and its alkaloids entitled *The Pharmacology of the Opium Alkaloids*, (two volumes) constitutes the second portion of the survey (Supplement No. 165 of the Public Health Reports). The responsibility for the preparation of this material was assumed by Dr. Eddy, as director of the experimental staff. He has done much more than prepare a composite picture of the effects of morphine as they have been established experimentally. The types of experimental work which have been done are described thoroughly, the net results are summarized, and the large gaps which still exist in our knowledge of this substance are indicated.

A feature of the book which proves of great value to anyone interested in the field is a very complete subject index, covering not only the text of the monograph itself, but also the main features of all of the papers in the enormous bibliography, papers all too numerous to have received notice in the text.

Its author and the Committee on Drug Addiction expressed the hope that this study of the literature,* presenting a picture of current knowledge of this subject, would prove of value to workers in the field as a starting point from which new investigations could be carried on.

Nine years of effort went into the preparation of this survey of the pharmacology of the opium alkaloids. Part 1 was published in 1941. Part 2 is contained in a separate volume published in 1943. It has a very extensive bibliography. The substances selected for inclusion in Part 2 are related to morphine. It surveys all that has been written on the physiological effects of these drugs and summarizes it without loss of anything but unimportant details. The material has been classified first according to drugs, next according to the same physiological divisions adopted for morphine, and finally according to the animals studied.

One interesting development of this study was the discovery

---

* The literature on addiction prior to 1940 has been summarized by Krueger, Eddy and Sumwalt in *The Pharmacology of the Opium Alkaloids*. The literature on addiction which had appeared since 1940 was reviewed by Isbell in the *Journal of Pharmacology and Experimental Therapeutics*, 99: 355-397, August, 1950.

of desomorphine, which is eight times more powerful than morphine, but unfortunately as addicting, so that its manufacture
has not been permitted in the United States.

Much of the work done by Doctors Eddy and Small has been
the basis for the recent development of new narcotics which
have proved very valuable in the practice of medicine.

NARCOTICS IN MEDICINE

In an effort to disseminate information to the medical profession concerning the use of various derivatives of opium in the
legitimate practice of medicine, first, from the standpoint of their
indispensable use, second, from their ill-advised use, and third,
from their abusive use, the American Medical Association published in their *Journal* a series of articles from March 14 to June
6, 1931, and subsequently published in book form, entitled *Indispensable Uses of Narcotics.*

DANGER OF OPIATES IN SEVERE ASTHMA

In an article entitled "Death from Asthma—A Warning" which
was published in *The Journal,* June 13, 1942, a warning is given
that the opiates should be rigorously avoided in the treatment
of severe asthma, and especially so since other drugs such as
ephedrine derivatives, epinephrine, and aminophylline are superior.

OPIATES IN CANCER CASES

A study entitled "The Relief of Pain in Cancer Patients" published by the United States Public Health Service in 1936, con-
cludes that a lesser amount of narcotic drugs is necessary in
cancer cases than is ordinarily supposed.

MORPHINE VS. OTHER REMEDIES

Morphine deadens pain of all descriptions (neuralgia, intestinal
pains, wounds, etc.) by diminishing the sensitiveness of the cer-

ebrum. In the same way it induces sleep, and is particularly effective when pain is the cause of sleeplessness. It is not, however,
necessary to use morphine for all pain, as there are many other
remedies. It is a medical malpractice to employ morphine simply
as a soporific. Morphine is often the only practical remedy for
excessive excitement produced by various causes. It also allays
irritation of the upper air passages, but, for this purpose, can
nearly always be replaced by codeine. Morphine has a powerful
influence on respiration; it reduces the rapidity of the breathing
and allows deeper breaths to be taken.

GUARDING AGAINST ADDICTION

In the hands of the physician, drugs are indispensable medicaments, while in the hands of the layman they spell ruin. All habit-
forming narcotic drugs have this in common—that their continued use and abuse in every case leads sooner or later to loss of
moral control and even to physical and mental collapse.

Whenever, in persons who are by constitution and general
predisposition mentally unstable, the balance of the mental and
physical functions is upset, this can be remedied by the use of
opium or morphine. In order, however, that these substances may
give this relief, these psychical conditions must be present; they
need not have manifested themselves actively, but may be latent
and may be brought into operation by the supply of morphine
to the system. The first effect of morphine upon such persons is
a feeling of extraordinary well-being and vigor, a state of euphoria which a man in an unbalanced psychical condition seeks to
recreate by further supplies of the drug. Later on, however, the
effect of the same dose is only to produce satisfaction at the feeling of "normal health" attained by the use of morphine. The
action of morphine on the addict may perhaps be conceived of
in this way—that it has become a factor in the process of cell
metabolism. If this factor is absent, the functions of the cells are
thrown out of gear. If the drug is supplied afresh, the functions
apparently become regular once more.

The intensity and duration of the condition induced by morphine vary from one individual to another. Many persons who

are used to taking morphine are content with relatively small amounts—in some cases, over longer periods at a stretch. In the majority of cases, however, increasingly numerous and stronger doses are needed to produce the illusion of approximately normal health or to avoid a feeling of depression. Any unnecessary excess over the quantity required to counteract that feeling—a luxury dose so to speak—may produce a real euphoria, in which morphine and opium act as a screen preventing the unpleasant impressions and the worries of life from reaching the surface of consciousness.

Such people are, of course, in special danger, for, with the prolonged use of morphine, habituation sets in, manifesting itself principally in an ever-growing craving and increased bodily tolerance. The tolerance shows itself in this way: that doses of morphine, toxic in themselves, are then tolerated without any of those acute symptoms of poisoning which would necessarily appear in persons not thus habituated. In order to alleviate pain and produce euphoria, increasingly large doses are needed. There is then an uncontrollable and tormenting desire for ever-larger quantities. Finally, the amount of morphine taken is so great that the cells can no longer assimilate it.

APPRAISAL OF VALUE OF NEW OPIATES

A thorough and exact study of the different properties of opiates—analgesic, cough-relieving, hypnotic, etc.—is always a matter of some difficulty, and this difficulty is greatly increased if account is taken of the individual's constitution and condition, the special reaction of his autonomic nervous system and the nature of his endocrine formula.

Appraisal of the value of new opiates calls for a comparative examination of the different pharmacological and chemical effects. Research on these lines will indicate the group of opiates to which the new drug should be assigned and show its peculiar reactions in the human body. Where drugs of the morphine group are concerned, this work of systematic comparison is the more needful, since those who prescribe or generally recommend them are taking a serious responsibility. However, the clinical examination, which is usually of primary importance, is particularly difficult in the case of these various substances, which are very similar in nearly all respects.

The effects on the respiratory centre are difficult to judge by experiment. The real value of a medicament as a cough-relieving agent can be tested only on the human body, because the animals which are habitually used for these experiments are not subject to coughs. Only recently have experimental conditions been produced in them which may be equivalent to the chronic irritation associated with a cough in the human patient.

Also, recently a way of objectively measuring the influence of any remedy on a cough has been found. In the main, however, the physician must fall back on observations carried out with the utmost care, and on the evidence of the patient. If optimum conditions are to be ensured, the research can only be reliably conducted on intelligent patients in a hospital.

The influence of new opiates on pain and sleep is relatively easier to assess, but here also we have to take into consideration individual response, and depend for our evidence on the intelligence and goodwill of the patient. To measure the intensity of pain in a patient, we have no objective scale, and none either for the degree of alleviation of pain. Furthermore, it is impossible to compare absolutely equal intensities of pain to assess the analgesic strength of two drugs. Finally, and this applies particularly to opiates, one can never be quite sure whether the patient's own judgment of the pain-stilling power of a drug is unaffected by any euphoric influence.

Whether a new drug is habit-forming or not can be judged only after collecting all the necessary facts. Whenever a new opiate comes on the market, it is often claimed to be non-habit-forming and not to have the undesirable by-effects commonly associated with the older drugs of the same group. One particularly famous example of this kind was that of a drug put on the market several decades ago—heroin; but there have been other instances in more recent times. The great difficulty in estimating the degree of euphoria arises from the observation, often repeated, that individuals vary in their reactions to drugs. Some of them feel unpleasant by-effects of morphine to a very high degree, and to such persons it would be almost impossible to administer morphine in an emergency. Others feel the typical effects of euphoria, and they return to the doctor to try to obtain more. These facts, known to every experienced physician, afford the best proof of the difficulties entailed in judging the comparative value of opiates.

SUBSTITUTES FOR MORPHINE

A brief consideration will be given of several of the other opium derivatives which have been used as substitutes for morphine—eucodal, dicodid, and dilaudid. The drugs will be considered in relation to morphine as a basis of comparison. This is only a study of the literature.

EUCODAL

Eucodal is regarded as a derivative of thebaine, but it has no longer the characteristics of this substance. It does not cause convulsions; on the contrary, it is as narcotic as morphine (and codeine). Its action is also based on a central effect, and, generally speaking, is not only much more powerful than that of codeine but may sometimes surpass even that of morphine.

As an analgesic, eucodal is superior to morphine. Order of decreasing strength: *heroin, eucodal, morphine, codeine, dionine.*

As a cough cure, eucodal is less potent than codeine and dionine. It seems that eucodal, like morphine, effects a reduction of the sensitiveness of the respiratory tract commensurate with the degree of narcosis produced. Order of decreasing strength: *codeine, dionine, heroin, eucodal, morphine.* Its ability to create euphoria is less pronounced than with morphine. Order of decreasing strength: *heroin, morphine, eucodal, codeine, dionine.*

The toxicity in the rabbit is reflected in the convulsive power. Order of decreasing strength: *heroin, dionine and eucodal, codeine, morphine.*

The toxicity for man is inferred from the depressing effect on the respiratory function of the rabbit. According to these observations, eucodal seems to be slightly more dangerous than morphine, but less to be feared than heroin. Order of decreasing strength: *heroin, eucodal, morphine, codeine, dionine.*

If we try to assign eucodal to its appropriate place in the opiate group, we have to put in between morphine and codeine; but it is closer to morphine in type of its effect. Its fundamental characteristics are very similar to those of morphine, but perhaps less pronounced, especially in the matter of concomitant effects, addiction properties, etc. (Kleinschmidt) W. E. Dixon is of opinion that eucodal is more similar to heroin than to morphine.

Eucodal frequently proves superior to morphine in swiftness of action and intensity of the effect, but the duration of the former is generally shorter—on the average 6 hours, instead of 12 with 0.02 gram of morphine (Pfeiler). Other authors have not observed this shortness of effect, e.g., Wohlgemuth. In many cases, eucodal seems at least equivalent to morphine, and in some even superior (Baumm).

If one should try to sum up in a general way the addiction properties of eucodal, one would say that the danger of contracting a habit through taking eucodal should not be thought to be a less serious matter than the risk of morphine addiction, a conclusion which is borne out by the evidence collected by means of a questionnaire and published in 1928 (P. Wolff).

DICODID

The second of the three newer habit-forming drugs under consideration, dicodid, has been known since 1923.

Dicodid is really a derivative of codeine, but with some of the characteristics changed, and occupying in the sequence of the opiates a position somewhat different from that of codeine.

Gottlieb came to the conclusion, in the light of his experiments on different animals, that dicodid should be placed—with respect to pharmacological character—between morphine and codeine. Eddy and Reid also judged that dicodid is more effective than codeine, but less so than morphine.

The main effect of dicodid is its sedative action on coughs.

The sedative effect of dicodid on the brain is similar to that of morphine, and much more distinct than that of codeine (Rickmann). In comparison with morphine, the general narcotic effect of dicodid is considerably less (Sametinger), whilst the soothing action on the respiration is more powerful than that of codeine, and the narcotic effect on the sensation of pain equal to that of morphine.

It is well known and recognized that dicodid creates euphoria and addiction, but the degree to which this is the case will now be explained more fully.

There is no question but that dicodid is able to create euphoria (Sametinger, Wehl, Simon, and others); it seems, however, that the euphoria is less intense than with morphine (Roller, Castelhun). R. F. Mayer states, on the other hand, that euphoria seemed to endure longer in his observations than that of morphine, because it does not have the same sleep-inducing effect as the latter. This slighter degree of euphoria may explain why the danger of contracting a habit seems to be less strong (Castelhun, Weinberg, Hecht, Bing). Furland and Schelenz state, accordingly, that the effect on coughs is not diminished by the administration of dicodid over a longer period. With dicodid, therefore, the danger of misuse seems to be considerably less than it is with morphine, even when dicodid is administered over lengthy periods (Sametinger). But there is no doubt, as has been said before, that cases of addiction to dicodid are known (Sametinger, Mueller de la Fuente). Dicodid has not been found to be an equivalent substitute for morphine (Castelhun). Abstinence symptoms are described as being relatively slight, passing off quickly (R. F. Mayer). The drug could always be withdrawn without great difficulty (Ries, Sametinger), even in cases of depression (Richtzenhain). Abstinence symptoms in animals are less pronounced than with morphine or dilaudid (Eddy and Reid).

Addiction to dicodid seems to be rarer and easier to combat than that of morphine or eucodal.

DILAUDID

The question of dilaudid has been studied with great care by R. B. King, C. K. Himmelsbach and B. S. Sanders as reported in *Supplement No. 113* of the United States Public Health *Reports,*

1935. From observations made on morphine addicts, involving the substitution of dilaudid for morphine, it was concluded that:

1. Dilaudid is an effective substitute for morphine.
2. Dilaudid possesses definite addiction liability.
3. Definite morphine-dilaudid cross-tolerance exists.
4. The potency of dilaudid is approximately four times that of morphine, but the duration of its action appears to be considerably less than that of morphine.
5. In the presence of a daily laxative, equally effective doses of dilaudid are as constipative as morphine.
6. In equally effective doses, dilaudid appears to effect sleep as does morphine.
7. Dilaudid appears to possess no therapeutic advantage over morphine.

FALLACY OF LEGALIZING DRUG ADDICTION

To carry into effect the Hague Convention of 1912 "to limit exclusively to medical and legitimate purposes the manufacture, sale and use of morphine, cocaine and their respective salts," the Congress of the United States enacted, in 1914, major legislation in the form of the Harrison Narcotic Act. It stopped the indiscriminate purchase across the counter in the United States of drugs for the purpose of satisfying drug addiction.

Under this law the responsibility for the proper prescribing and dispensing of narcotic drugs, rests upon the physician in charge of any given case. Without reference to the question of addiction, a physician acting in accordance with proper medical practice may prescribe or dispense narcotics for the relief of acute pain or for any acute condition. Mere addiction alone is not recognized as an incurable disease.

THE CLINIC PLAN

The *clinic* plan recently advocated by a small minority group in one section of the country, would radically change the present plan of enforcement and revert to dispensing narcotic drugs to drug addicts for the purpose of maintaining addiction. Under this plan anyone who is now or who later becomes a drug addict would apply to the clinic and receive the amount of narcotic drug sufficient to maintain his customary use. The proponents of the plan claim that the "dope peddler" would thus be put out of business.

This plan would elevate a most despicable trade to the avowed status of an honorable business, nay, to the status of practice of a time-honored profession; and drug addicts would multiply unrestrained, to the irrevocable impairment of the moral fiber and physical welfare of the American people.

Any plan which, like the one under discussion, tends to maintain and increase the spread of drug addiction is not only in direct contravention of the spirit and purpose of the international drug conventions, which the United States solemnly entered into along with *seventy-two other nations of the world*, but also constitutes a complete reversal of settled national policy of more than twenty years standing with respect to narcotic drug traffic control. This national policy is firmly rooted in the national legislation as interpreted by the highest Federal Court, and supplemented by concomitant State narcotic legislation.

The supplying of narcotics to addicts merely for the purpose of maintaining addiction certainly constitutes distribution for abusive use even if taken over by practitioners, and to recognize such procedure as legal would be not only a gross repudiation of our international obligations, but also a reversion to conditions prior to the enactment of national control legislation and a surrender of the benefits of twenty-four years of progress in controlling this evil, in which control the United States has been a pioneer among nations.

The answer to the problem is not, therefore, to accept narcotic drug addiction as a necessary evil and calmly proceed to ration with a daily supply each and every person who applies for the ration. It should rather be the provision by the States of facilities for scientific treatment of these unfortunates, looking toward a cure, coupled with vigorous and unremitting efforts toward elimination of improper sources of supply so as to facilitate complete rehabilitation of the reclaimed addict and *prevent the addition of recruits to the ranks of these unfortunates*. By scientific treatment is meant that professional treatment which includes confinement or restraint upon the addict to insure that no surreptitious source of supply is available to him that would defeat the purpose of the attending physician.

COURT DECISION ON THE NATURE OF PRESCRIPTIONS

One of the provisions of the Harrison Narcotic Law makes it unlawful to sell, barter, exchange, or give away the specified narcotic drugs except pursuant to an official order form, but there is an exception to the requirement of an official order form in the case of a practitioner who prescribes or dispenses to a patient "in the course of professional practice only." Within a very few years of the date the Harrison Law became effective, the United States Supreme Court was called upon to rule upon the application of this exception to the prescribing by a physician of narcotic drugs to an addict merely to gratify drug addiction. In the case of *Webb and Goldbaum vs. United States* (1919) 249 U. S. 96, the following question was propounded to the Supreme Court:

If a practicing and registered physician issues an order for morphine to an habitual user thereof, the order not being issued by him in the course of professional treatment in the attempted cure of the habit, but being issued for the purpose of providing the user with morphine sufficient to keep him comfortable by maintaining his customary use, is such order a physician's prescription under exception (b) of section 2 (of the Harrison Narcotic Law)?

In reply to this question, the United States Supreme Court held that

To call such an order for the use of morphine a physician's prescription would be so plain a perversion of meaning that no discussion of the subject is required. That question should be answered in the negative.

It is pertinent in this connection to quote from a report of a special committee of physicians, which was adopted by the American Medical Association and printed in *The Journal* of that Association June 14, 1924, reading in part as follows:

Your committee desires to place on record its firm conviction that any method of treatment for narcotic drug addiction, whether private, institutional, official or governmental, which permits the addicted person to dose himself with the habit forming narcotic drugs placed in his hands for self-administration, is an unsatisfactory treatment of addiction, begets deception, extends the abuse of habit-forming narcotic drugs, and causes an increase in crime. Therefore, your committee recommends that the American Medical Association urge both federal and state governments to exert their full powers and authority to put an end to all manner of such so-called ambulatory methods of treatment of narcotic drug addiction, whether practiced by the private physician or by the so-called "narcotic clinic" or dispensary.

In the opinion of your committee, the only proper and scientific method of treating narcotic drug addiction is under such conditions of control of both the addict and the drug, that any administration of a habit-forming narcotic drug must be by, or under the direct personal authority of the physician, with no chance of any distribution of the drug of addiction to others, or opportunity for the same person to procure any of the drug from any source other than from the physician directly responsible for the addict's treatment.

The Federal Bureau of Narcotics has never approved ambulatory treatment for drug addiction, for the reason that experience has shown where the addict controls the dosage he will not be benefited or cured. Medical authorities agree that the treatment of addiction with the view toward effecting a cure, which makes no provision for confinement while the drug is being withdrawn is a failure, except in a relatively small number of cases where the addict is possessed of a much greater degree of will-power than that of the average addict.

ABUSE UNDER THE CLINIC PLAN

The clinic plan for dealing with the narcotic addict problem is not a new development, as stated in the League of Nations Document O. C. 1614. A number of clinics were opened in various cities in the United States during and after the year 1919 in an effort to deal with the problem, but whether or not the original intention was to attempt a cure of the so-called patients, it soon developed that the average clinic merely represented a supply depot for drug addicts. In some cases, so far from a reduction in treatment, it was found that so-called patients were actually receiving increased dosage from the clinic and in one case where a peddler was convicted in Texas for a violation of the Harrison Law it was shown that he had gone directly from Leavenworth Penitentiary to the clinic at Shreveport, Louisiana, in order to gain access to a cheap supply of morphine.

In an investigation of the alleged patients of one of the clinics many were found to have criminal records and perhaps the majority of the so-called patients were not local residents but were individuals who had been attracted to the city by the cheap source of supply for morphine and who managed to make a living, including the price of the drug, by petty thievery, panhandling, and other anti-social and parasitic activities. With literally hundreds of so-called patients on the rolls of the clinic, it is obvious that this large group could not receive anything approaching proper attention from the few physicians assigned to the clinic and even if a conscientious attempt were made at giving the reductive ambulatory treatment, the plan was foredoomed to failure because of the fundamental inefficiency of this treatment. By the end of 1925 most, if not all, of these clinics had been closed because the State authorities themselves had realized the failure of the plan. Not only did the clinic plan fail to solve the narcotic drug addict problem but it actually introduced new problems involving the public welfare.

At a session of the Opium Advisory Committee of the League of Nations, the question of clinics and the rationing of drug addicts was brought up and it was the consensus of the many nations there assembled that to establish clinics in countries which have a narcotic drug problem would be as sane as to establish infection centers during a smallpox epidemic. The rationing of addicts has been frowned upon by the signatories to the narcotic conventions, and the only place in the world where such a policy is now in force is in the Far East.

THE FORMOSA PLAN

With regard to the plan which is in effect in Formosa, we have a valuable and informing contribution to our knowledge on the subject by Dr. Tsungming To, Health Commission of Formosa. After classifying 57,073 crimes committed during seven years by natives of Formosa, his records show that based upon the relative proportion of opium users to non-users we find 70.83% *crim-*

inality among opium users as against 29.17% criminality among non-users. In Formosa, opium smoking is licensed and the cost of opium is very small. *Under these conditions the only attributable cause for greater criminality among narcotic addicts than non-addicts is the direct effect of the use of narcotics upon the character of the user.* Dr. To gives us the answer. It is because drug addiction causes a relentless destruction of character and releases criminal tendencies.

ASSOCIATION AS CAUSE OF ADDICTION

In a certain city in our country, during a recent period when there occurred an influx of criminal addicts from neighboring cities and States to obtain narcotic drugs from several doctors and druggists, highway robbery increased from 55 cases in the corresponding period of the previous years to 97 cases; larceny from 738 to 1,025; and burglary from 11 to 58. In another city, the chief of police reported that theft and burglary complaints dropped noticeably following a narcotic clean-up. Thus it will be seen that from a business, social, and moral standpoint, the presence and contact of narcotic addicts in American communities is a potential danger. One survey showed that 67½ percent of the addicts under observation had criminal records. Here too it might be stated that association is the largest single cause of drug addiction—all authentic surveys on the subject have shown that 50 percent or more of the addicts acquired their habit through association with other addicts.

The consensus of world-wide study of work and solutions pertaining to narcotic drug addiction gives no credence to any school of thought which fosters the rationing of drug addicts under the so-called clinic system. The problem is one which cannot safely be temporized with. The American Government could not advocate or approve any policy that would tend to make easier the access to narcotic drugs by a group which has proved itself, both by habit and precept, lacking in the physical willpower and mental stamina necessary to solve the problems which led them to drug addiction in the first place, much less to solve the addiction itself.

It is believed that easy or unrestricted access to drugs tends materially to increase addiction. In the light of present and past knowledge, the very best thing that can be offered to a drug addict, for his own good as well as for the good of society, is confinement and treatment with a view to cure and rehabilitation.

CONCLUSION

The United States has spared neither time nor money in getting at the basic truth in regard to drug addiction and every effort has been made to help the addict, but it is known that the narcotic clinic has been of no avail. The clinic idea, which simply supplies the addict with his drug for an indefinite period, creates a vicious circle. In this connection, it is interesting to note that most of the advocates of this system do not even go so far as to advocate a "cure." It is simply set forth as a plan whereby the addict maintains his old habit and invariably returns to the clinic where a fresh supply is administered or given to him for a small sum, and the victim again set at large to contaminate others to his ranks; this procedure to be continued indefinitely.

This method of treatment has never yet proved successful anywhere in the world, and it has been given sufficient trials that would have shown the merits if any had existed. Certainly anyone with even cursory knowledge of the situation realizes the complete futility of the narcotic clinic. The American Government would never tolerate such a system based on the degradation of its citizens.

As earlier stated, to conform to the clinic idea, it would be necessary to abrogate the treaties into which the United States solemnly entered along with sixty-four other nations of the civilized world. This Government has received many tributes of admiration for its leadership in narcotic control work, and if it hopes for the continued approval of the world, it cannot afford to compromise or slip from the high pinnacle it has attained and now occupies in the family of nations.

NARCOTIC CLINICS IN THE UNITED STATES

During and after the year 1919, forty-four or more narcotic clinics or dispensaries were opened by municipal or state health officials in large cities throughout the United States in an experiment which it was thought might present a simple and easy solution of the problems arising from narcotic drug addiction. Drugs were sold to addicts at prices as low as two cents a grain.

There seems to be no doubt that the clinics were started in good faith but at that time there was a general lack of familiarity with the facts regarding the addiction evil and, according to a report made in 1921 by a member of the Committee on Narcotic Drugs of the American Medical Association, it had not been realized that:

The vice that causes degeneration of the moral sense and spreads through social contact, readily infects the entire community, saps its moral fiber, and contaminates the individual members one after another, like the rotten apple in a barrel of sound ones.

The 1921 report continues:

Public opinion regarding the vice of drug addiction has been deliberately and consistently corrupted through propaganda. Cleverly devised appeals to that universal human instinct whereby the emotions are stirred by abhorrence of human suffering in any form, or by whatever may appear like persecution of helpless human beings; lurid portrayals of alleged "horrible suffering inflicted" on addicts through being deprived of their drug; adroit misrepresentation of fact; plausible reiteration of certain pseudoscientific fallacies designed to confuse the unscientific mind; downright false statement, and insidious innuendoes assiduously propagated are brought to bear on an unsuspecting public to encourage it to feel pity for the miserable wretches, "whose name is legion" we are told, and whose "sufferings," hysterically exaggerated, are graphically served up to be looked on as if they were actually being made "victims of persecution" by the authorities, who would deprive the wretches of even the drug they crave.

The shallow pretense that drug addiction is "a disease" which the specialist must be allowed to "treat," which pretended treatment consists in supplying its victims with the drug that has caused their physical and moral debauchery, . . . has been asserted and urged in volumes of "literature" by the self-styled "specialists."

Significant articles of sensational character dealing with narcotic addiction have appeared in the public press during recent months, denouncing the alleged "persecution" of the addict and . . . well calculated to create in their favor popular prejudice.

This same line of thought which prompted the clinic experiment in the early days of narcotic law enforcement has recently been exploited again as a solution of the present narcotic addiction problem.

The clinics were operated for varying periods and in one city as long as four years. The most comprehensive series of facts, having real scientific value that had then been compiled anywhere in the world, was embraced in the published statistics gathered from analytical study of the nearly 8,000 cases of addiction registered and cared for in narcotic clinics during about ten months by the Department of Health of the City of New York. These cases were subjected to most careful observation and study by specialists qualified to make scientific analysis and arrive at sound conclusions. They reported, "We have given the clinic a careful and thorough as well as a lengthy trial and we honestly believe it is unwise to maintain it any longer."

In some clinics careful physical examinations were given addicts before enrollment, and various methods of registration were practiced, including the furnishing of identification cards containing physical descriptions, photographs, and fingerprints of the addicts. (In clinics where the addicts were fingerprinted, numerous fugitive criminals were located and returned to the States where they were wanted.)

In some clinics addicts were given diminishing amounts of narcotics until reaching a minimum dosage which would prevent withdrawal symptoms; in others, cures of addiction were attempted in hospitals operated in conjunction with the clinics, as in New York City, if the addict would submit himself to treatment. In still others, the customary dosage was maintained or often increased upon the demands of addicts. Administration of drugs to addicts on the premises was attempted and proved to be completely unworkable because the addicts were unwilling to go the required distances to the clinics every six or eight hours during the day and night when they wanted a shot.

By the end of 1925 all of these clinics had been closed by the various State authorities for the reasons quoted herein.

As an indication of the vast extent of addiction during the several years around 1920, four hospitals in New York and the U. S.

Penitentiary at Atlanta, Georgia, reported 25,000 cases of drug addiction; and the New York City Prison reported 12,000 cases. (In all of the 25,000 cases where immediate and absolute withdrawal of the drug was routine practice there were no deaths resulting.)

At Sing Sing Prison in 1920, the number of drug addicts received increased over 100 percent; in 1922 they increased over 500 percent; and in 1923 the increase was over 900 percent.

In 1922, 20 percent of the prisoners incarcerated in the Atlanta Penitentiary were drug addicts; at the Woman's Workhouse, Blackwell's Island, New York, practically all prostitutes committed were drug addicts; and from 60 to 80 percent of all committed there were drug addicts.

This illustrates the situation with regard to crime and drug addiction during the period when the narcotic clinics were in operation.

In 1952, 7.8 percent (1,157) of the prisoners committed to Federal institutions were narcotic addicts, and 1.4 percent were marihuana addicts.

In New York City it was stated by the Department of Health that "the purpose of this narcotic clinic is to provide temporary care for addicts who have been patronizing profiteer doctors and druggists." The clinics practically eliminated this profiteering practice, but there suddenly mushroomed and thrived in its place a tremendous illicit traffic in narcotics which supplemented and nullified the reduction treatments of addicts in attendance at the clinics.

In a one-year period in the early 1920's when these clinics were in operation, the volume of illicit peddling of narcotics reached the point where an incredibly large amount of 71,151 ounces of narcotic drugs was seized in the domestic illicit traffic—or more than fourteen times as much as was seized in 1952.

In New York State alone, when sixteen or more narcotic clinics were in operation throughout the State, almost 4,000 ounces of narcotic drugs were seized in illicit channels during a year or almost as much as was seized in the entire United States during 1952.

THE NEW YORK CITY NARCOTIC CLINIC

Excerpts from Report published February, 1920, by S. Dana Hubbard, M.D., Acting Director, Bureau of Public Health Education, Department of Health, City of New York:

The arrest of several trafficking physicians and druggists (in the spring of 1919) for violating the narcotic laws caused the Department of Health to open a relief clinic, which began as an emergency and was expected, naturally, to be only a temporary experiment, but the necessity was so acute and attracted so much attention from those interested that the Commissioner of Health decided to continue it for some time, in order to study this subject and obtain data regarding the problem.

We feel that we have had an unusually wide and peculiarly general experience with drug addicts of all classes—classes so large as to make us think that others' experience in this form of practice has not been nearly so extensive.

The public narcotic clinic is a new thing. In fact there are only a very few in existence and, if we may judge from our experience, they are not desirable and do not satisfactorily deal with this problem. We have given the clinic a careful and thorough as well as a lengthy trial and we honestly believe it is unwise to maintain it longer.

The clinic has been found to possess all the objectionable features characteristic of the so-called "ambulatory" treatment, as practiced by the trafficking physicians.

From our experience with narcotic relief and registration in New York City, we now are of the opinion that the present law—the Harrison Act—should be strictly and uniformly enforced. To do so would bring these tipplers in drugs to the front and would hurt no one, not even the users themselves. These opinions, while radical, are not given to belittle the opinions previously expressed by persons supposedly well-informed on this matter, but are the results of an actual practical and intimate working knowledge of this subject.

Most—in fact 70 percent—of the addicts, in our clinic, are young people; (9 *percent, or 743 out of a total of 7,464, were in the 15-19 age group*) they have had no really serious experiences—surely none sufficient to occasion a desire to escape all of life's responsibilities by recourse to the dreams of narcotic drugs; therefore the one and only conclusion that we can arrive at is that the acquirement of this practice—drug addiction—is incident to propinquity, bad associates, taken together with weak vacillating dispositions, making a successful combination in favor of the acquirement of such a habit. Being with companions who have those habits, they, in their curiosity, give it a trial (similar to the acquirement of cigarette smoking in our young) and soon have to travel the same road to their own regret. (Reasons assigned by addicts for acquiring the habit were: Bad Associates . . . 5,190 or 69 percent; Illness . . . 1,994 or 26 percent; Other Causes . . . 280 or 5 percent.)

The emergency relief narcotic clinic has brought out a mass of material, from which it is possible to study this problem, heretofore more or less vaguely thought about and on which there were but few statistical data.

Habits usually only affect the individual but, in drug addiction, indulgence appears to react on the community. The effect on the community is evidenced by debauching of its citizenry, by increase of crime and antisocial vices. The extent also spreads like a pestilential disease.

There may be those who say drug addiction is a mysterious disease; that it creates a disease mechanism; that it is not a matter for the authorities, particularly for the Department of Health;

Our opinion is that this habit is not a mysterious disease; there is a very general and complete understanding of drug addiction from the therapeutic standpoint among all who have dealt with it in institutions. In our opinion, drug addiction is simply a degrading, debasing habit, and it is not necessary to consider this indulgence in any other light than an antisocial one, and that those who are charged with correcting and preventing such tendencies should be stimulated to do so to their utmost, and all efforts exerted in this direction should be free from restraint, absolutely unhampered, and that all physicians interested in the general welfare of the people should earnestly encourage such action.

There may be other views regarding the control and prevention of drug addiction, but we opine that this is the natural and sane one to be generally expressed. It can be safely said, without contradiction, that drug addiction, per se, is not a disease, nor to be so regarded any more than excessive indulgence in cigarettes (to which all of these addicts appear to be committed), or an overindulgence in alcohol (which but few of them require). Experience in our clinic appears to indicate that drug addiction affects the human economy in about the same way as does any vicious abuse, excess, or bad practice, each attacking and weakening along the channels most susceptible.

The practice of the clinic was not to prescribe for any new applicant an amount over 15 grains—10 grains being the usual amount. Reduction was by a gradual daily lessening of the amount prescribed. It was found that some could be reduced to as low as 2 or 3 grains. Others, disloyal to the clinic and themselves, would, when deprived by the clinic, refuse to accept our regulation and would buy additional amounts outside.

Many addicts endeavored to get from the clinic actually more than they themselves needed. The drug was sold much below the general retail price—the price at drug stores was 7 to 11 cents a grain to the addict; while, at the clinic, the maximum price was 3 cents a grain and later this was reduced to 2 cents.

Some individuals would endeavor to deceive and actually would go through registration and examination in order to obtain the drug to sell to addicts at an advance of the clinic price.

Having demonstrated certain peculiar conditions regarding the narcotic drug addict, with a study of over seven thousand, covering a long period, and after consultation with many well informed on this subject (and who were not in any way economically concerned except for social betterment of individuals), we concluded that narcotic drug addiction serves no useful purpose; that there is no justifiable reason at all for its continuance, and that the certainty with which this indulgence benumbs and blunts moral fiber, the practice being indulged in the majority of instances (69 percent) by the young boy or girl, makes its control absolutely necessary. That ambulatory treatment is farcical and useless, and is only putting off what should be immediately done. Physicians should not be permitted, under guise of treatment, to prescribe narcotics for such indulgence. Laws should be so amended that the narcotic addict, when determined, should be sent by due process of commitment to a suitable institution and held there until a medical officer considers it safe for him to return to society.

Narcotic indulgence in the young adult exists without adequate reason, and the mere fact that such a habit has been acquired innocently is not an adequate reason for condoning this fault. Formerly many held the opinion that it was difficult, unsafe, and required expert care to cure an addict, but it is not so by any manner of means. A plan called by the addicts "cold turkey"—abrupt withdrawal (practiced in Kings County Hospital, and without a death)—is not only possible but practical. It does occasion some suffering, . . . We hold no brief for either plan, but we state with positiveness that the plans are simple, but to be successful absolute control of the addict in preventing renewal of supply is the essential factor.

From an experience with many hundreds passing through our clinic and hospital (when the addicts approached the "irreducible minimum" of the drug they were sent to the hospital for cure), it is our firm opinion that entire withdrawal may, in many instances, be successfully performed. That all that is needed is to have the withdrawal supervised by a physician, so that those who need medical care may get it when it is required.

Strict, adequate, and proper as well as uniform enforcement of the law—the Harrison Act—throughout this city and country is now demanded and is essential towards preventing recruits to these miserable ranks. Drug addiction spreads like a pestilence through association. In a study of over 7,500 addicts in this city exemptions requested for persons ill of some malady numbered less than 250.

The practices of drug addicts to meet the demands of their depraved appetites causes financial embarrassment, and to meet these desires the addicts become immoral and antisocial. When in need of the drug, or overstimulated from indulgence, all moral influence and self-control are lost.

These individuals either in need of the drug or under its stimulating influence are a distinct menace to society. They will commit the most revolting of crimes in cold blood.

Drug addiction is not a mysterious disease. From a purely scientific point of view it would be interesting to have more light on the problem of tolerance, but on therapeutic indications and possibilities there is but little difference of opinion.

Drug addicts, under careful medical and supervisory nursing, present no pathological condition—only a disturbed or perverted functioning.

The action of internal organs is inhibited or functionally disturbed, but, when these influences are removed and normal action permitted, this derangement quickly disappears.

It is our opinion that any form of cure can take an addict off his drug provided this is done promptly. This was done at Riverside Hospital, in 3 to 5 days, without discomfort to the patient.

From information obtained from the large number of addicts who have come to our clinic, most of whom have taken various methods of our cure, it may be concluded that all methods of withdrawal are equally efficacious and only differ in regard to the comfort of the addict while taking the cure. Aftercare is always essential.

Treatment of the narcotic drug addict by private physicians prescribing and druggists dispensing, while the individual is going about, is wrong. The giving of a narcotic drug into the possession of an addict for self-administration should be forbidden.

The case of drug addiction that can be cured by ambulatory treatment is the rare exception and so unusual as to make one think it impossible.

Physicians generally are of the opinion that ambulatory treatment is not good practice, and few doctors use this form of treating addicts; it is believed that those so doing must be either ignorant of proper methods or do so in bad faith.

Our study of this problem in this city indicates, most positively, the necessity for the general and uniform enforcement of the Harrison Act.

The clinic is not the solution.

A number of clinics were established by the Commissioner of the State Narcotic Drug Control Commission in the State of New York. There was no legal authority for the establishment of these clinics, and in appointing physicians to conduct them the Commissioner of the State Narcotic Drug Control Commission "usurped the authority."

ALBANY, N. Y. (Estimated cost for one year for prescriptions and narcotics for 120 addicts, $52,000.00. Two doctors running the clinic had total weekly income of $429 from narcotic prescriptions; the profits made by the drugstore which filled prescriptions netted $17,000 yearly.)

Police gave information that most of the addicts attending this clinic had criminal records; many of the women were prostitutes, and some of the men were living from the earnings of the women; many others were engaged in selling narcotics in the underworld.

A number of the addicts stated that they were not addicted to the use of cocaine prior to attending the clinic. The youngest addict attending the clinic in 1920 was 21 years of age.

No cures were effected at this clinic. Criminal addicts and women prostitutes were drawn to this clinic from Detroit, Michigan; Cincinnati, Ohio; Pittsburgh, Pennsylvania; New York City and Utica, New York. The following are comments made by members of the Police Department concerning the clinic:

Capt. F. L. "The Narcotic clinic is a crime. Criminal addicts are attracted from all parts of the country."

Capt. G. P. "I am opposed to the clinic. The addicts turn to the easiest way of getting the amount of money they need, which is dangerous to any community they may be in."

Detec. A. G. "The clinic is no good. It is a disgrace. Certain women addicts solicit men on the streets in order to get their money for morphine and cocaine at the clinic. Some of the addicts in attendance are peddling dope and others are buying additional quantities from peddlers. Most addicts reported getting at the clinic more narcotics than they needed."

ROCHESTER, N. Y. Sixty-five addicts were in attendance at the clinic. The profit of the doctor operating it was around $7,000 per annum and it was said he devoted from 9 to 10 hours time weekly to the clinic. Assuming that he spent ten hours weekly, fifty-two weeks a year, 520 hours or 52 days, ten hours each, his compensation was therefore $7,000 for 52 days' work. He supplied addicts with narcotic drugs sufficient to last them for periods ranging from 2 to 10 days. This clinic, like most others of the ambulatory type, was condemned by men high in medical authority.

Police had required 24 of the addicts attending the clinic to leave the city. There were a great many narcotic peddlers in the city who were selling drugs to some of the addicts obtaining only a limited supply of morphine at the clinic. Several of the addicts attending the clinic were peddling drugs smuggled from Canada. There were at least 45 addicts in Rochester who were not enrolled at the clinic and who obtained supplies from peddlers.

The clinic had been located at three different addresses due to the fact that the landlords of two buildings where it was previously located considered it undesirable to have addicts coming in and out of their buildings.

Statements concerning narcotic clinics in other States:

NEW HAVEN, CONNECTICUT. Four physicians connected with the clinic stated that it was not probable for any cures to be effected by the ambulatory treatment. They all agreed that the majority of the addicts enjoyed good health other than the ill effects brought about by their addiction. They also agreed that in their opinion many of the addicts obtaining morphine at the clinic disposed of it illegally among other addicts.

A number of known addicts residing in New Haven were not enrolled at the clinic and obtained their supplies from illicit sources. There were peddlers in New Haven all the time the clinic was in operation. Dr. S. L. Spier stated that occasionally he learned of an addict who supplemented his supply of drugs which he obtained at the New Haven clinic by visiting other clinics.

At the New Haven clinic it was disclosed that one addict operated a railroad signal switch tower, working on the midnight shift, and that he was in control of the most important switches on the main line of this railroad. The throwing of a wrong switch might cause a serious train wreck and the loss of many lives.

Another addict was engaged in the delivery and taxi business. He was unable to obtain a driver's state license under his own name as he was a known addict, and as a subterfuge he used a fictitious name under which he secured the license.

PROVIDENCE, RHODE ISLAND. Dr. Clifford Griffin, police surgeon in charge of the clinic, stated that no cures could be effected in their clinic and that "Isolation is absolutely necessary if an attempt is to be made at a cure. This means restraint in an institution. Most cases must be restrained by legal commitment to be held until a cure has been satisfactorily effected."

Peter F. Gilmartin, Superintendent of the Police Department, stated that he was very much opposed to the clinic because it effected no cures and only fed the addicts, making it attractive for their remaining in Providence; and that the only way to successfully treat and cure an addict was to put him in an institution.

One addict who obtained morphine from this clinic was under Federal indictment for having sold morphine so obtained.

Another addict stated that it was not an uncommon practice for some of the addicts obtaining daily amounts of morphine of seven grains, or even less, on prescriptions at the Providence narcotic clinic, to peddle part of the drug so obtained. This man had been discharged from Blackwell's Island Hospital, New York City, and pronounced cured of drug addiction. As soon as he returned to Providence he resumed the habit by visiting the clinic and persuading the physician to issue him prescriptions.

ATLANTA, GEORGIA. Many known drug peddlers were patronizing the clinic and receiving their supply which was freely peddled. Drug peddling in Atlanta was exceedingly prevalent notwithstanding the clinics in that city.

At this clinic there were no records of cures by the ambulatory reductive method.

Ten of the addicts attending the clinic volunteered to be sentenced for a term of one year to the Federal penitentiary for the purpose of curing their addiction to drugs.

One addict attending the Atlanta clinic received a prescription for morphine daily. While attending the clinic he was indicted by the Federal grand jury for having 20 ounces of morphine in his possession.

A young woman attending the clinic stated that she married her husband when a young healthy girl; that he was an addict and taught her to use the drug, after which he sent her to rooming houses to obtain money through prostitution.

Several of the addicts attending this clinic were working in positions hazardous to public safety, such as railroad switchmen and chauffeurs.

Many of the addicts sold and exchanged drugs among themselves. Most of them were of the underworld type.

No cocaine was prescribed by the physicians in charge of the clinic, which caused the addicts to purchase that drug from peddlers, as well as additional quantities of morphine.

The city health authorities stated that the clinic system was a nuisance, that clinics were generally abused with bad practices, and that they were a burden on the city.

Dr. F. K. Boland, President of the Fulton County Medical Society, stated that he did not approve of an ambulatory clinic; that institutional treatment is the only method; and that the narcotic clinic was of no benefit to drug addicts or to the community.

Two City Physicians stated that the only effective treatment for drug addicts is confinement, and that the clinic system was of no benefit to the city.

Dr. T. F. Abercrombie, Secretary of the Georgia State Board of Health stated that the narcotic clinic was not beneficial to anyone and on the contrary drew narcotic peddlers and many undesirables to the city; that the addicts should be placed in an institution.

Mayor James Key of Atlanta stated that the clinic system was very bad and that he could not think of anything that could be worse.

Chief of Police Lamarr Poole stated that the clinic does not benefit the addict or the community, but attracts many thieves to the city; that it is difficult to handle the thieves when the city authorities were providing narcotics for them. He urged that clinics be abolished. The narcotic clinic or dispensary operated under seemingly legal authority tended to approve and encourage rather than discourage the drug habit.

Eighty-five of the 190 addicts served at the clinic had police records and two were known dope peddlers.

Practically all in attendance at the clinic were without visible means of support.

SHREVEPORT, LOUISIANA. It was estimated that 75 percent of the drug addicts in Texas made their headquarters at Shreveport following the operation of that clinic. One addict in Texas was apprehended receiving a package through the mail containing 8 grains of morphine sulphate bearing the label of the Shreveport Clinic. The defendant stated that he had a friend in Shreveport who obtained 20 grains of morphine from the clinic daily and that he always received half of it.

Forty percent of the addicts gave a history of venereal disease or examinations showed its presence

In this clinic many fugitive offenders were caught by the police and sent back to places where they were wanted.

The clinic sold monthly $2500 worth of narcotics, at a monthly profit of about $1800.

Several prostitutes attended the clinic and plied their trade on the streets of Shreveport. One, 19 years of age, and another, 23, had never been addicts until they registered at the clinic.

The addicts said they would take less drugs if the cost were higher; in some cases daily amounts were increased from 5 or 8 grains to 10 grains daily. Addicts who had used 2 grains daily before coming to the clinic were demanding 10 grains. Addicts who got supplies at the clinic sold to other addicts who would not attend. Some of the addicts were also buying narcotics from peddlers while attending the clinic. Many of the addicts came from distant States and said they would be off the drugs if it were not so easy to procure them. One addict who had never taken drugs previously was induced to buy drugs from an addict in attendance at the clinic and later persuaded to accompany her to the clinic. The former made a regular practice of selling narcotics she got from the clinic and of getting morphine from other persons she persuaded to go to the clinic.

One citizen of Shreveport stated: "The clinic is an outrage; it should be discontinued; it brings a lot of bums here; nothing is safe on the streets, and the quicker the clinic is closed the better." Another stated:

"One of the greatest things that can be done for this community is to close the narcotic clinic." These statements were typical of the public opinion on the subject.

Evidence showed a continuous traffic in narcotics between clinic patients and others, and that numerous persons who had never used drugs previously, or who had been cured of addiction over several-year periods, registered at the clinic and started using as high as 10 grains daily. Many of the persons used fictitious names and addresses, and were without visible means of support. One addict stated that when he came to Shreveport before the clinics were established, the same doctor who was in charge of the clinic had cured him of drug addiction, after which he had discontinued the use of drugs for 18 months. As soon as the clinic went into operation he applied for 8 grains of morphine a day, and when his case was investigated he was receiving 12 grains daily at the clinic from the same doctor who had previously cured him of addiction. Another addict who had been cured of addiction before he registered at the clinic stated that "It would be one of the finest things that ever happened if there were not a grain of morphine obtainable because the only reason that myself and others are addicts is due to the fact that the 'stuff' is so easy to get in Shreveport."

One addict went direct to Shreveport from Leavenworth Penitentiary where he had served a year for narcotic law violations. He was put on the clinic register and given 10 grains of morphine daily. A woman who had been off drugs for a considerable length of time before she went to the clinic was receiving 11 grains of morphine daily.

There was a continuous illicit narcotic traffic being carried on in Shreveport, both in supplies procured from the clinic and in narcotics obtained elsewhere by peddlers. It was never possible to procure evidence of illicit sales of drugs as agents were always confronted with bottles bearing the clinic label.

This clinic was conducted not only in violation of the Harrison Act but in defiance of orders of the Louisiana State Board of Health after a thorough investigation approved by the Louisiana Medical Association a year prior to the date in 1923 when it finally ceased operations.

ALEXANDRIA, LOUISIANA. This narcotic dispensary was closed by the Louisiana State Board of Health for the reasons heretofore mentioned.

LOS ANGELES, CALIFORNIA.

Addict No. 101 received 8 grains on his first visit to the clinic; this amount was later increased to 12 grains instead of being reduced. He admitted he had been purchasing as much as a dram a week on the outside from peddlers.

Addict No. 131, an actor addicted to morphine for ten years, obtained sufficient morphine to give 6 grains daily to another actor.

Addict No. 17, using 8 grains daily, returned to the clinic several times stating he had broken the bottle and requested an additional supply, which was furnished to him.

Dr. J. W. Nedins, in charge of the clinic, stated that he had never made any special study of drug addiction but expressed doubts if any cures would be effected by clinic treatment, and advocated institutional treatment for satisfactory cures.

Dr. James T. Fisher, a neurologist, head of the clinic board, stated that the so-called clinic was nothing more than a dope supply house for addicts and should have been closed a long time ago; further that no attempts at cure were being made at the clinic, that none could be effected, and the quicker it was closed the better.

Dr. E. H. Williams, a member of the Board of Supervisors, stated that the clinic only touched about 30 percent of the actual addicts in the district, and the other 70 percent would not present themselves at a public clinic.

EXCERPTS FROM THE LOS ANGELES EXAMINER: "The Municipal Narcotic Clinics of both Los Angeles and San Diego have been officially ordered closed finally and the wholesale traffic in dope which has been carried on by the municipal clinic for half a year will be a thing of the past.

"Action follows Examiner exposé. Again the Examiner has been vindicated!

"Months ago the Examiner exposed the evils, the immorality, the illegality of the municipal narcotic clinic.

"Even were the operation of these clinics legal, they are morally wrong, inadequate, ineffective, and the clinics themselves, not only here, but elsewhere, are failures. They have made an earnest effort to make the clinic a success, but we know that no clinic of an ambulatory nature ever can be successful. The only practicable treatment is that in which the patient is confined in a hospital or sanatarium and is under the thumb of the physician at all times.

"The best known clinic, that established in New York, was soon found a failure. Men high in the medical profession, like Dr. S. Dana

Hubbard of New York Department of Health, who himself conducted the New York clinic, which was closed; Dr. Oscar F. Dowling, president of the Louisiana State Board of Health, and many others, all condemned these clinics. The ambulatory treatment of drug addiction was emphatically denounced.

"This clinic has resulted in numerous dope fiends flocking here from other cities, among them many criminals. When I came in today I met one hop-head on the train who admitted that he was coming here from San Francisco to get dope at the clinic. And a few minutes later I met another at the clinic.

"I have been informed that Chief of Police Patrick of San Diego said that he was not in favor of the clinic there, that it did more harm than good, and it was only a means for furnishing addicts with dope. He further added that twice as many addicts were in that city as before the clinic opened. I know that conditions here parallel those at San Diego.

"All clinics should—and they will—be closed. They are indefensible from either a legal or a moral viewpoint."

Dr. Paschal, the Assistant Health Commissioner, stated that in his opinion the clinic not only accomplished no good but that it actually tended to condone the use of drugs by the addicts.

The extent of operations of this clinic is shown by the fact that several hundred thousands of grains of morphine were sold to addicts in four months at a clear profit for the city of more than eleven thousand dollars from sales at ten cents per grain.

The police records of Los Angeles revealed that "not only has the so-called crime wave not diminished since the establishment of the clinic, but on the contrary, it has increased to a very great degree."

CLINICS IN CANADA

A formidable opponent of the ambulatory treatment of drug addiction in Canada is Colonel C. H. L. Sharman, former chief of the Canadian Narcotic Service, a member of the former Opium Advisory Committee of the League of Nations, Canadian Representative on the United Nations Commission on Narcotic Drugs and member of the Supervisory Body located at Geneva, Switzerland. Colonel Sharman is a distinguished international drug expert and has had remarkable success in reducing drug addiction in Canada. He shared the views expressed by R. S. S. Wilson, former superintendent of the Royal Mounted Canadian Police who is a veteran drug fighter of many years.

Excerpts from Mr. Wilson's analysis follow:

The solution to the narcotic problem does not lie in the creation of government clinics where narcotic injections are given to addicts at cost price. This amounts to nothing more than officially condoning drug addiction and placing the stamp of public approval upon a vicious and soul-destroying habit, and comes close to realization of the addict's dream of a "barrel of heroin on every street corner."

It would no more stop drug addiction than the legal sale of opium in government dispensaries has stopped the drug traffic or stamped out narcotic addiction in the Far East.

The sale of alcoholic beverages in government liquor stores helps to control bootlegging but it does not stop it nor does it solve the problem of the chronic alcoholic.

ABSTINENCE ONLY SALVATION

The only hope for his salvation lies in complete abstinence. A person addicted to alcohol would never be satisfied with a "minimum required dosage" of liquor a day even if he could purchase it for a few cents at a government-operated clinic. Certainly, he would be glad to take the alcohol so generously provided by the government, but would promptly thereafter resort to the nearest illicit source for an additional supply.

In many ways—and the leading medical authorities are in agreement in this—there is a close similarity between addiction to alcohol and addiction to narcotic drugs. The same authorities likewise agree that there is only one cure in either case—complete and unqualified abstinence.

Contrary to what the committee seems to think, the addict who received a daily "shot" in a government clinic would not be satisfied with this, but would seek an additional supply from illicit sources. In other words, the government clinic would merely fill the role of another drug peddler. . . . Because it did not furnish all the addict's requirements there would still be peddlers catering to his wants.

This means that the addict would continue to be an addict and would still be obliged to resort to crime to obtain the money with which to purchase his narcotics.

No medical practitioner could ascertain the exact quantity of a drug which, administered, say three times a day, would stabilize the addict unless the person in question were confined under close supervision for several days in a hospital.

EVER INCREASING DOSES?

The addict derives no relief (which he terms "pleasure") from the underlying emotional instability which led to his becoming an addict in the first place. If he can't get the additional drug at the clinic, the addict will seek it elsewhere, of that we may be sure.

Will the clinic cater to the addict's wants by giving him ever increasing doses of the drug until he reaches the saturation point and dies of acute narcotic poisoning?

Where, before the war Canadian addicts used opium and morphine, they are now almost 100 percent addicted to heroin, a drug so deadly in its habit-forming characteristics that its medical use is forbidden throughout the United States and in all hospitals in this country operated by the Department of Veterans Affairs.

Does the committee propose administering heroin to our addicts? I can hardly credit the thought. But if they do not, and resort to the considerably milder morphine or codeine, the addicts will most definitely not be satisfied and, more than ever, will seek to get "high" or "steamed up" on illegally procured heroin.

To be quite frank, I cannot visualize the Government of Canada, as it is obliged to do by international treaty, including in its annual estimates of internal consumption to the United Nations Narcotic Commission an item covering the legal administration of morphine, much less heroin, to Canadian drug addicts.

Insofar as heroin is concerned, the system of international control is so strict that countries, such as Canada, which do not produce it have to make a special request to the government of the exporting country.

Moreover, import certificates covering heroin can be issued only in favor of a government department and in this way the importing government assumes special responsibility in respect to heroin and undertakes to supervise strictly its subsequent distribution.

There are a number of other reasons I could advance, if space permitted, why the whole idea of government-operated narcotic clinics is, in my opinion, quite impractical.

PSYCHOLOGIC FACTORS VITAL

However, of far greater importance is the fact that we should remember that we are not treating with ordinary every-day sick people when we are dealing with drug addicts. As one eminent authority, Dr. J. H. W. Rhein, puts it: "Any effort to correct the evils of drug addiction must be based on a thorough understanding of the psychologic factors underlying the cause. The cause of development of the habit is inherent in the individual. The drug addict is a psychopath before he acquires the habit. He is a person who cannot face, unassisted, painful situations; he resents suffering, physical, mental or moral; he has not adjusted himself to his emotional reactions. The most common symptom that requires relief is a feeling of inadequacy; an inability to cope with difficulties. These conditions call for an easy and rapid method of relief which is found in the use of drugs."

Habitual criminals are psychopaths, and psychopaths are abnormal individuals who, because of their abnormality, are especially liable to become addicts.

To such persons drug addiction is merely an incident in their delinquent careers, and the crimes they commit, even though they be to obtain money with which to buy narcotics, are not directly attributable to the fact that they are drug addicts.

More than 95 percent of all drug addicts are the criminal addicts whose addiction in its inception and in its continuance is due to vice, vicious environment, and criminal associations. Experience definitely shows that in nearly all cases the addict was a criminal *before* he became addicted.

That is the actual situation as it exists here in Canada and it is useless to draw comparisons with other countries which are not faced with a drug problem and to say that such countries do not understand our concept of the criminal addict because their addicts "are not driven to crime in order to support their addiction."

One would gather from this statement that drug addicts were originally quite decent people who have been forced into a life of crime as a result of becoming addicted.

This is not so and the fact that in nearly all cases the addict was a criminal before he became addicted must be constantly borne in mind if we ever hope to make a realistic approach to the solution of the narcotic problem in Canada.

It has been amply demonstrated in the past that addiction cannot be cured by the ambulatory method, that is, by the administration to the addict of gradually decreasing quantities of narcotics by a physician in his office.

This holds true not only for the main bulk of the addict population, which is made up of thieves, shop-lifters, prostitutes, forgers and such like underworld characters, but also for the tiny remaining non-criminal fraction.

FORCED COMMITTAL BETTER

It has been found that far better results in effecting cures are obtained in the case of prisoners who are compulsorily committed for treatment and subsequently released on parole, than in the case of the "voluntary committals" who enter the hospital of their own volition and may leave whenever they please.

The latter (and the same would hold true here in Canada) largely treat the hospital as a "rest-centre" where they may with a minimum of physical discomfort cut down their drug habits to a manageable level.

While a comprehensive follow-up service is essential, this will not work without compulsion. The history of institutional treatment of drug addiction by the federal government in the United States not only shows that compulsory treatment is much more effective than voluntary treatment, but also that the lack of completely satisfactory results in that country is largely attributable to the absence of stringent and legally enforceable parole regulations, with recommittal the penalty for their violation, governing all cases after release from treatment.

In actual point of fact, a drug addict can be cured. However, due to the present lack of adequate provision in this country for the treatment of drug addiction, there is only one class of addict for whom there is any hope of a permanent cure.

These are the relatively few professional and business men who have families and business and social responsibilities. Such individuals, upon their release from a mental hospital or private sanitarium, return to their daily work and surroundings freed from the contaminating influence of contact with other addicts; they usually are of superior mental attainments and have a definite incentive—their home, families and business—to fight against any reversion to the habit.

In Canada there are today well over 150 members of one group alone who although previously addicted, are now leading normal lives and have been doing so for periods of from two to 14 years. The successful results achieved in the federal narcotic hospitals in the United States, and in this country when dealing with cases where there is no underworld association, proves conclusively the incorrectness of the general belief that a drug addict can never be cured.

White-flowered Papaver somniferum is the main source of opium; the widely-grown and colorful garden poppy is P. orientale. (An old print)

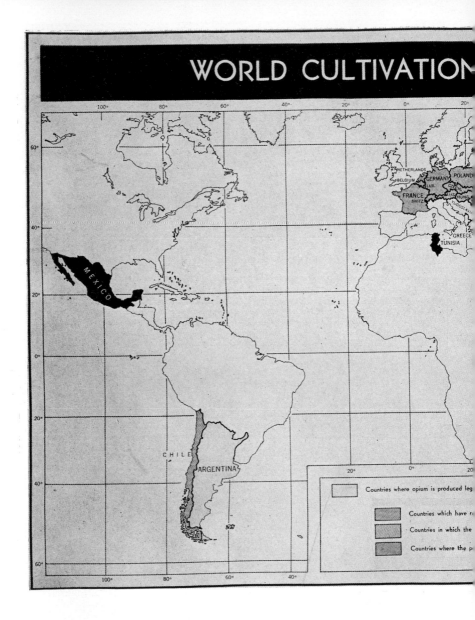

This map reflects the information collected by the various pertinent committees of the United Nations. It will be observed that the cultivation areas represented, by both legal and illegal production, do not necessarily correlate with the volume of the illicit traffic, although they do indicate the potential sources of it. This picturization, there-

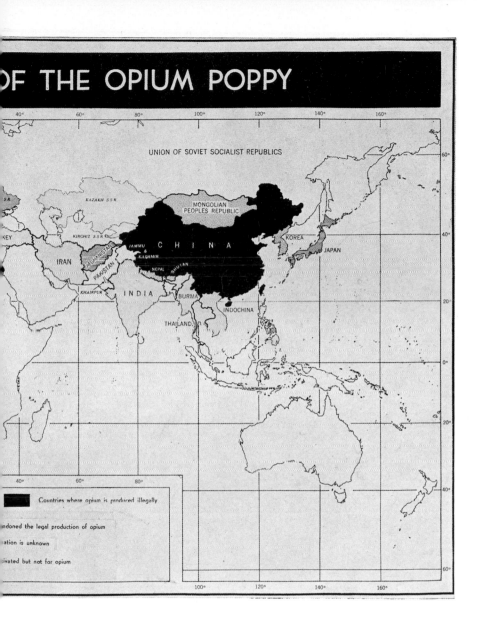

OF THE OPIUM POPPY

fore, must be used in conjunction with the text of this book in under-
standing the international aspects of the problem. * Note that in the
USSR legal cultivation for opium production is limited to the Kirghiz
SSR and the Kazakh SSR, and in Pakistan, is limited to the state of
Khairpur. Courtesy of United Nations Presentation, September 1949.

A symbolic depiction of narcotic fantasy, the artist unknown; the
brilliantly-colored original painting was seized during a narcotic raid.

The age-old caravan (Yünnan Province, China) plies its trade today in a country where opium is produced illegally. The sign is from a shop in India where opium is legally produced and publicly sold.

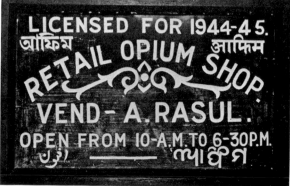

LICENSED FOR 1944-45.
আফিম RETAIL OPIUM SHOP আফিম
VEND - A. RASUL.
OPEN FROM 10-A.M. TO 6-30 P.M.

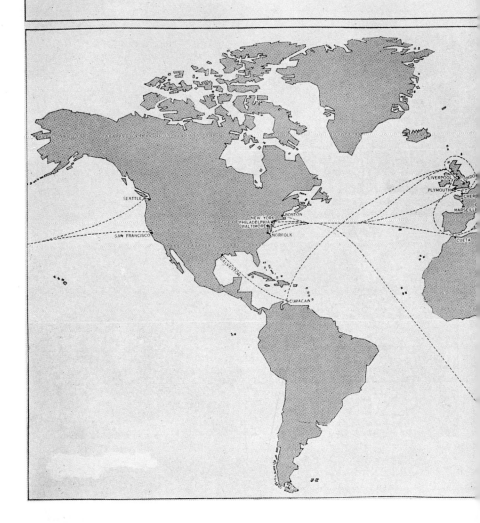

The sea routes lead to ports of entry and thus emphasize these population concentrations as centers of criminal activity and as places of notable addiction. The network for distribution fans out inland: conversely, the areas of production feed into these coastal points of dis-

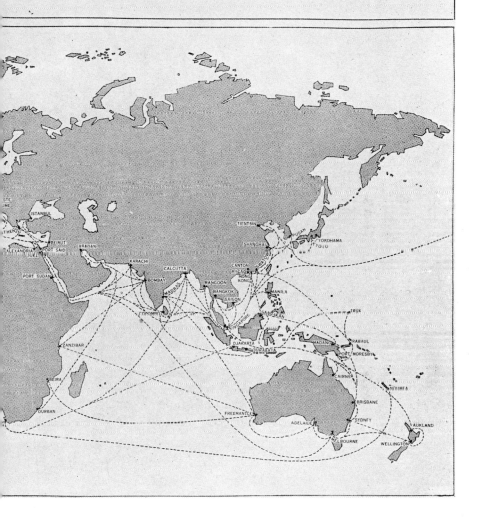

tribution. The air routes have recently been added in the pattern of the illicit traffic. The importance of international cooperation in the control of the traffic in narcotics is fully discussed in the text of this book. Courtesy of United Nations Presentation, December 1950.

Marihuana (Indian hemp): male and female flowers and leaf. Below, harvesting the ten- to twelve-foot plants for commercial fiber.

CONCENTRATE ON ADDICTS

If we accept the proposition that the narcotic problem is capable of solution, and no right thinking man would wish otherwise, how then should we proceed?

It is my definite and considered opinion that drug addiction as we know it today, with all its attendant crime and evil, can be wiped out in Canada within a very few years if we are but willing to face the facts and attack the problem from a realistic point of view.

We can stop the drug traffic in Canada if we will do three things:
1. Maintain international and domestic control over the legal traffic.
2. Continue to wage war on narcotic smuggler and internal traffickers.
3. Cure and permanently control the drug addict.

Mental disease is not an ordinary ailment which can be treated at home or in jail. Society recognizes that the mentally ill must be forcibly confined and consequently we have enacted legislation providing for their committal to proper institutions.

In the old days lunatics were punished because it was believed their infirmity was self-imposed through deliberate association with evil spirits. But today we would regard as morally indefensible any attempt to punish an insane person, even though his affliction were self-imposed, as for example general paresis, which is a direct result of self-imposed vice, namely venereal disease.

However, we have made no such progress when it comes to drug addiction. Yet the drug addict, even though he be a criminal who deliberately addicted himself, is essentially a psychopath whose addiction is actually due to his underlying mental instability.

If we are prepared to accept the proposition that there is a close similarity between insanity and narcotic addiction, then we should be willing to take the next step and provide the necessary legislation for the enforced committal and control of the drug addict.

It is the opinion of the writer that the Opium and Narcotic Drug Act should be amended to provide that a drug addict, after certification as such by three physicians, must be committed for a period of not less than 10 years to a narcotic hospital operated by the Federal Government.

The act should further provide that the first year of the 10-year committal period must be spent in the hospital as an in-patient, but that after the expiration of the first year the addict would be eligible for release on parole.

The narcotic hospital would be competently staffed and the emphasis would be on mental cure and rehabilitation and training for a useful occupation. There would be no suggestion of punishment.

The hospital would provide the very latest medical techniques for withdrawal of the drug of addiction and restoration of the patient to normal physical health.

The second and more protracted stage of mental rehabilitation would be accomplished through up-to-date methods of psychotherapy designed to treat the underlying psychopathic condition which led the patient to become an addict and to reeducate and reconstruct his personality so that he can learn to adapt himself to his emotional reactions.

Combined with this treatment would be occupational therapy to ensure that the patient's physical and mental energies were directed into channels best suited to his needs and most likely to make him into a useful and self-supporting member of society.

After the expiration of one year in the hospital the patient would be released, but only on parole and to outside employment. Unless the patient were willing to go to the job provided him and signed an undertaking to remain on that job and otherwise to abide implicitly by the terms of his parole, he would not be released.

Such terms would provide that the parolee report regularly to the parole officer, that he not associate with members of the criminal classes or visit persons or places where there was any possibility of narcotic contamination, that he not change his employment or place of abode without prior report to and approval of the parole officer, and that he undergo periodical medical re-checks.

"LIFE" AFTER 2 RE-COMMITTALS

Parole would continue until the expiration of the 10-year period, unless the individual violated the conditions of his parole, in which case a warrant would automatically be issued for his re-committal.

In the event an addict were re-committed on two occasions he would be classed as incurable and sent for life to a special institution reserved for such cases. There he would once more be physically cured and given an opportunity to follow a useful avocation, but permanently within the confines of the institution.

IX

NARCOTICS, CRIME, AND PUBLICITY

FOR THE PAST SEVERAL YEARS, THE GENERAL PUBLIC HAS BEEN BOM-
barded with stories, articles, pictures, programs, discussions, and
speeches dealing with all phases of drug addiction. Headlines
such as "Twenty-five Housebreaks are Charged to Drug Addict,"
"Doped by Marihuana, Youth 'Goes Crazy' in County Jail Cell,"
"Charge Husband Killed Wife During Marihuana Brawl," "Teen-
Age Drug Addict Ring Uncovered," "Gang of Marihuana-Crazed
Hoodlums Leaves Bloody Trail," "Accused Killer Tells of 'Marihuana Fog,'" "Killer Tells of Smoking Marihuana Before Hold-
Up," and "Police Seize 'Reefers' in Gang Raid," have become
commonplace in our daily press. Radio and television shows have
featured the dope fiend, and publishers of cheap fiction have not
hesitated to use indefensible and lurid stories involving addicts
to enhance their sales. The wrong kind of publicity on narcotics
might be divided into three classes:

1. Sensational material designed to promote sales;
2. Misguided use of material;
3. Inaccurate reporting.

SENSATIONALISM

Morally, there is no excuse for the existence of the first type,
and it exists legally because of the traditional American distaste
for censorship. Those who publish such material are fully aware
of the nature of their acts but, as practical men, know that there
are ten weak souls who will devour such droppings as against

one alert citizen who will be sufficiently aroused to complain. Such promotors know only too well how valuable from a sales angle an official condemnation can be. One candidly admitted, "We do anything to provoke some criticism because that always makes the sales rocket."

In recent months, a Congressional Committee conducted hearings in connection with some of these indefensible publications. Among the sordid collection of books was one which was termed "a manual for potential drug addicts." Publications directed to the sensory and bestial characteristics of humanity are unquestionably degrading, but when they embark on a field of material which can cause impressionable young people to acquire the most degenerate habit known to man, it is time to call a halt. If our lawmakers cannot remedy the situation, a tight embargo by the general public on the particular company or author will. Fiction alone has no monopoly in this field, because the purveyors of corruption have not hesitated for a moment to invade the youngster's comic books and "funny" sheets. Furthermore, sponsors and radio stations who should know better, on occasion have foisted amazingly disreputable "dope fiend" pictures into the living room.

MISUSE OF MATERIAL

By misguided material is meant writings or pictures which are well intended but which, through inherent flaws or inaccuracies, hinder rather than help the over-all situation. The bulk of the material in this class consists of writings intended for education and educational films and while the sales aspect is generally secondary, it is undeniably there. If the many good people who desire to help eradicate the evil would only realize first that this is a highly specialized problem susceptible to discussion only after thorough and intense research, they would commence with a far firmer foundation. This is not a subject where writing flows without careful thought. It is no field in which to experiment with unproved ideas, fanciful suggestions, or curbstone opinions. One of the more unfortunate aspects of the whole situation has been created by the outpourings from pseudo-experts since the problem of drug addiction has become widely publicized. A few normally intelligent educators, who should know better, after a cursory study, came forward with unbelievable conclusions and suggestions, some of which were diametrically opposite to the views of life-long students of the subject. However, the impact of their views has been very small.

Fortunately for the welfare of our country, the Motion Picture Producers Association of America has a provision in their code governing the industry to the effect that its members cannot produce films showing the narcotic traffic or drug addiction in any form. Were it not for this commendable self-imposed restriction by the motion-picture industry, the public would be continually subjected to the presentation of numerous motion pictures with a narcotic theme, with a strong potential increase in drug addiction.

From time to time a few motion pictures on narcotics are made outside the code, but their showing evokes so much protest from civic-minded individuals and groups that they are usually withdrawn from circulation before they do much damage.

As a case in point a highly reputable firm recently produced a film (not approved by the Motion Picture Producers Association of America) avowedly aimed at the problem of drug addiction and represented as propaganda against the use of narcotics. The film was intended for showing in secondary schools. It opens with an intended educational approach in that it portrays the plants opium, coca, and marihuana and explains the derivation of the narcotic principles. Then a happy school environment is portrayed while the commentator builds up the menace of drug addiction. Next is seen experimentation by groups of young people and progression from marihuana smoking (including some technique) to "mainline" use of heroin. Scenes follow this phase depicting the necessity of obtaining money to sustain addiction by displaying the techniques of mugging and assaulting, and shoplifting, proceeding to the furtive meetings of drug peddler and addict, and the coercion of the addict into becoming a seller to support his addiction. Comparatively mild withdrawal symptoms are displayed as the compelling reason for continuance of the addiction. The addict "hero" is pictured as a good boy with a kind, sympathetic mother. He has strayed into bad company ultimately leading to his downfall, arrest for shoplifting, and discovery on his person of his "works" and some capsules of heroin. Arraigned before the Juvenile Court in a tearful scene, he is placed on probation to undergo a cure. The impression gained of the cure is that it is pleasant, quick and certain, featuring desirable occupational therapy, followed by a return to his former environment where he is shunned by the good boys and girls.

Bearing in mind that the production of this film was motivated by people of integrity and with the best of intentions, it is unsuitable for exhibition to either parents or children. Among the inherent weaknesses of this approach are the following:

1. It vividly pictures the appearance of growing marihuana which might lead some youngsters to experiment.
2. It portrays addiction as a disease of youth which might accidentally occur in a normal and healthy environment. This is inaccurate.
3. It teaches the technique of mugging, robbing, shoplifting, and the peddling of drugs.
4. It shows the technique for smoking marihuana.
5. It depicts the withdrawal of drugs as a mildly uncomfortable affair rather than in its true, vicious light.
6. It shows treatment merely as a pleasant occupational therapy.
7. It conveys the impression that addiction can be cured like the measles which is wholly incorrect. The statistics on recidivism alone shatter that conclusion.

A lot more could be said, but it would be redundant. However, it seems reasonable to inquire why it is necessary to produce such a picture. Does a solution to this terrible problem demand that the general public and our youth be saturated with knowledge no matter how indiscriminately it is ladled out? Does this subject necessitate lurid and sensational treatment rather than the careful and considered discussions attendant on such ills as sex perversion and syphilis? Certainly no one would want to drench the American public with illustrations concerning the techniques of sex perversion. Then why single out drug addiction? Drug addiction is sporadic and not widespread in the United States. Consequently, an avalanche of educational material is unnecessary; it too often arouses curiosity and leads to addiction.

PROBLEMS OF REPORTING

Inaccurate reporting generally stems from a definite lack of knowledge concerning narcotics, incorrect sources of information, or a desire to put color in an otherwise drab story.

Many stories have been founded on bad information, which is certainly no news to anyone. However, in addition to the usual unintentional misinformation which can befall any reporter, there have been many cases where an accused or his legal advisor has purposely conveyed the impression that the culprit was under the influence of dope when the crime occurred.

In one absolutely unjustifiable killing of an aged grocer and the wounding of his wife and a customer in the store during the hold-up, no mention of marihuana use or influence was made until the defendants retained counsel to defend them against the State's demand for a death penalty. Newspapermen, leaping to the bait, immediately began to write positive stories blaming the crime on marihuana, and within a few days it became an accepted fact that the root of the crime had been marihuana. Worse yet, there was even a demand from one civic group that the defendants be treated as sick people rather than criminals—that they be hospitalized rather than tried for murder. The true fact, as admitted later, was that defense counsel saw no way to avert a conviction, and hence was trying to save his clients from the death penalty by injecting the alibi that the crime had been committed while they were under the influence of marihuana and hence were not responsible for their acts. Ultimately, the alibi collapsed for want of proof and the defendants were sentenced to death.

This story is not an isolated example of felons attempting to claim the use of marihuana as the escape hatch from an extreme penalty, for official files are replete with them. But it does point up the need for more diligent investigation on the part of reporters. City editors who find a speculative mention of marihuana in a reporter's story would be doing a great public service if they would refuse to use it in their headlines. One reporter on a Southwestern newspaper pointed out that there was a suspicion of marihuana use in a case. Next day the headlines read, "Gang of Marihuana Crazed Hoodlums Leave Bloody Trail." Questioned, the scribe had nothing tangible on the marihuana angle and claimed that the heading had been composed in the editorial room.

Several years ago a story appeared in a Midwestern paper headlined, "Doped by Marihuana, Youth 'Goes Crazy' in County Jail Cell." It sounded interesting in print and quoted the jailor at length on the evils of marihuana. When checked the jailor denied even mentioning marihuana and the reporter stated that he had had no information regarding marihuana but had simply written the story as a humor story because the jailor was "quite a character."

The foregoing comments are predicated on actual case histories and exemplify publicity of a type certainly not designed to help law enforcement officials or allay public hysteria. Fortunately, this type of publicity has been in the minority. Obviously, the few sensationalists whose only interest in the subject of addiction is measured by its value to their sales, will never stop such nefarious writings. However, reporters, newscasters, publishers, writers, movie and television producers can help if they so desire. They can help by being sure they have all the true facts before a story is published and by weighing carefully its news value against the impact it will have on the public's well-being. Before making a martyr out of a marihuana killer, his record should be checked, for the chances are that he will have had criminal tendencies long before marihuana appeared in the picture.

One final thought for both producers and sponsors—stop building detective stories around drug addicts. Generally the facts are distorted, the plots abominable, and the youngsters' curiosity improperly and unduly aroused thereby. One fact is inescapable—unless the subject of narcotics and its criminal offshoots are treated with utmost care and accuracy, more damage than good can result.

REPORTS AND RESOLUTIONS

EXCERPTS FROM O. C. 1642, DATED GENEVA, MAY 18, 1936

LEAGUE OF NATIONS ADVISORY COMMITTEE ON TRAFFIC IN OPIUM AND OTHER DANGEROUS DRUGS

Anti-Narcotic Education and Propaganda

The most striking feature of the replies from the governments * interested in measures for combating drug addiction is the divergence of opinion as to the direct and indirect means of action. For instance, the Government of *Siam* in its Annual Report for 1933 felt that direct propaganda by means of posters, films, and lectures was not likely to be successful, quite apart from the expenditure incurred, but was more likely to stimulate unwholesome curiosity than to act as a salutary warning. This being so, no propaganda was done in *Siam*

In the *Straits Settlements* and the *Federated Malay States,* as also in *Siam,* the Government does not resort to direct action or propaganda but adopts indirect methods, the improvement of social conditions and the provision of playing fields—measures which the authorities believe to be really effective. As regards this negative attitude towards direct propaganda, the Commission of Enquiry into the Control of Opium Smoking in the Far East was informed in the official reply of the Burmese authorities that no educational measures had been taken to discourage the smoking of opium. Such steps were considered undesirable as they might advertise the use of opium for smoking and stimulate curiosity as to the effects.

In the *Straits Settlements,* The Director of Education of the colony also expressed the view at that time "that it would be a mistake to carry on propaganda by education against opium smoking among boys, which would have the reverse effect of that intended."

Lastly, the authorities in *Siam* told the Commission that anti-opium education would be unnecessary, would do no good and might do some harm by attracting attention to opium smoking.

As will be seen, there is a divergence of opinion as to direct and indirect means, even in the territories in which the opium problem is of primary importance. It is not surprising, therefore, that in the

* The Advisory Committee secured lengthy reports on the subject from the 68 Governments parties to the 1931 Convention To Limit the Manufacture of Narcotic Drugs, before the Committee reached a decision.

countries in which opium and drug addiction are far less widespread all educational methods or direct propaganda should be open to controversy and grave objection.

EXCERPT OF REPORT BY
UNITED NATIONS COMMISSION ON NARCOTIC DRUGS
TO THE ECONOMIC AND SOCIAL COUNCIL, MAY 2, 1951
*Education and Propaganda
Against the Use of Narcotic Drugs*

On the basis of a draft resolution submitted by the representative of France, the Commission discussed the advisability of education and propaganda against the use of narcotic drugs. After a general discussion, the representative of the Secretary-General gave the Commission an account of the work done by the League of Nations on the problem, with special reference to the resolution adopted by the Advisory Committee on Traffic in Opium and Other Dangerous Drugs on June 2, 1936, in which it was stated ". . . that propaganda in schools and other direct propaganda should only be practiced in certain countries where addiction is a substantial problem. In other countries where addiction is, on the contrary, sporadic, such propaganda would be definitely dangerous . . ." (League of Nations Document C.290.M. 176.1936.XI.) The Commission, after introducing some amendments into the draft with the object of bringing its terms into conformity with the point of view expressed by the Advisory Committee, decided by 10 votes in favor and 1 (Russia) against to recommend to the Council the adoption of the following resolution:

EDUCATION AND PROPAGANDA
AGAINST THE USE OF NARCOTIC DRUGS

The Economic and Social Council,
Being informed that the question of anti-narcotic education and propaganda has arisen in various countries,
1. *Considers* it advisable to restate the principle adopted by the Advisory Committee on Opium and Other Dangerous Drugs of the League of Nations, namely, that propaganda in schools and other forms of direct propaganda can be with advantage employed only in certain countries where drug addiction has assumed widespread proportions (China, Iran, India, and Thailand); and that in other countries where it is of a more sporadic

character (European countries and countries of the North American continent), such measures would be definitely dangerous, and

2. Draws the attention of governments to this principle.

RESOLUTION

Passed by National Convention of

NATIONAL WOMAN'S CHRISTIAN TEMPERANCE UNION

at Denver, Colorado,

September 1950.

NARCOTICS—WHEREAS, during the past year the narcotic drug theme as presented to the public in numerous motion pictures, radio and television programs, and magazine and newspaper articles, has deteriorated to the point where public welfare is being endangered; and

WHEREAS, the indiscriminate dissemination, particularly to the youth, of material dramatizing the use of narcotic drugs and traffic therein, serves no purpose except to satisfy morbid curiosity, and is and always has been considered contrary to the public interest in the United States; since its effect is the reverse of that intended because it advertises the use of narcotics for non-medical purposes, thus developing unwholesome interest regarding the effect of narcotics, on the part of impressionable persons who would not otherwise be inclined to pursue the subject or to experiment with such dangerous substances; and

WHEREAS, the international authorities on narcotic drug control likewise have always maintained that direct propaganda on the subject should be used only in countries like those in the Far East where addiction is rampant, but in countries like the United States direct propaganda is dangerous because, instead of diverting young people from addiction, it tends to awaken interest and arouse undue curiosity, thus defeating its own object; and

WHEREAS, the United States Bureau of Narcotics reports that the results they have noted of the recent distribution of "educational" material on the narcotic drug traffic have served to emphasize the soundness and desirability of these views;

THEREFORE, BE IT RESOLVED, THAT THE NATIONAL WOMAN'S CHRISTIAN TEMPERANCE UNION use its influence wherever possible to discourage the indiscriminate use of stories based on the narcotic theme as presently exploited in motion pictures, radio and television programs and in certain types of magazine and newspaper articles, all of which have the effect of increasing rather than lessening the hazards which lead to drug addiction.

Similar policy statements have been adopted by Parents-Teacher Associations, General Federation of Womens Clubs, by the City Council of Baltimore, Maryland, and others.

For those who decide to go ahead with an educational program, the Bureau of Narcotics recommends a booklet "Living Death—The Truth about Drug Addiction," as the most suitable material available. This booklet can be obtained free of cost from the Bureau in Washington.

X

THE INDIVIDUAL: METHODS OF TREATMENT

DRUG ADDICTION IS FUNDAMENTALLY A SYMPTOM OF A PERSONALITY disturbance, and Kolb and Felix have set forth four general personality types as examples of the kinds of personality disorders upon which addiction is based.

Briefly, the first group consists of what is generally known as the *medical addict*—persons who have been introduced to drugs through treatment and who have continued using the drug after the termination of the treatment. While, like the other types, there is some basic emotional problem underlying their continued use of the drugs, the difference lies only in that they first encountered the drugs in the course of medical treatment.

The second group embraces those having psychoneurotic disorders who take the drugs for relief of anxiety or whatever symptoms they may have.

In the third and largest group are found the psychopaths. These make up the bulk of the addict population and generally are created by infectious contact with persons already drug-conditioned. They seek the drug for its euphoric value and for the pleasure and relief they believe they secure from it.

Lastly is drug addiction with psychosis in which group are encountered those mentally ill.

(Further analysis will be found in Medical Aspects of Addiction, later in this Chapter.)

223

WHAT THE PHYSICIAN SHOULD UNDERSTAND ABOUT ADDICTS

Generally, a normal, healthy person receives no specific psy-chological sensation from an opiate and will regard it simply as something to relieve pain. When the pain is alleviated, therefore, no need exists for its further use. However, extended use could result in the euphorizing effects taking hold, creating an ac-cidental or medical addict. It is for this reason that doctors avoid the use of addicting drugs where a substitute can accomplish the purpose.

However, where a serious flaw exists in an individual's person-ality such as a neurosis, nervous hypertension, psychological mal-adjustment, or a psychopathic disorder, the drug will have a stronger and more rapid effect with euphoria occurring much sooner.

Erich Hesse very lucidly describes the impact of the addicting drugs on these types of individuals. Hesse states,* "Their minds feel at ease. The victim experiences a sensation of happiness, of freedom from all troubles, which makes him forget all his worries and his mental restlessness, or at least makes these appear insignificant (Peters, Steil, Geilen). Such an experience may be a sufficient motive for weak characters to enjoy a second intoxica-tion soon after the first one."

Sensory perception decreases during the intoxication. In the initial stage of the addiction, volitional processes are not so strongly impaired as to make a voluntary renunciation of mor-phine impossible. Peters describes two such cases. One of them was a man known for his weak will power, who used morphine daily for three weeks, and then made up his mind to give it up, which he did. The other was a member of a nursing order, whose nerves had been frayed by his exhausting duty day and night. At first he would only occasionally reach for the morphine syr-inge. Then he took the drug daily for eight consecutive days. His superiors learned about it, and forbade him the further use of morphine. He actually kept his promise to stay away from the drug, for several years, at least.

* Erich Hesse—*Narcotics and Drug Addiction.*

Voluntary escape from the clutches of the poison is no longer possible after real addiction has developed. In this stage the alkaloid is the only thing capable of keeping the addict in a bearable physical and mental condition. If the drug level in the blood and in the tissues is lowered, the abstinence phenomena will set in. The addict becomes irritable, moody, depressed, and once again will reach for the narcotic in order to escape from this unpleasant state. His affective and emotional life now undergoes a basic change. If he had been sociable, now he shuns company. Preoccupied with himself, he keeps to himself, avoids people, and becomes disinterested in his environment and the outer world. His mind is dominated by only one thought, the desire for morphine or other narcotic drug, whose toxin alone is capable of making his life bearable. His will power is limited and the autistic attitude of the addict projects it in the direction of the alkaloid exclusively.

There begins the transition to the marantic stage. Periods of moodiness, delusions, lack of self-confidence, negligence of duties, moral aberration, and finally acute psychoses may set in. Morality wanes. Unscrupulousness, carelessness, negligence, lying, forgery of prescriptions, embezzlement of money, burglary, and other criminal acts may now be expected from the addict. Frequently the desire to secure the drug is the motive behind the illicit acts. Such individuals, now turned completely asocial, are responsible for the most horrifying human tragedies within their spheres of activity. The final stage begins with the negligence of physical cleanliness, and it ends with complete physical decay, preceded by various somatic symptoms; paleness, strong perspiration upon the slightest stimulus, skin rashes, sexual disturbances with dysmenorrhea and amenorrhea or decrease of potency.

THE CHARACTER OF THE ADDICT PERSONALITY

Hesse, citing Bonhoeffer, points out that only 10-15 percent of all addicts are non-psychopaths. Thus in approximately 85-90 percent of the cases are found individuals suffering from psychoneuroses, character disorders, and other problems ranging through the whole series of psychiatric ailments. While there is no typical addict personality, it is safe to say that there are numerous addiction-prone people with personality disturbances who could easily succumb to the drug habit.

The fact that the overwhelming number of drug addicts suffer from a character disorder points up these salient facts. First of all, an individual far more threatening to society is created when psychopathic tendencies are blended with drug addiction. The innate viciousness of drug addiction with its iron grasp on such an individual predisposes a dangerous result. Too frequently, altruists gloss over and generalize by classifying all drug addicts as sick persons—persons whom treatment will cure and rehabilitate. Too frequently the impression is conveyed that the drug addict population consists of unfortunate people who fell into a bad habit that could have occurred to anyone.

Too infrequently are we told that the chances of a complete cure are not good, that those addicted a relatively short time represent most of those cured, and that relapse is frequent. Too infrequently are we advised that we are in the main not dealing with average citizens who have suddenly been smitten with drug addiction, but in fact with people who had unpleasant and troublesome tendencies before drug addiction was superimposed. And too infrequently are we informed that many cases warrant strong corrective action because of some basic disturbance which drugs have awakened, or simply because of prior antisocial behavior. A spot check of any police record bureau will disclose the fact that many addicts were criminal offenders, long before taking on the drug habit. Make no mistake about it—we're not dealing with something hospitalization alone will cure but a dreaded scourge that penetrates infinitely deeper and requires a much greater effort to uproot. And in too many cases, we are confronted with some inherently bad patients.

TREATMENT AND CONTROL

An old time narcotic agent once summed up the subject of treatment by describing it thus: "About ten days in the 'shot room' to get off the drugs, four to six months of work under healthy conditions, after which it becomes a mental problem which the patient, now discharged, must overcome for himself."

There isn't a great deal to quarrel with in that succinct analysis.

Actual withdrawal of drugs can be accomplished either abruptly or gradually. The abrupt method, sometimes referred to as the cold-turkey treatment, is still used on occasion, but it is generally not preferred by a majority of the medical authorities. The weakness of this method in addition to its inhumaneness is that a particular patient's condition might be such that immediate and complete withdrawal might kill him, and futhermore, rapid sudden withdrawals only serve to create added burdens of anxiety and hostility to the overtaxed emotional state of the addict. It is safe to say that few hospitals or physicians employ this method today.

The cornerstone of successful treatment must be laid in a drug-free environment. Anyone who believes that the ambulatory method of treatment will succeed only deludes himself, as it has been proved a failure. A wise judge or probation officer will never countenance that type of treatment. Hospitalization presents the best guarantee of securing the important factors of proper control, thorough observation and complete medical care. Upon leaving the hospital, the vitally important factor of care after discharge arises.

Control of the addict cannot be overemphasized. As Dr. Reichard* so aptly stated: "Control of the addict for a period of at least one year is imperative. Sometimes the period of control must be longer; for a few, such control must be life-long." Control does not mean confinement in an institution. That is necessary for some months at the beginning of treatment. Supervision in the community, with the ability on the part of someone with the proper training to return the patient to an institution for further intensive treatment when necessary, is a type of control that is greatly needed.

The development and utilization by communities of legal methods of restricting the personal liberty of the addict, analogous to those now functioning for psychotic persons, is highly desirable. Since most definitions of addiction include loss of self-

---

* "Addiction: Some Theoretical Considerations as to its Nature, Cause, Prevention and Treatment" by J. D. Reichard, *American Journal of Psychiatry*, Vol. 103, No. 6, May, 1947.

control, it seems unrealistic to expect an addict to exhibit enough control to remain voluntarily in a drug-free environment.

We should, by obtaining the cooperation of our colleagues in the legal profession and of our legislators, endeavor to work out a more adequate method of control. Control, particularly after discharge, is imperative.

Proper treatment dictates that the drugs be withdrawn humanely and gradually from the patient followed by rehabilitative and psychiatric treatment. Generally the best plan for withdrawal involves the substitution of Methadon for whatever drug the addict has been using, followed by a reduction of the dosage of Methadon over a period of approximately ten days.

After withdrawal has been accomplished, any chance of cure requires a prolonged period of institutional rehabilitation under closest surveillance. The individual should be enabled to engage in useful work each day and occupational therapy should be geared to bring out and implement any talents or skills which are present. It is important that all patients, including those with chronic diseases, be required to participate in some type of useful endeavor. Recreational facilities, such as movies, athletics, games, reading rooms, and music should also be provided.

Psychotherapy, of great importance in the effort to avoid relapse, must be adequate. The treatment parallels that given to non-addicted persons suffering from psychoneuroses and other character disorders with a view to obtaining as high a degree of mental and emotional stabilization as possible. Unfortunately, adequate personnel is lacking to care for all those who require psychotherapy.

NEED FOR AN INTELLIGENT PUBLIC ATTITUDE

After discharge from the hospital, the most precarious period commences, and it is for this reason an adequate program of follow-up treatment is needed. Unfortunately there is very little opportunity for the addict to obtain this care. Too many free mental health clinics are disinterested in drug addicts. It is clear that welfare groups, churches, hospitals, and local government agencies must take a more affirmative interest in the returning drug addict. Nobody suggests a parade with ticker tape for the returned addict, but no community can be excused for failure to be interested or for failure to help. For those who regard it from a dollars-and-cents viewpoint, remember that a cured addict no longer is a taxpayer's burden. When an addict is cured, the underworld has lost one of its best customers.

FACILITIES FOR TREATMENT

A word about the facilities for treatment. With the exception of the hospital for teen-age addicts opened in 1952 in New York City and the clinics established at Chicago, Illinois, very little, if anything, has been done below the Federal level. The great majority of State and local governments continue refusing to assume any responsibility for the cure of drug addiction. Care for the insane? Yes. Tuberculars? Yes. Sex offenders? Yes. Epilepsy? Yes. Drug addicts? No! A truly indefensible situation!

Facilities at the two United States Public Health Service Hospitals—one located at Lexington, Kentucky, and the other at Fort Worth, Texas—permit patients to remain under treatment for the necessary length of time. The larger hospital at Lexington, opened in 1935, was the first of its kind in the world and unique in the combined program of research and treatment. Subsequently, the additional hospital in Fort Worth was constructed in 1938. Thus today there are approximately 2,200 beds for the treatment of narcotic addicts in these Federal hospitals.

Every year approximately 3,000 men and women receive treatment at the hospital at Lexington. Staffed by over 500 medical and other hospital personnel, it is located on 1,250 acres of Kentucky blue-grass farm land where the farm, dairy, and building maintenance, in addition to the furniture factory and garment shop, offer splendid occupational training opportunities. For physical recreation a baseball diamond, gymnasium, tennis courts, and bowling alleys are provided. Weekly motion pictures and stage shows are shown in the auditorium, and there are regular school classes, an excellent library, and a music department with a band and orchestra. Church services are conducted each week in the hospital chapel by Protestant, Catholic, and Jewish Chaplains.

Admission to the hospital is limited to those men and women who have become addicted to narcotic drugs as defined by Federal law which reads as follows:

The term *addict* means any person who habitually uses any habit-forming narcotic drugs so as to endanger the public morals, health, safety, or welfare, or who is or has been so far addicted to the use of such habit-forming narcotic drugs as to have lost the power of self-control with reference to his addiction.

The term *habit-forming narcotic drug* or *narcotic* means opium and coca leaves and the several alkaloids derived therefrom, the best known of these alkaloids being morphia, heroin, and codeine, obtained from opium, and cocaine derived from the coca plant; all compounds, salts, preparations, or other derivatives obtained either from the raw material or from the various alkaloids; Indian hemp and its various derivatives, compounds, and preparations, and peyote in its various forms; isonipecaine and its derivatives, compounds, salts, and preparations; opiates (as defined in Section 3228(f) of Title 26).

BASIC PRINCIPLES FOR THE PHYSICIAN

In discussing the individual physician's role in connection with the problem of drug addiction, three principles should be expressed at the outset:

1. The physician should familiarize himself thoroughly with the Federal laws and regulations as well as State laws and regulations, remembering that the laws of each State vary, as do Federal and State enactments.
2. Ambulatory treatment of drug addiction should not be tried. Institutional treatment is always required.
3. An addict should never be given drugs for self-administration.

A previous chapter has discussed the physician's legal obligations.

"WHAT TO DO WITH A DRUG ADDICT"

An excellent statement* has been prepared by the Committee on Drug Addiction and Narcotics of the National Research

* *Journal* of the American Medical Association, July 26, 1952, page 1220.

Council,* assisted by Dr. Harris Isbell, Director, National Institute of Mental Health, Addiction Research Center, United States Public Health Service Hospital, Lexington, Kentucky, and it contains some pertinent advice concerning treatment, some excerpts from which are here presented.

Diagnosis of Addiction

Most frequently, addicts who appear in a physician's office are transients who are unknown to the physician. Such persons are likely to appear when circuses and carnivals are present in a community. Less commonly, addicts may be nontransient persons who are fairly well known to the physician. Frequently, nontransient addicts are neurotic persons or are patients who are known to have been chronic alcoholics. It is not unusual for the nontransient addict to be a physician. In recent years, it has not been unusual in certain areas for an adolescent boy or girl to be brought to the physician by relatives or by representatives of social organizations for advice relative to the treatment of addiction.

Most frequently, the diagnosis of addiction is made at the onset of the interview by the patient's statement that he is addicted to and needs drugs. The addict may attempt to conceal his addiction and may present a glib story of some physical illness; most frequently mentioned are atypical angina pectoris, kidney colic, migraine, or hemorrhoids. Generally, the story culminates with the suggestion that other physicians have found that the only adequate remedy is a prescription for narcotic drugs. Frequently, addicts of this type may appear armed with a formula which they state was given to them by another physician and which they have found very effective for the relief of their alleged symptoms. The formula will usually contain morphine, laudanum, or cocaine. If refused morphine, many addicts will ask for either methadone or meperidine. They will state that these drugs are not opiates but are synthetic drugs and are nonaddicting. All too frequently, uninformed physicians will be taken in by this story and will prescribe the synthetic analgesics. It is not unusual for addicts to attempt to obtain narcotics on the basis of some mild, chronic, nonfatal disease, such as asthma, arthritis, or chronic osteomyelitis, for which narcotics are not usually required or given. They will state that these diseases cause them terrible pain, that physicians

* See Appendix II for the composition, purposes and functioning of this Committee.

in another town have been prescribing narcotics, and that their own physician is away and they need drugs only until he returns. Occasionally, transient addicts may appear who are suffering with serious physical diseases, such as advanced cardiovascular diseases or emphysema. These cases present particularly difficult problems and treatment since the stress of abrupt withdrawal might prove fatal.

Nontransient addicts who are well known to the physician sometimes attempt to develop stories similar to those used by the transient, veteran, criminal type of addict. Nontransient addicts, however, are more likely to be sincere than the transient addict. Many such patients truly desire to be cured of their addiction and should be given all possible help. All too frequently, a nontransient addict will be a physician or a nurse. In such cases, the most likely drug of addiction is now meperidine largely because of the widespread belief among the medical profession that this substance is not addicting.

The presenting situation may also be that of an adolescent girl or boy who is brought to the physician by his parents or by other responsible persons. Generally, such adolescents will admit the use of drugs and present no particular problem in diagnosis. In such cases, the physician should exercise a certain degree of care, since because of the widespread publicity concerning addiction in adolescents, many parents may wrongly attribute normal or abnormal adolescent behavior to drug addiction.

When the history leads one to suspect addiction, a complete physical examination is of the utmost importance. A transient addict is frequently surprised when the physician indicates a desire to perform a complete physical examination and may refuse the examination and immediately leave the office. It is important to realize that there are no pathognomonic physical signs of addiction. The opiate drugs do not cause drunkenness as do the barbiturates and alcohol, so mental confusion, emotional instability, nystagmus, and ataxia are not to be expected. Since complete or partial tolerance to many of the effects of morphine develops during the course of addiction, doctors must not expect that addicts presenting themselves in their offices will show the same effects as might be expected in persons not addicted, namely, constriction of the pupils and sedative effects. An addict may or may not show pupillary constriction depending on how recently he has received a dose of morphine. Superficially, tolerant addicts will appear to be physically and mentally normal unless they have been without drugs for some time and signs of abstinence have appeared.

The most important findings are the presence of old and recent needlemarks. These needlemarks should be sought over the veins in the antecubital spaces, the deltoid region, the abdomen, the anterior surface of the thighs, and along the veins of the legs and hands. Multiple abscesses or old abscess scars are also suggestive. Miosis is not a completely reliable sign since partial tolerance to pupillary constriction caused by morphine develops during addiction. Addicts who are using either meperidine or methadone are likely to have induration and inflammation of large areas of the skin, particularly over the deltoid region and the anterior surface of the thighs. Presence of long scars or tattooing over superficial veins is extremely suggestive, particularly if fresh needlemarks are present. One important feature may be that no physical findings are present which satisfactorily explain the serious symptoms detailed by the patient when the history was taken.

Occasionally, persons who are suspected of taking cocaine or marihuana are brought to the physician for an opinion. Neither cocaine nor marihuana produces physical dependence. Since such patients are usually brought to the physician long after the drug effects have worn off, findings are generally scanty. The signs of cocaine intoxication, however, include mydriasis, sweating, tachycardia, increase in blood pressure, increase of deep tendon reflexes, nervousness, tremor, an unblinking stare, and auditory and visual hallucinations. Intoxication with marihuana is characterized by injection of the conjunctivae, a sleepy appearance, excessive giggling, silly behavior, absence of marked ataxia, and a strong odor on the breath resembling that of cubeb cigarettes.

There are no laboratory procedures generally available to the average physician which are helpful in the diagnosis of addiction. Reliable tests for the presence of morphine and cocaine in the urine have been developed, but these methods are quite complex and are not suitable for use in the ordinary laboratory. There are no methods available for the detection of morphine in blood and no laboratory procedures which are sufficiently specific for the detection of synthetic analgesics and marihuana in either blood or urine. Furthermore, if such procedures were available, a positive test of the presence of drugs in the urine would mean only that the person had recently taken or been given a dose of a drug and would not necessarily mean that he was addicted to that drug.

A definitive diagnosis of addiction to morphine or similar drugs depends upon the demonstration of the characteristic signs of abstinence following complete and abrupt withdrawal of drugs. In order to prove the presence of physical dependence, the addict must be isolated in an environment so well controlled that there is no possibility of any narcotic drugs, other than those prescribed, being obtained by the addict. If such an environment is available, isolation of the addict and withholding of all narcotics will prove the presence or absence of dependence on these drugs. The detection of physical dependence requires familiarity with the signs of abstinence from morphine.

If morphine is abruptly withdrawn from a patient who has been receiving as much as 0.26 to 0.39 gm. (4 to 6 grains) daily for a period of 30 days or more, few signs are observed during the first 16 hours of abstinence. The patient is likely to go into a restless tossing sleep which may last for several hours. About 14 to 18 hours after the last dose of the drug was given, the addict will begin to yawn; rhinorrhea, perspiration, and lacrimation will appear. These mild signs increase in intensity during the first 24 hours of abstinence; thereafter, they become constant. Dilatation of the pupils then appears and, on close observation, recurring waves of gooseflesh will be seen. About 36 hours after the last dose of morphine was given, uncontrollable twitching of the muscles occurs. The patient will become extremely restless, will move from side to side in bed, and tremor of the face and tongue will be evident. The patient will complain of severe cramps in his legs, abdomen, and back; he will be unable to eat or to sleep for any period of time and vomiting and diarrhea frequently occur. Rectal temperature rises about 2 F, respiratory rate is usually elevated to 20 to 30 per minute and is increased in depth. Systolic blood pressure is usually elevated about 15 mm. of mercury, and patients will lose 5 to 15 pounds of weight during the second 24 hours of abstinence. A reduction in eosinpohils per cubic millimeter of blood closely parallels the intensity of abstinence symptoms, and, at the peak intensity of the withdrawal illness, the eosinophil count will be nearly zero. This constellation of signs and symptoms constitutes as clear-cut and well delineated a syndrome as is ever seen in clinical medicine. Once it has been observed, it scarcely can be mistaken for any other condition. Acute signs and symptoms reach maximum intensity 48 hours after the last dose of morphine has been given and will remain intense until 72 hours have passed. Thereafter, they gradually subside and, after 50 to 10 days, completely disappear, although the addict may still be weak and sleeping poorly.

It is necessary to remember that the intensity of the abstinence syndrome varies from person to person and is, within limits, dependent on the dose that the addict has been receiving. Not all patients will exhibit all the signs of abstinence listed above. Severe grades of abstinence symptoms are practically always seen in addicts who have been receiving as much as 60 to 90 gm. (1 to 1.5 grains) of morphine four or more times daily. The intensity of abstinence symptoms becomes milder as the average daily dose declines. Since most adolescent addicts actually have been receiving only small amounts of opiates, the effects of abstinence are usually quite mild in juvenile addicts and very close examination may be required to detect the minor signs which are present.

Symptoms of abstinence from other opiates and the synthetic analgesics differ from morphine chiefly in intensity and duration. Effects of abstinence from heroin, dihydromorphinone, and metopon appear very rapidly, reach maximum intensity in 12 hours or less, are somewhat more severe than those from morphine, and subside more rapidly. Abstinence symptoms from codeine appear slowly and are more prolonged than those from morphine. Abstinence symptoms from dihydrocodeinone and eukodal are less intense than those from morphine, but more intense than those from codeine. The symptoms from Dromoran are quite similar in course and intensity to those from morphine.

Effects of abstinence from meperidine appear rapidly and are detectable two to three hours after the last dose of meperidine has been administered. Abstinence from meperidine has an effect somewhat similar to that of abstinence from morphine, but restlessness is even greater, and uncontrollable twitching and jerking of the muscles is extreme. The course of abstinence from meperidine is quite short and symptoms usually disappear two to three days following withdrawal.

Signs of abstinence from methadone come on slowly and are usually not detectable until the third or fourth day after the last dose of the drug has been given. Autonomic signs, such as sweating and mydriasis, are not very prominent. For this reason, the detection of abstinence symptoms is more difficult. The course of abstinence from methadone, however, is quite prolonged. Because of this, withdrawal of methadone is regarded by many addicts as being more uncomfortable than abstinence from morphine.

Frequently, because of the lack of suitable facilities, it may not be possible to isolate the addict and prove the presence of addiction by allowing the signs of abstinence to appear. It is almost useless to attempt to carry out diagnostic withdrawal in a general hospital, or even in mental hospitals, since addicts frequently manage to smuggle drugs into these environments. Diagnostic withdrawal may also be impossible because of the addict's refusal to undergo the procedure and, in certain cases, it may be unwise if the patient has some serious physical disease.

Where adequate isolation for diagnostic withdrawal is not possible, the diagnosis of addiction can be established only tentatively.

A new drug, N-allylnormorphine, which is a very effective antidote for morphine, has recently been shown to precipitate signs of abstinence in addicted persons within 15 minutes following its administration. This agent, therefore, may provide a means of quickly establishing the presence and degree of physical dependence on opiate drugs, but sufficient information on the safety and reliability of the procedure is not available at this time to permit a recommendation for general use of N-allylnormorphine as a diagnostic agent in suspected addiction.

Reporting of Addicts

The physician is under no legal obligation to report cases of addiction to Federal officials. The Bureau of Narcotics, however, welcomes voluntary reporting of addicts by physicians.

Disposition of the Addict

Once a tentative diagnosis of addiction has been made, the physician would be well advised to seek consultation for confirmation. The problem then becomes one of advising the addict in accordance with the two cardinal principles of treatment set forth above—institutional treatment is necessary, and drugs must not be given to the addict for self-adminisration. The addict must be advised to seek admission to an institution for treatment. If he will not accept this advice, the physician may ethically refuse to take any further action. If the patient indicates willingness to undergo institutional treatment, steps should be taken immediately to obtain admission to the nearest and most available institution. Frequently, this can be accomplished immediately by telephoning the institution selected. The physician should refuse to administer any narcotics unless the patient shows the utmost diligence in obtaining entrance into an institution. Such excuses as time for arranging business and personal affairs or preference for one institution over another should not be accepted as reasons for the administration of narcotics; nor should the presence of signs of abstinence be a valid reason for immediate administration of narcotics unless the patient has such serious physical disease that stress of abstinence might prove fatal.

The physician must be prepared to resist the demands of addicts for narcotics and must exercise great care and judgment in determining whether physical disease which requires the immediate administration of opiates is present. If a physician yields to the importunities of an addict and gives him morphine for mild asthma, his waiting room will soon be cluttered with other addicts, all of them complaining that they have asthma or some similar condition. Such a situation can lead only to embarrassment to the physician and, perhaps, to difficulties with the authorities.

When the patient has agreed to go to an institution and has presented satisfactory evidence that he has taken steps to obtain admission (mere statement of the addict is not sufficient evidence of this), the problem is then reduced to the immediate management of the patient. The second principle, drugs should not be given to the addict for self-administration, applies here. It may be possible to place the patient in a general hospital where narcotics can be administered under direct supervision while final arrangements for entrance to the specialized institution are being made. The physician, in any event, should not give the addict a prescription for narcotics but should administer personally such drugs as are appropriate for immediate need only. It may be emphasized that it is always wise to seek consultation with another physician relative to the diagnosis of addiction and/or the presence of serious physical disease. A special record of narcotics administered should be kept, and, as has been previously mentioned, temporary administration of drugs should not be extended beyond the minimum time absolutely necessary for arrangements for admission to an institution to be completed. When the addict leaves his home community, he should be accompanied to the institution, whenever possible, by some responsible person, preferably a physician or a nurse.

No absolute rule can be laid down for the amount of narcotics to be given during the time arrangements for admission to a proper institution are being made. However, no amount of narcotic should be used in excess of that necessary for the immediate need of the patient. Either morphine or methadone may be used since these two drugs will adequately control abstinence from any of the other narcotics. It is advisable to limit the initial dose to 16 mg. (1/4 grain) of morphine or 10 mg. (1/6 grain) of methadone. It practically never should be necessary to exceed as a single dose 60 mg. (1 grain) of morphine or 30 mg. (1/2 grain) of methadone. Even in patients with very severe heart disease, there is little danger of abstinence from morphine causing death if the above dosage schedule is followed. The type of drug given and the dose should be unknown to the addict and all possible precautions should be taken to prevent the addict from obtaining narcotics from other sources.

The Adolescent Addict with or without Demonstrable Dependence on Narcotic Drugs

Despite their ages, adolescent addicts must be separated from their usual environments. Institutional treatment for adolescents with demonstrable dependence is just as necessary as for adult addicts and the same procedures should be followed. Adolescents without physical dependence might possibly be sent to a camp, farm, or some other environment where rehabilitative treatment may be attained rather than sent to institutions where contact with older, more hardened addicts is unavoidable.

Patients with Incurable, Fatal, Painful Diseases

Persons in this class are usually patients who are dying with advanced carcinoma, tuberculosis, or some other chronic disease. The problem in such instances is completely different from those described above. The physician is properly concerned, primarily, with relieving suffering and, only secondarily, with the addiction. Federal and State narcotic laws were not designed to prevent narcotics from being prescribed in such cases. Proper, ethical medical practice, however, demands that certain principles be followed.

Physicians prescribing narcotics for such patients should personally be attending the patient. A diagnosis of a painful, incurable disease should be confirmed by consultation with another physician. All means of relieving pain other than prescription of narcotics should be exhausted. Such measures include the use of drugs other than narcotics, physical therapy, and surgical procedures designed to relieve pain. When administration of narcotics becomes necessary, the physician should initially use drugs of lesser potency, such as codeine. When use of more potent narcotics is required, they should be given in the smallest possible dose and the interval of administration should be as long as possible. Precautions should be taken to ensure that the amounts of narcotics prescribed are no greater than those actually required for the particular patient so that there will be no surplus for diversion to illicit use. Whenever possible, the drugs should be given orally rather than hypodermically. Drugs should not be given directly to the patient for self-administration. The status of the patient and his disease should be reviewed periodically to make certain that the diagnosis is correct and that definitive, curative therapy is not possible.

Cocaine and Marihuana Addicts

Since physical dependence on these drugs does not develop and there is no withdrawal illness, the patient should simply be advised to seek treatment in a properly staffed institution. Hospitalization until admission to an institution can be obtained but is not necessary or advisable.

Choice of Institution

The choice of an institution depends upon the type of case, the financial situation of the patient, and other factors. Many private sanatoriums in the United States make a specialty of the treatment of narcotic drug addiction. Advice concerning these institutions can be obtained from local medical societies, the American Hospital Association, The American Psychiatric Association, or the American Medical Association. Alternatively, the physician may investigate the possibilities of having the patient admitted to a public, local, or State institution. Information concerning such institutions can be obtained by contacting local or State health departments. Lack of suitable local facilities remains one of the difficulties in the treatment of addiction. Physicians should support the establishment of such facilities in States in which no provision for addicts has yet been made.

Where local facilities are not available, addicts can be referred to the two federal hospitals maintained by the U. S. Public Health Service at Lexington, Kentucky, and Forth Worth, Texas. Persons addicted to opiates, synthetic analgesics, cocaine, and marihuana are eligible for admission to these institutions. Patients who are addicted to alcohol, barbiturates, or bromides are not eligible for admission to these federal hospitals unless they are also addicted to morphine, synthetic analgesics, marihuana, or cocaine. If the patient is indigent, treatment is available without charge. If the patient has funds, he is required to pay $5.00 daily for his treatment. Addicts entering these institutions are asked to remain at least 135 days before being discharged. Ordinarily, there is no waiting list for male patients and admission can be arranged readily by writing or telephoning the Medical Officer in Charge of either hospital. Only the institution in Lexington has facilities for female patients, consequently, women usually must wait for a short time before they can be admitted.

The Need for Compulsion

Unfortunately, many addicts will not go to an institution or remain there until treatment is completed unless compelled to do so by legal means. There is a great need for legislation in most of the States which would make it possible to commit addicts to institutions where they would be forced to remain until maximum benefit of treatment had been obtained. The Federal Bureau of Narcotics has drafted a text of such a proposed law and will distribute copies to interested persons on request. Legislation has also been proposed which would make it possible for the two U. S. Public Health Service Hospitals that treat addicts to accept and hold addicts committed under State laws. Passage of such laws deserves the support of all physicians.

Treatment Following Discharge from Institution

The follow-up treatment after the patient has been discharged from an institution is usually the weakest link in the overall treatment of addiction, and it is in this particular phase of the problem that the ordinary physician can make the greatest contribution. The physician should do what he can to assist the addict to find a job following discharge from an institution. He can attempt to make arrangements, utilizing such social agencies as are available, to separate the addict from the environment which played a role in engendering the addiction. He should encourage the former addict to participate in the activities of community groups, such as churches and clubs. The physician can advise the relatives of a former addict respecting environmental and familial factors which may be contributing to the patient's difficulties. He can also administer such forms of psychotherapy as he is qualified to carry out. When suitable facilities are available, intensive psychotherapy by a qualified psychiatrist is of great value provided the patient is willing to accept such treatment. The addict should remain under close supervision for at least two years following discharge from an institution. Although the tendency to relapse is very great in addiction, the physician should maintain an optimistic attitude even in the face of repeated recurrence and should continually encourage and support the addict.

Management of Disease in Former Addicts

When a person who formerly has been addicted to morphine becomes afflicted with a disease for which narcotics are usually prescribed (this situation usually develops when a surgical operation becomes necessary), he should be handled just as if he had never been addicted. Since the former addict has been withdrawn from narcotics and has lost his tolerance to them, narcotics should be prescribed in the same doses and at the same intervals as is customary with persons who have never been addicted. Larger doses are not required. Narcotics should never be given to the former addict for self-administration, and use of narcotics should be discontinued as soon as possible. The addict should then be supervised closely for a month or so in order to avert relapse to uncontrolled use of drugs.

Management of Addicts Who Have Relapsed

The management of patients who have relapsed to abusive use of narcotic drugs should follow the same lines as detailed above. The only difference is that the period of supervision following discharge from an institution should be extended.

Can the addict be cured? Yes and no, depending on individual circumstances. Young people and those addicted a short time are the best prospects. There is at Lexington the finest hospital of its kind in the world. Many experts will cite an over-all rate of 25 percent cures; cynics off the record will claim that it actually is no more than 2 percent. At the best, there are harsh statistics. The bright side, however, is the Lexington story. From 1935 to 1952, 18,000 addicts were admitted for treatment. Of these, 64 percent never returned for treatment, 21 percent returned a second time, 6 percent a third time, and 9 percent four or more times. These figures should give everyone confidence that the U. S. Public Health Service Hospitals can secure good results in one of medicine's most tremendously difficult tasks. The hospitals and their great staffs have proved that the addict can be rehabilitated. Complete and unselfish support by the general public will certainly increase the number of addicts who can be made into useful members of society. That support is merited.

One final word. Those who fight drug addiction are fighting uphill with the odds very much against them. There is no sure cure, no complete knowledge, and the chances of winning are definitely not too good. It may very well be the beginning of the end—a short and horrible existence. The best cure for addiction? Never let it happen!

MEDICAL ASPECTS OF ADDICTION TO ANALGESIC DRUGS

The following discussion has been extracted from an article by Dr. Victor H. Vogel and Dr. Harris Isbell of the United States Public Health Service Hospital at Lexington, Kentucky, on this subject published in the *United Nations Bulletin on Narcotics,* Vol. II, No. 4, October, 1950.

Before discussing a subject it is necessary to define it. In the past the most widely used definition of addiction has been that formulated by pharmacologists which states that addiction is a condition brought about by the repeated administration of a drug such that its use becomes necessary and cessation of it causes mental and physical disturbances. The symptoms which appear following withdrawal of morphine indicate the development of a state called "dependence" on the drug. Dependence may be emotional, physical, or both. However satisfactory this definition may be to pharmacologists, who are concerned only with the effects of drugs, it is not acceptable to persons who actually have to handle the human beings who are addicted. The pharmacological definition of addiction puts the cart before the horse because one has to take morphine for at least two or three weeks before any dependence is developed. Moreover, if dependence were the only important factor in addiction the solution of the problem would be very easy. One simply would permit addicts to have drugs so that their dependence would be continuously satisfied. It should also be noted that this definition makes coffee, tea and tobacco addicting substances because emotional dependence on these substances is just as marked as it is on cocaine or marihuana which are regarded as addicting drugs by practically all societies.

Any definition which makes dependence the central feature of the definition is undesirable because of the public's reaction to the term addiction. Laymen and even physicians believe that the use of an "addicting" drug is an extremely bad thing. Contrariwise, the habitual use of a "non-addicting" drug is not nearly so reprehensible and is not a matter of public concern. Actually, we are concerned about addiction and attempts to regulate the use of addicting drugs, not because individuals who use the drugs become dependent upon them, but, because the effects of the drug are harmful both to the individual and to society. The harm which the use of various drugs may cause arises in a number of ways. It may be due to a decrease in the potential social productivity of the addict as occurs during addiction to morphine and similar drugs, to the precipitation of undesirable and dangerous behaviour (even of temporary insanity) as may occur with the abuse of cocaine and marihuana, or to the mental confusion and impairment of motor function which are prominent features of addiction to either alcohol or the barbiturates. Dependence is important in addiction but it is important chiefly because it tends to make the addiction continuous rather than periodic and so increases the amount of harm which the addiction produces.

In recent years a number of psychiatrically oriented workers in the United States have formulated a definition which makes loss of self-control with reference to the use of the drug and harm to the individual or to society the essential features. This point of view was accepted in part by the Drug Addiction Committee of the National Research Council who, after long discussion, recently adopted the following definition: "Addiction is a state of periodic or chronic intoxication which is detrimental to the individual and to society which is produced by the repeated administration of a drug. Its characteristics are a compulsion to continue taking the drug and to increase the dose with the development of psychic and, sometimes, physical dependence on the drug's effects. Finally, the development of means to continue administration of the drug becomes an important motive in the addict's existence." One should note that the leading sentence of this definition makes "detriment to the individual and to society" necessary to the definition of addiction and that the development of physical dependence is not a necessary characteristic of the term.

Under the terms of this definition, many drugs would be considered addicting. They include opium and some of its derivatives (morphine, heroin, dihydromorphinone [dilaudid], codeine, methyldihydromorphinone [metopon], dihydrocodeinone and eucodal); the synthetic drugs with morphine-like actions (meperidine [demerol or dolantin] and its derivatives, methadone [amidone, dolophine, "10820," physepteone] and all derivatives of methadone including isomethadone and heptazone [CB-11]); cocaine; hashish in any form; barbiturates; bromides; alcohol; peyote (mescaline); and amphetamine. Coffee, tobacco, and tea cause little harm and are culturally acceptable in most societies and are not regarded as addicting substances. In this article we will be concerned only with the medical aspects of addiction to the analgesic, or pain-relieving drugs.

The Harm Produced by Addiction to Analgesic Drugs

Many of the popular notions concerning the damage caused by addiction to analgesic drugs are completely erroneous. These drugs do not make individuals who use them into supermen. . . . Moreover, individuals who are tolerant to opiates show no outward evidence of intoxication and are very difficult to differentiate from persons who are not taking drugs. Individuals who are addicted to these drugs maintain good muscular co-ordination and, if sufficiently strongly motivated, can continue to work, although the amount of work produced is definitely impaired by addiction. It is perfectly correct to state that the physical effects of addiction to a narcotic drug are much less damaging than are the effects of addiction to barbiturates or coca leaves. What then is the damage which these drugs produce and why are we concerned with them? The harm caused by addiction to analgesic drugs has been best described by Kolb who said "When taken in large doses they (the opiates) sap the physical and mental energy; lethargy is produced, ambition is lessened and the pleasurable feeling already described—that all is well—makes the addict contented. These various facts cause him to pay less attention to work than formerly; consequently they tend to become idlers by these means alone . . .

"The dreamy satisfaction and the pleasurable physical thrill produced by opium in many addicts in their earlier experiences with it are of themselves forms of dissipation which tend to cause moral deterioration." . . .

Characteristics of Addiction to Analgesics

Addiction to opium and similar drugs is usually described as embracing three intimately related but distinct phenomena: (1) tolerance, (2) physical dependence, and (3) habituation. It is wise to keep in mind that these terms are descriptive and do not constitute a definition of addiction.

Tolerance is defined as a diminishing effect in repetition of the same dose of the drug over a period of time or, conversely, a necessity to increase the dose to obtain an effect equivalent to the original dose. *Physical dependence* refers to an altered physiological state brought about by the repeated administration of the drug which necessitates the continued use of the drug to prevent the occurrence of the characteristic illness which is termed an abstinence syndrome. *Habituation* refers to emotional and psychological dependence on the drug—substitution of the drug for other types of adaptive behaviour. Habituation is closely related to the euphoric effect of the drug; that is, the relief of pain or emotional discomfort.

The mechanism of the development of *tolerance* to the analgesic drugs is unknown. The older theories of the mechanism have been reviewed by Eddy. Most of them are unsatisfactory. Marme believed that morphine was oxidized in the body to a substance called oxydimorphine and that oxydimorphine had effects which opposed the actions of morphine. Other investigators have been unable to confirm Marme's theory. Gioffredi thought that prolonged administration of morphine caused the production of a substance which was a specific antitoxin for morphine but, in carefully controlled experiments, Du Mez and Kolb were unable to find any evidence of the presence of any antimorphine substance in the serum of monkeys who were tolerant to morphine. Other investigators have felt that increased destruction and excretion of morphine by the body might account for tolerance. This is quite unlikely since tolerance develops to some effects of morphine at varying rates and on the other hand tolerance to certain effects never develops. Since morphine simultaneously stimulates and depresses different parts of the nervous system of animals, and since the stimulant effects outlast the depressant effects, Tatum, Seevers and Collins postulated that, as addiction proceeds, there is an increment of stimulant effects which oppose the depressant action of morphine thus bringing about tolerance. Amsler stated that morphine produced a persistent change in the cells of the body which rendered the cells more sensitive to the stimulant effects of morphine and more resistant to the depressant effects of the drug. Cloetta and others have postulated that there is some increase in resistance of the reactive cells to morphine but do not explain how this increased resistance is brought about. The hypothesis which is most widely held at present states that administration of morphine brings into play certain physiological responses which oppose some of the actions of morphine. Repeated administration of morphine strengthens the physiological counter responses and diminishes the effect of the drug. Wikler believes that these enhanced physiological responses are actually conditioned reflexes.

Physical dependence is one of the most striking characteristics of addiction to analgesic drugs and its importance in the total picture of addiction has both been over-emphasized and minimized. Pharmacologists are prone to regard physical dependence as the primary and only distinguishing characteristic of an addicting drug. The reasons for rejecting this view have been stated above. Other individuals have denied the existence of physical dependence and have attributed with-drawal phenomena to anxiety or malingering. This latter view is cer-tainly not tenable because physical dependence has been produced in dogs, monkeys and chimpanzees, and Wikler has shown that physical dependence can be observed in the paralysed extremities of dogs whose spinal cord has been severed as well as in dogs from whom all of the cerebral cortex (the part of the brain involved in thinking and emotions) has been removed.

The course of abstinence from morphine has been described in great detail by Himmelsbach. If morphine is abruptly withdrawn from an individual who has been taking as much as 0.26 to 0.39 grammes daily for a period of 30 days or more, few signs are seen in the first 8 to 16 hours of abstinence. The patient is likely to go into a restless, tossing sleep which lasts several hours. About 12 to 18 hours after the last dose of the drug has been given, the patient begins to yawn, his nose begins to run, he starts to sweat and large tears form and run down his face. These signs increase in intensity and, during the second 24 hours of abstinence, the pupils of the eyes become widely dilated, the patients complain of "hot and cold" flashes and, on careful obser-vation, one can see recurrent waves of gooseflesh on the skin. The gooseflesh resembles the skin of a plucked turkey and accounts for the origin of the term "cold turkey" which is used by the addicts in the United States to describe abrupt and complete withdrawal from drugs.

Thirty-six hours after the last dose of morphine has been given, uncontrollable twitching of the muscles begins. This twitching and jerking accounts for the term "kicking their habit." Severe muscular cramps develop in the legs, abdomen and back. Anorexia and insomnia become prominent. Vomiting and diarrhoea are frequently seen. The patient has a mild fever, the respiratory rate rises to 25 or 30 per minute and becomes irregular and sighing in character, and the blood pressure is slightly elevated. The addict is unable to eat and will probably lose five or six pounds during the second and third days of abstinence. The acute signs and symptoms reach their height 48 hours after the last dose of morphine was taken and remain at the peak until the 72nd hour of abstinence. Thereafter, all signs gradually subside and after 5 to 10 days the addict, though weak and shaky, is almost well. Difficulties in sleeping and small changes in pulse rate, temperature, and in the blood can be detected as long as three to four months after withdrawal. Thereafter, the physical state of the addict becomes completely normal unless he is suffering from some other disease.

The intensity of the withdrawal sickness is more dependent on the dose of morphine the addict has been receiving than any single factor. Mild grades of abstinence can be detected in former morphine addicts after the administration of as little as 20 mgm. of morphine four times daily for 30 days. Grades of abstinence which are as intense as any which can be developed with any drug for any period of time can be produced by the administration of 60 to 90 mgm. of morphine four times daily for 30 days. The picture of abstinence from opium (either smoked or eaten), heroin, dihydromorphinone and metopon is qualitatively similar to that of abstinence from morphine and the intensity is just as great. Abstinence from opium develops at about the same rate as abstinence from morphine, whereas, abstinence from the other drugs mentioned above comes on more rapidly than does abstinence from morphine and subsides somewhat more quickly. Abstinence from codeine, though quite definite, is less intense than abstinence from morphine, comes on more slowly and subsides more slowly. Abstinence from dihydrocodeinone is somewhat more intense than abstinence from codeine but less intense than abstinence from morphine. Abstinence from meperidine (demerol or dolantin) is milder than abstinence from morphine but comes on more rapidly and subsides more quickly than abstinence from morphine. Abstinence from methadone comes on rather slowly, is mild in intensity, and subsides quite slowly. Abstinence from methadone is qualitatively different from abstinence from morphine in that few of the signs which indicate involvement of the autonomic nervous system (yawning, running nose, tearing, dilatation of the pupils, and vomiting) are seen.

The mechanism of physical dependence, like that of tolerance, is still unknown. It is certainly not due to anatomical alterations in the cells. Many of the theories which have been proposed to explain the manifestations of physical dependence are identical with those advanced as explanations of tolerance. These include the oxydimorphine, antitoxic and pathobiotic hypotheses. Theories which are based on changes in the way in which the body handles water, theories involving reversible coagulation of the proteins of the cell, and theories involving the replacement of a cell constituent have all been shown to be without basis. The excitation theory of Tatum, Seevers and Collins has had considerable vogue. According to this hypothesis, withdrawal signs are due to the stimulant actions of morphine outlasting the depressant actions. There are however a number of objections to the theory of Tatum, Seevers and Collins. Signs of abstinence from morphine in all species of animals are different from the signs produced by the stimulant actions of the drug. For example, these authors state that constriction of the pupil and slowing of the pulse are the result of stimulant actions. During withdrawal, instead of pupillary constriction and slowing of the pulse, dilatation of the pupils and increase in the pulse rate occur. Convulsions, which are one of the most striking stimulant actions of morphine in the dog, are not a feature of abstinence in this species. The stimulant actions of codeine are greater in proportion to its depressant actions than are those of morphine. One would therefore expect, on the basis of the theory of Tatum, Seevers and Collins, that dependence on codeine would be more severe than on morphine. The reverse is the case. The results of Wikler and Frank on the reflexes in the paralysed hindlimbs of addicted chronic spinal dogs also do not support the views of Tatum and Seevers. The hypothesis, which is currently favoured by most authorities, states that signs of abstinence represent a release of the enhanced physiological mechanisms which oppose the actions of morphine from the brake imposed by the continuing presence of morphine in the body. This particular idea appears to fit the known facts better than any other hypothesis yet advanced. Many of the signs of abstinence from morphine are qualitatively the opposites of many of the acute effects of morphine. Morphine depresses body temperature and during abstinence one sees fever. Morphine constricts the pupils and during abstinence one sees mydriasis. Himmelsbach suggested that the homeostatic responses which oppose the actions of morphine are mediated largely by the hypothalamus (the portion of the brain which is largely concerned with the regulations of temperature, blood pressure, etc.) via the autonomic nervous system. While this may be true, the experiments of Wikler show that other parts of the nervous system are also involved.

Habituation has been described by Himmelsbach as the psychical phenomena of adaptation and mental conditioning to the repetition of an effect. In more simple language, this means that the addict comes to use the drug as the answer to all of life's stresses. Rather than taking positive and definite actions about his difficulties, the addict temporarily defers the need for a solution of the problems by taking a dose of his favourite opiate. The directly pleasurable effects of the opiates are strongly reinforced in individuals who have been addicted by the relief which the drug affords from the symptoms of abstinence. Having once experienced the relief of abstinence by morphine, the addict comes to think of the drug as possessing magical qualities. He refers to it as "God's own medicine" and comes to believe that it is a "cure" for all mental and physical ailments.

The Cause of Addiction

In order to produce addiction a drug must have effects which certain persons regard as pleasurable. Kolb distinguishes two types of pleasure following the use of morphine. Negative pleasure refers to relief of either physical pain or psychic tension while positive pleasure refers to elevation of the individual above his usual emotional plane. The pleasure which morphine induces in susceptible individuals is one of the most subtle and enjoyable sensations known to man. As mentioned above, the drug does not increase the efficiency of the individual, does not make him more courageous, and does not permit him to engage in long continued effort. Actually, morphine produces a sensation of pleasant relaxation, ease, and warmth. It resembles the feeling one gains after working in the garden or completing some other pleasant task. In this state, all worries vanish and the individual can sit and dream deferring all decisions until tomorrow. One should keep in mind that in taking drugs to induce this state, the addict is seeking the same thing we all desire—peace and comfort. He is merely going about attaining this universal human desire in a way which provides only temporary peace and which is in itself pathological. If the drug is taken intravenously, a pleasant tingling spreads through the entire body. This sensation is most marked in the abdominal region and has been compared by some addicts to the sensation of a sexual orgasm. Intravenous injection appears to be especially attractive to individuals with psychopathic personalities.

The meaning which the effects of morphine have for a given individual is dependent upon his personality characteristics. Psychically normal individuals do not have psychic tension, are already at ease, and are not impressed by the effects of the drug. To put it differently, they cannot be, or feel no need to be, raised above their usual emotional plane. If such persons are suffering from physical pain, the relief of the pain by morphine may be very impressive and may be interpreted as pleasure. Psychically normal individuals, however, feel no need for the drug once the physical disease which was responsible for their pain has disappeared. Individuals who are fundamentally emotionally immature childlike persons that have never made a proper adaptation to the problems of living are, however, greatly pleased by the effects of the drug. They find that morphine gives them a sense of relief comparable to the solution of a difficult problem or the shaking off of a heavy responsibility. Many of them feel that their efficiency is increased and that they can meet better adjusted people on equal terms. For a time, morphine seems to be the answer to their difficulties, but as they develop tolerance they find that they must take more and more to induce the desired effects. Finally, the drug will not produce the desired sensations at all, and the addict finds himself taking it to prevent the discomfort of withdrawal.

It follows, from what was said above, that the effects of morphine are much more pleasurable to individuals who have some type of psychic maladjustment than it is to psychically normal individuals. The types of individuals who are especially prone to addiction have been well described by Kolb and Felix who list four general personality patterns.

The first personality group consists of cases who, during the course of a physical illness, received drugs over an extended period of time, and, following relief of their ailment, continued to use the drug. These persons are frequently termed "accidental" or "medical" addicts. Such persons are regarded by some authors as constituting a special group of addicts who differ from persons who began the use of drugs as a result of thrill and pleasure seeking and association with persons who were already addicted. In our experience, all "medical" addicts have some fundamental emotional problem which causes them to continue the use of drugs beyond the period of medical need. There is, then, no basic difference between "medical" and "non-medical" addicts except in the mode of their original contact with drugs. In persons with stable personalities, social pressures, conscience, and a well balanced make-up negate the pleasure produced by drugs sufficiently to prevent their continued use.

The second group consists of persons with all types of psychoneurotic disorders. Included in this classification are people who have a great deal of anxiety, are nervous, tense, and frightened or worried by minor matters; people who feel compelled to do things in a certain way and who become very uncomfortable if their routines are upset; and individuals who have strange inexplicable types of paralyses or losses of sensation in their extremities (hysterical persons). Individuals of this class begin the use of morphine because it relieves their anxiety and takes away whatever symptoms they may have. Even in the beginning, the drug is used to induce "negative" pleasure. Such persons do not ordinarily increase the dosage of narcotics as rapidly as do psychopaths and may remain on low dosages of morphine for years.

These people usually have no criminal records prior to addiction, and their illegitimate activities after addiction usually are of a minor kind which are generally traceable to their great need for drugs. They are certainly deserving of pity and need treatment more than punishment.

The third group consists of psychopathic persons who ordinarily become addicted through contact and association with persons who already are using drugs. They are generally emotionally undeveloped, aggressive and hostile persons who take drugs for the pleasure arising from the relief of the tension arising from their unconscious aggressive drives. In many of these people, the use of morphine represents a means of expressing hostility and resentment against society. Many of these individuals are basically amoral and addiction is merely an incident in their criminal careers. . . .

The fourth, and smallest group, is made up of individuals who are insane (psychotic) and who are also drug addicts. The mental illness in many of the persons in this classification is mild in degree and some of these persons seem to be able to make a better adjustment while taking drugs. It is often difficult to determine whether these individuals are actually insane while they are actively using morphine since signs of the psychosis do not become apparent until the drug is withdrawn.

Many addicts are difficult to classify exactly as to personality type. Many of them exhibit much of the overt behaviour pattern of the psychopath but, when studied more carefully, are found to possess psychoneurotic characteristics as well. Kolb originally described such persons as suffering from a vague, poorly crystallized personality defect which he termed a psychopathic diathesis. They are now classified under the terms of behaviour or character disorders. Types of individuals who fall into this bordedline class include persons who unconsciously wish to be sheltered and protected, shy, withdrawn individuals who feel the world is against them, and people who seem to have never grown up. Most of the persons in this group make a marginal adjustment to life before becoming acquainted with narcotics. Once they begin the use of drugs they lose part of their normal adaptive patterns of adjustment and become parasites on society. This regression of personality and loss of social adaptation represents the greatest danger in drug addiction.

The mode of contact with a drug determines to a great extent whether an individual with a susceptible personality will become addicted. If contact with a drug results from legitimate medical administration during the course of illness, addiction seldom occurs. In fact, less than 5 per cent of addicts become addicted by this means. Contact with the drug through addict friends as a result of curiosity, association, thrill and pleasure seeking is a much more potent cause of addiction. This fact explains why so many individuals who have personality characteristics similar to those of addicts never become addicted. They do not have addict acquaintances.

Abuse of all types of drugs is based on the same personality factors, so that addiction to one drug predisposes to addiction to another. Thus an individual who abuses alcohol and receives morphine for the relief of symptoms of alcoholic debauches is very likely to change his addiction to morphine. Persons who smoke marihuana are frequently thrown into close contact with narcotic drug addicts and, as a result of the association, change from marihuana to heroin or morphine. . . .

Addiction to opiate drugs is continuous and not intermittent as is frequently the case with alcohol, cocaine and barbiturates. This is usually interpreted as indicating that the addict fears the abstinence symptoms and continues to take the drug to avoid the pain of withdrawal. Wikler believes that, in addition to the avoidance of pain, the relief of abstinence symptoms by morphine represents the satisfaction of a biologically determined need which is similar to the relief of other biologically determined needs such as hunger or thirst and is therefore pleasurable in a positive sense. This idea implies that addicts enjoy being dependent upon drugs so that they can experience the pleasure of the relief of the abstinence symptoms by morphine. It is possible that both mechanisms operate simultaneously in the same individual.

The tendency to relapse is also a striking characteristic of addiction to narcotic drugs. According to most authorities, the tendency to relapse is due to the fact that once drugs are withdrawn the same personality characteristics which predisposed the individual to addiction are still present. The proneness to addiction caused by these personality traits is greatly reinforced by the phenomenon of habituation, or emotional dependence. As Kolb says, the addict is so conditioned that he thinks of taking a dose of morphine when he is exhilarated or depressed. If an individual who has been an addict meets a friend on the street he is pleased and this leads to the idea of a "shot" to celebrate the event. If he becomes depressed or upset by any matter, no matter how minor, he is inclined to take the drug so that he can forget the problem or defer its solution until the following day. If he develops some illness and is uncomfortable, he remembers the relief which morphine gave when he was ill from lack of the drug and feels that he must have some of his magical "cure-all" to alleviate the manifestations of his present illness.

Diagnosis of Opiate Addiction

The appearance and behaviour of addicts who have developed a high degree of tolerance to morphine may be indistinguishable from the appearance and behaviour of individuals who are not taking drugs. Morphine does not produce staggering, slurring of speech or as great a degree of impairment of intellectual functioning as does alcohol or the barbiturates so that, so far as can be ascertained by casual examination, the addict may appear to be completely normal. The presence of numerous abscess scars in the skin and the finding of needle marks, particularly in the form of tattooing over the veins, are very suggestive. Emaciation arises only when the addict is in poor financial circumstances and spends all his available income for drugs rather than for food. Frequently it is necessary to isolate a person suspected of being an addict and allow him no drugs in order to determine whether he is actually physically dependent on drugs. If the characteristic signs of abstinence appear, the question is immediately settled. Tests are available for the detection of morphine and other drugs in the urine, but these tests are difficult to carry out and are not available to most physicians.

The appearance and behaviour of individuals who are addicted to methadone is identical with that of individuals who are addicted to morphine. Marked induration and inflammation of the skin over the sites where the drug is usually injected is a characteristic finding in addiction to methadone. Individuals who are taking large amounts of meperidine (demerol) may exhibit marked dilatation of the pupils, inco-ordination, uncontrollable muscle twitching and even convulsions. In the amounts taken by addicts, chronic intoxication with meperidine is even more undesirable than is addiction to morphine.

Treatment of Drug Addiction

Treatment of drug addiction can be divided into two phases; withdrawal of drugs, and rehabilitative therapy. Withdrawal is necessary and is the first step in treatment but is much less important than rehabilitative therapy and is the only part of the treatment of drug addiction which is easily accomplished.

Withdrawal of drugs from narcotic addicts on an outpatient or office basis should not be undertaken as it almost surely will fail. Withdrawal in any environment except that of a well managed institution under the control of persons trained in the treatment of addiction is difficult to accomplish. Withdrawal should be carried on in the quickest, smoothest and most humane manner possible so as to establish good rapport between the patient and the physician on which to base subsequent psychotherapy and rehabilitation. Abrupt and complete withdrawal of narcotic drugs carries a certain degree of danger and is unnecessarily cruel. This type of treatment tends to foster an attitude of resentment and hostility in the addict which greatly hampers efforts for his continued treatment. A withdrawal which is conducted too slowly tends to keep the addict mildly uncomfortable for long periods of time. He is, therefore, likely to become discouraged and to discontinue treatment. Simple reduction of the dosage of drugs over a period of 7 to 14 days represents a good method of denarcotizing the addict. Recently it has been found that methadone can be substituted for morphine without signs of abstinence appearing and that the symptoms which do appear during reduction of methadone are milder than those accompanying reduction of morphine. This latter method of withdrawal has, therefore, become quite popular.

Many physicians who do not have a complete understanding of the problem of drug addiction have devised various schemes of withdrawing drugs. About ten new methods are advocated each year and frequently these are spoken of as "cures." This fixation on withdrawal therapy is probably traceable to the idea that addiction is merely a matter of physical dependence and all that one has to do is to withdraw the drug. Many of these methods have been based on erroneous theories of addiction, are illogical and more dangerous than abrupt withdrawal of morphine. We are referring here to treatments which involve intensive purgation, inductions of convulsions by electric shock, raising huge blisters on the skin and injecting the blister fluid into the addicts, the use of scopolamine or hyoscine which makes the patient psychotic, the use of atropine, the use of insulin and of heavy sedation with barbiturates. As Kolb has pointed out, abstinence from morphine is a self-limited illness, and any withdrawal method which involves taking away the addict's drug will succeed unless the patient is killed in the process.

Adjunctive treatment during withdrawal includes the use of small doses of sedative drugs. It is important not to use large amounts of these agents since excessive sedation seems to accentuate the development of emotional upsets during withdrawal. Furthermore, the use of sedative drugs prolongs emotional dependence on drug therapy and one may succeed in transferring the addiction to barbiturates which is a far more damaging and serious matter than is addiction to morphine. Hydrotherapy in the form of continuous warm tepid baths is helpful in relieving excessive nervousness. Maintenance of a sufficient fluid intake is very important and a light ample diet should be supplied.

Emotional reactions to withdrawal are frequently much more difficult to handle than are the physical symptoms. Excessive anxiety, hysterical reactions, and attempts at malingering frequently occur. These must be handled by appropriate psychotherapeutic techniques as they arise. Generally, simple reassurance will suffice. Individuals undergoing withdrawal of drugs seldom become psychotic.

It has recently been both reported and denied that the operation of prefrontal lobotomy prevents the appearance of abstinence signs following withdrawal of drugs from addicted individuals. This operation consists of severing the frontal lobes from the other parts of the brain. It is difficult to understand how this operation would prevent the appearance of withdrawal signs since Wikler has shown that severe abstinence occurs in dogs from whom all the cerebral cortex has been removed. In any event, the operation produces considerable intellectual impairment and personality change and would not be justified merely on the basis of preventing signs of abstinence. Its use in addiction should probably be limited to the treatment of individuals with intractable pain. Whether the operation will so alter the personality of the addict that he will not relapse to the use of drugs has not been determined.

Rehabilitative Therapy

Whenever possible, any physical disease which the addict may have should be removed by appropriate therapeutic procedures after withdrawal has been completed. In cases of addiction associated with chronic diseases which are not completely curable, the treatment should be designed to produce the maximum possible degree of improvement and to teach the individual to manage his disease without resort to narcotics. In cases in which intractable pain plays a part in causing the addiction, appropriate surgical procedures designed to relieve the pain should be considered.

Time is an extremely important factor in handling drug addicts. Time is necessary not only to allow the altered physiology of the addict to return to normal (this requires about three to six months) but also time is necessary to break up his established habit patterns of using drugs as the answer to all his problems. The addict must learn to work, play, and sleep without drugs. Since time is such an important factor, some kind of coercion is frequently necessary. Many addicts may begin treatment with the best intentions in the world, but after a few days their basic personality difficulties assert themselves and they discontinue treatment. Coercion may take the form of pressure from friends, relatives or law enforcement officers. Frequently these measures fail and some type of legal action becomes necessary.

An adequate programme of occupational therapy is extremely important. Occupational therapy should not be a matter of weaving rugs, but should be so designed as to permit every patient who is capable of it an opportunity to perform at least eight hours of useful productive work daily. Whenever possible, the types of occupations available should maintain and add to any skills which the addict may possess so that following discharge he will be well prepared to take a useful place in society. Individuals with physical handicaps should not be allowed to vegetate on infirmary wards but should do as much work as the limits imposed by their disabilities will permit.

Whenever possible, addicts should receive psychotherapy designed to remove or lessen their personality problems. The first decision is whether psychotherapy should be offered at all. The emotional development of many addicts was arrested at a very early stage and such individuals are very resistant to psychotherapy of any type. About all that can be done in such cases is to provide a short period of institutional supervision followed by a long period of supervision of the patient by his family, friends, minister, or probation officer following discharge from the institution. Other individuals who reached a greater level of emotional maturity prior to addiction should be offered intensive psychotherapy. Psychotherapy is an individual matter which is dependent not only upon personality characteristics of the patient but on the training, orientation, and skill of the person who administers the treatment. It is in no wise different from psychotherapy administered to non-addicts and complete description is beyond the bounds of this article. There are, unfortunately, not enough psychiatrists to administer psychotherapy to all addicts who need and will accept it. This deficiency in therapeutic facilities perhaps can be partially bridged by organizing group therepeutic sessions. . . .

Prior to discharge from an institution the patient should make a plan. If possible, he should have a definite place to go, a job, and friends to whom he can turn. He should remain under some type of supervision for several years. In planning and conducting this phase of treatment, the resources of a good social service department are invaluable.

Prevention of Drug Addiction

. . . . Prior to the passage of the Harrison Narcotic Act in 1914, it was estimated that there were from 150,000 to 200,000 narcotic addicts, mostly women, in the United States. By 1948, the number of addicts in the United States had been reduced to approximately 48,000, mostly men. The Geneva Convention of the League of Nations had also operated to reduce world-wide production and refining of opium and therefore addiction. Further progress in the control of production and distribution of narcotics under the ægis of the United Nations is to be expected.

Although legal control of narcotics represents an effective means of reducing addiction, these laws can hardly be regarded as completely just unless some provision is made for the addict who is the person chiefly affected by the passage of such laws. Since many addicts are not criminals, they should not be incarcerated in ordinary penal institutions merely because they are addicted. Special institutions which view addiction as a medical problem should be provided for the care of such persons. Addicts who are basically criminals should, however, not be treated in hospitals but should be sent to the usual penal institutions.

In the United States, the addict was at first neglected following enactment of the Harrison Narcotic Act and was sent to penal institutions along with criminals. The realization . . . led to the establishment of two hospitals, one at Lexington, Kentucky, and the other at Fort Worth, Texas, which specialize in the care of narcotic addicts. The Lexington Hospital has been in operation since 1935 and the results obtained in treating addicts at this institution show that the effort has been well worthwhile. Of 11,041 addicts admitted between May 1, 1935 and January 1, 1949, 6,788 or 61.4 per cent have been admitted to the institution only once. Stated in another way, the known relapse rate is only 39.6 per cent. Although this rate indicates that the treatment of drug addiction is still far from completely satisfactory, it also shows that the treatment of drug addicts is far from the hopeless proposition which so many persons have thought it to be. Many addicts, who do relapse, remain abstinent for many years before returning to the use of drugs and such period of abstinence should be regarded as a considerable gain just as a long remission is counted a gain in other chronic relapsing diseases such as tuberculosis or arthritis.

The treatment of drug addicts also contributes to the prevention of addiction. Since addiction spreads from person to person like an infectious disease, isolation of the addict from susceptible individuals during his treatment prevents the spread of addiction. Cure of an addict, like cure of a tuberculous patient, removes an infectious focus.

Continuing improvement in the results of the treatment of drug addicts is dependent more upon advances in our knowledge of mental disease than it is upon any other factor. The intensification of research in this field gives us every reason to hope that new knowledge, which will lead to great improvement in the results of the treatment of addiction, will soon be uncovered.

DECEPTIONS BY ADDICTS TO OBTAIN NARCOTICS FROM PHYSICIANS AND DRUGGISTS

Curtailment of illicit supplies of narcotics has placed great pressure on legal stocks. The Bureau of Narcotics with the assistance of the local police and the medical and pharmaceutical associations had diligently pursued a campaign for the safeguarding of narcotic stocks. The holding of large drug stocks in exposed places has been discouraged, and safeguarding by electrical alarm systems has been recommended wherever substantial supplies are stored. The result has been that, while burglaries, robberies, and larcenies of drug stock occur in considerable numbers, the proceeds from individual thefts are usually small.

The narcotic addict already skilled in confidence games and similar dissimulations in evading the law has had to intensify and improve on many time-honored dodges for obtaining illicit drugs.

The schemes are sometimes of a rather elaborate confidence type. In one case addicts secured a series of narcotic prescriptions from a physician for a non-existent female patient and went so far as to have the doctor reserve hospital facilities for a proposed operation on the supposed patient. Some devices are much more simple. A successful *modus operandi* is for the addict or confederate, usually a woman, to walk into a drugstore

–generally when the proprietor or clerk is alone–and make a purchase of a personal appliance, asking permission to use the prescription room. After this customer has left the store the narcotic cabinet is found to have been pilfered.

The relative scarcity of narcotics has resulted in a great deal of pressure on physicians by addicts in order to obtain narcotic supplies. Simulating illness with a plausible story, these addicts are sometimes able to deceive inexperienced medical men into furnishing narcotics or prescriptions calling for them. Living in a world of deception, the addict often develops unusual acting ability. He becomes a specialist in whatever disease he decides to suffer from, reads everything about his "ailment" in the medical journals, learns every symptom, knows precisely when to twinge with pain at the doctor's touch.

Some addicts go to almost unbelievable lengths to carry out their deceptions. One had been operated upon years ago for a kidney ailment. In his efforts to obtain narcotics from a physician he would claim severe pain from a kidney stone. Whenever the physician insisted upon taking an X-ray, the addict would conceal in his hand an ordinary small stone. After being prepared for the X-ray, he would then secrete the stone in a pocket of the scar tissue on his back, in the exact position of a kidney stone, thus disclosing a stone in the X-ray. On his last attempt the stone fell out and was retrieved by the technician, resulting in his prosecution and conviction to a term of a year and a day for obtaining narcotics by fraud. Some inflict wounds on themselves to simulate postoperative scars. Others use some material which will produce a real coughing fit.

There have also been several instances of vicious assaults by criminal addicts on physicians and druggists in attempts to secure narcotics; one addict attacked a seventy-two-year-old physician and his elderly housekeeper with a knife.

Doctors who leave medical bags or kits in parked automobiles really are inviting predatory addicts to break into the vehicles for the narcotics that may be found in the bags. In these cases the addicts will often wantonly throw away or dispose of valuable medical instruments.

In Celina, Texas, a burglar entered the storage room of a drug store before closing time and hid in the rafters until the store was locked. He then removed the narcotics from a wooden cabinet and left the store.

In Dallas, Texas, a burglar gained entrance to a drug store by sawing boards which covered the skylight and he then used an explosive on the safe in which the narcotics were kept, damaging the safe beyond repair. In Central City, Kentucky, a pharmacy was burglarized twice in five weeks for narcotics. The drugs were stored in an unlocked cabinet.

Two addicts, brothers, staged an armed robbery of a drug store in Memphis, Tennessee, to obtain a supply of narcotic drugs. Due to the fast thinking of the pharmacists on duty in the store, other drugs were given to the robbers in place of narcotics, and they failed to get any narcotic drugs other than a small amount of Empirin with codeine. The robbers were both under the influence of narcotics at the time of the holdup.

In Houston, Texas, in August 1952, a druggist who was fed up with burglars, shot to death an ex-convict who was trying to force open the door of his pharmacy. The store had been burglarized at least eight times in the past few years. When the druggist heard someone trying to force the door open, he went out and fired a shotgun and a pistol. The burglar, a narcotic addict, was dead on arrival at a Houston hospital.

In a daylight robbery early on Sunday afternoon, September 14, 1952, at Seattle, Washington, a big stock of narcotic drugs was taken from the largest exclusive prescription pharmacy in the city. At gun point, the pharmacist and a porter were directed to lie face down on the prescription room floor. A second robber forced a customer to lie on the floor beside the other men, and the hands of all three were tied behind them. The robbers then asked where the narcotics were stored and when told where the stock was kept they asked where the rest of the stock was. The pharmacist replied that it was upstairs in the safe but that he did not know how to open it, an explanation which was accepted for some unknown reason.

The door of a midwest drug store opened one day in January a few years ago, and the proprietor saw a middle aged woman somewhat shabbily dressed, approaching the counter. The thin worn cloth coat certainly didn't provide much protection from the sub-zero weather the area was undergoing, but what particularly aroused the pharmacist's pity was the cumbersome and uncomfortable neck brace the woman was wearing. A fractured vertebrae, she said as she laid her torn gloves on the glass counter together with a prescription for some morphine sulphate tablets. It was particularly cruel because the injury had forced her to discontinue working and she just didn't know how she could make ends meet. The druggist felt a twinge of conscience for accepting the price of the tablets as he punched the register and watched the woman leave the store and start down the street. Unconsciously his eyes followed her, and to his complete amazement, he saw her enter an automobile, and sliding behind the wheel, whip off the brace and toss it into the back seat. As she drove off, the surprised druggist noted the license number and immediately advised the Federal Bureau of Narcotics. A brief investigation was quickly made, and the woman arrested. Of course she was a drug addict. She had to have drugs, and the neck brace had surely deceived a lot of people—several doctors and druggists. So well taken in were some of them that they even refused to accept payment for their services.

The old man was sitting on a park bench staring into space. Dirty, disheveled, unshaven, and worse yet, broke. His main concern was tonight's lodging. Just then he noticed a rather attractive young lady approaching and much to his surprise, as she drew abreast of him, she spoke. Would he like to earn five dollars? It was very easy and it would not take long. Ten minutes later the two of them were sitting in a doctor's office. Poor father was suffering severe pains from cancer of the rectum, and a prescription for morphine was necessary. And since it was so difficult for him to get to the doctor, would it be all right if the young lady simply picked up the prescriptions in the future. Assured that it was, they departed.

A year later the doctor encountered the young lady on the street. "How is your Dad these days?" "Still in great pain" was the response. "Well you better bring him in and let me look him over next week," said the doctor.

This presented quite a quandary for the young lady for she had not the slightest idea of the whereabouts of her alleged father. But she needed drugs badly. Down town she went, searched around, hired another old bum, visited the doctor, who after a short chat, issued another prescription and continued to issue them as previously. And he might be issuing them today if our young lady drug addict had not been arrested for forging a prescription in another city. The doctor was a mighty surprised individual when Federal agents unveiled the whole story for him.

The man handed the Minnesota doctor the certificate from the *Mayo Clinik* and the doctor noted that it was signed by the chief surgeon. That was good enough for him and within a matter of minutes, the patient was departing with a prescription for narcotics nestling in his pocket. Of course the doctor had made no physical examination. A great many doctors saw this certificate, and many of the drug stores in the area were divested of their narcotics supply before agents of the Federal Bureau of Narcotics caught up with a couple of drug addicts who were using the counterfeit certificate to satisfy their craving for drugs. The incredible fact, however, is that not one doctor noticed that the word clinic had been misspelled.

The reason for setting forth these cases is to show to what length addicts will go to procure drugs to satisfy their craving and also to show how physicians and druggists may be deluded into helping them.

Addicts are both ingenious and crafty, and it has been the aim of this chapter to attempt to supply information which will assist physicians and druggists in dealing with this type of individual.

XI

SOCIOLOGICAL IMPLICATIONS

THIS CHAPTER CALLS ATTENTION TO CERTAIN FACTORS INHERENT IN the over-all picture of Narcotics. Besides surveying addiction in the United States historically and outlining the general situation today, there will be found in the latter section—in the form of a discussion—a review of the world situation and the questions that are being currently raised looking to a better solution to the problem.

DRUG ADDICTION IN THE UNITED STATES

Three quarters of a century ago, narcotic addiction in the United States was almost eight times as prevalent as it is today. In 1877, the estimated number of narcotic users was 1 in every 400 of the population; in 1952, the number was not more than one out of every 3,000.

In 1909, when the first deterrent anti-opium law was passed in the United States, addiction to narcotics had become so widespread that imports of opium had reached the almost incredible figure of 628,177 pounds annually for a population of 50,000,000 people. Today, when the population is 155,000,000, annual consumption averages less than 361,000 pounds.

When the Harrison Act was passed in 1914, there were perhaps 150,000 to 200,000 narcotic addicts in the United States, or about 1 in every 460.

Remedial legislation had the effect of scaling down addiction until in World War I, only one man in 1,500 drafted was found to be a drug addict. (There was a deviation from a straight decline in a rather sharp upsurge after World War I, and in 1924 it was estimated by the United States Public Health Service that there was 1 addict in every 1,000 of the population.)

As the result of vigorous enforcement of the Federal narcotic laws, the figure had droped to 1 man in 10,000 in World War II. When that war ended, addiction was probably at the irreducible minimum. A temporary upswing in addiction occurred again in the postwar period, as predicted by the Federal Bureau of Narcotics. (See The Police and Narcotic Enforcement in Chapter VIII for discussion of teen-age addiction.)

When hearings produced substantial evidence that stiffer sentences reduce both drug traffic and addiction, and that sentences had been getting progressively lighter to the point where they were no deterrent, Congress passed the Boggs Act which was approved by the President on November 2, 1951. Until passage of this law, the maximum sentence was ten years but the average sentence served was a year and a half; no distinction was made between first and subsequent offenses. The Boggs Act makes mandatory minimum sentences of two, five, and ten years in Federal convictions for drug trafficking—with no parole, probation, or suspended sentences for second or third offenses.

The action of Congress in providing more adequate Federal penalty legislation and in restoring the enforcement personnel quota of the Bureau of Narcotics to prewar strength was of great help in halting the increase in drug addiction which, fortunately, was not general throughout the United States but was confined for the most part to the large cities in some six States.

After the peak of the postwar increase in addiction had been passed (1950), the Bureau reported in 1952, with a reasonable degree of certainty, that the ratio of addiction was not more than 1 out of every 3,000 of the population. The drug addict population of the United States Public Health Service Hospitals was decreasing, and fewer juvenile addicts were coming to the attention of the authorities.

Details regarding addiction surveys are given below.

PREVALENCE OF DRUG ADDICTION IN 1877

In a survey conducted in 1877 in Michigan by the State Board of Health, it was estimated that the total number of drug addicts in that State was 7,763 when the State's population was 1,334,031, or 516 per 100,000. It was estimated that there were in the entire United States 117,000 addicts in a population of 46,000,000, or 1 in every 400. (In 1877 in Adrian, Michigan, there were 116 drug addicts out of a population of 10,235, or 1 in every 100 of the general population. In a survey made in 1938 by the Federal Bureau of Narcotics, no nonmedical drug addicts could be found in Adrian.)

ARMY FIGURES ON DRUG ADDICTION IN WORLD WAR I COMPARED WITH WORLD WAR II

In a letter dated September 28, 1945, addressed to the Commissioner of Narcotics from Major Harold F. Dorn, Director, Medical Statistics Division, Army Service Forces, it was reported that roughly 1 man in 10,000 selective service registrants examined for military duty during World War II was rejected primarily because of drug addiction. This was a reliable indication of an impressive decrease in drug addiction, in comparison with World War I figures, when there were 3,000 rejections for drug addiction in an army of 4,500,000 men, or 1 man in 1,500.

DRUG ADDICTION IN 1924

In 1924, the United States Public Health Service made a survey on the prevalence and trend of drug addiction in the United States which indicated that there was at that time 1 addict supplied by the illicit traffic in every 1,000 of the general population.

DRUG ADDICTION IN 1937-1938

During these years the Federal Bureau of Narcotics conducted a survey on the prevalence of drug addiction which showed that addiction had decreased to the extent that there were then less than 2 nonmedical drug addicts known to the authorities in every 10,000 of the population.

While an actual count was not made in every State in the

Union, it was considered that the extent of drug addiction shown in the following 15 States, representing 25 percent of the area and 27 percent of the population of the continental United States, was fairly representative of the remainder of the country:

State	Population	Addicts	Addicts per 10,000
Connecticut	1,741,000	251	1.44
New York (excluding N.Y.C.)	5,824,345	593	1.02
Delaware	261,000	62	2.38
District of Columbia	627,000	231	3.68
North Carolina	3,492,000	501	1.43
Georgia	3,085,000	286	.93
Kentucky	2,920,000	584	2.00
Indiana	3,474,000	206	.59
Michigan	4,830,000	821	1.67
Minnesota	2,652,000	323	1.22
Mississippi	2,023,000	458	2.26
Oklahoma	2,548,000	787	3.09
Utah	519,000	27	.52
Nevada	101,000	102	10.09
Washington	1,658,000	250	1.51
Totals	35,755,345	5,482	1.53

PRINCIPAL AREAS OF ADDICTION THROUGHOUT THE WORLD

Heroin	Opium Smoking	Opium Eating	Cocaine	Marihuana (Hashish)
1. Turkey	1. China	1. India	1. Germany	1. India
2. China	2. Iran		2. Czecho-slovakia	2. Egypt
3. United States	3. India and Pakistan		3. Poland	3. Turkey
4. Japan	4. Thailand		4. Italy	4. Tunisia
5. Canada	5. Burma		5. India	5. French Morocco
6. Egypt	6. Straits Settlement		6. Peru	6. Africa
7. Hong Kong	7. Hong Kong		7. Chile	7. Mexico
8. Macao			8. Argentina	8. United States
			9. Cuba	

	Opium	*Opium*		*Marihuana*
Heroin	*Smoking*	*Eating*	*Cocaine*	*(Hashish)*
9. France	8. Macao		10. United	9. Brazil
10. Cuba	9. USSR		States	10. Canada
	10. Indonesia		11. Canada	11. United
	11. Egypt			Kingdom
	12. Nether-			12. Cuba
	lands			
	13. United			
	States			
	14. Canada			

NARCOTICS AND CRIME; ITS IMPACT ON SOCIETY

The most valuable and informative contribution to our knowledge of the relationship between drug addiction and crime is the statistical research conducted prior to World War II regarding opium smokers of the Japanese Colony of Formosa by Dr. Tsungming To of the Health Commission of Formosa, who is now a member of the faculty of Medicine, National Taiwan University, Taipeh, Formosa.

After classifying 57,073 crimes committed during a seven year period by natives of Formosa, his records show that based upon the relative proportion of opium smokers to non-smokers, 70.83 percent criminality was found among opium smokers as against 29.17 percent criminality among non-smokers.

In Formosa during the period covered by the survey, opium smoking was legalized and its users licensed by the government. The cost of the opium was a few cents a day. Under these conditions the only attributable cause for greater criminality among narcotic addicts than nonaddicts is the direct effect of the use of narcotics upon the moral fiber of the addict.

Dr. To concluded that drug addiction causes a relentless destruction of character and releases criminal tendencies. This is particularly interesting in view of the fact that some persons in this country claim that addicts become antisocial after addiction because the high cost of contraband drugs practically forces individuals of marginal economic status to resort to illegal sources of income, usually through the sale of narcotics or larceny.

The records of the Federal Bureau of Narcotics show a strong relationship between crime and drug addiction, both before and after the individual becomes addicted. The underworld has been for many years the principal recruiting ground for new addicts.

In studies made of representative groups of narcotic law violators by the Bureau, it has been found that many criminals who had long previous police records of a nonnarcotic nature later became drug addicts.

(a) Records selected at random from files of 119 narcotic trafficker addicts showed that 83 percent had previous criminal records, some of them exceedingly lengthy, for other offenses before the first narcotic crime was committed.

(b) In another study by the Bureau, it was noted that of all narcotic violators (except under the marihuana law) sentenced during a six-month period (1,268) 33 percent of the non-addicts had records (of violations of laws other than narcotic laws), while 67 percent of the addicts had such records; in other words, from these cases it appeared that the addict is twice as likely as the non-addict to have had a criminal record before the first narcotic offense.

BY WAY OF ILLUSTRATION

As illustrations of criminal records of addicts (before addiction), the following are cited:

Edward W.—First arrest, 1906, for juvenile delinquency at age of thirteen; 11 additional arrests in different States in the ensuing twelve years, 8 of which were for larceny and housebreaking. W. became addicted to drugs in 1918. He was arrested 36 times, escaped 5 times, since 1918 on various charges not connected with drugs.

Oscar B., drug addict, thirty-five years of age, confessed on November 23, 1939, to the slaying of a man during a hold-up one week previously. B. was later sentenced to serve 199 years imprisonment for murder. An examination of the killer showed on the veins of both arms and hands many needle scars from injections of drugs. He stated he had been addicted to the use of heroin for approximately three years. Prior to his addiction, B. had a record of 3 arrests on larceny and burglary charges.

Louis M., when arrested for his first narcotic offense had a record of 14 arrests prior to his addiction to drugs. At the time of his arrest he was under parole on a murder charge for which he had been sentenced to serve twenty years in the penitentiary. Other offenses had been assault, carrying of concealed weapons, larceny, and pocket picking.

In the records of 2,047 narcotic cases showing one or more prior convictions of the violators, there were shown 5,669 prior convictions of *major offenses,* and 2,309 prior convictions of minor offenses, or a total number of 7,978 prior convictions.

Narcotic agents and detectives of the New York City Narcotic Squad arrested Charles A., Joseph I., and Patsy N., for possession of 130 grains of smoking opium and a complete smoking opium outfit. A. had in his possession a loaded revolver. All of these defendants were addicts, and had long and varied criminal records. A. was wanted for hold-up of a Washington bank, and was at liberty under a two and a half year parole from Sing Sing Prison. He was described as a dangerous criminal, usually armed, and an habitual opium smoker. His record extended back to 1922, with convictions and sentences served for about eight different offenses, including safe blowing. N. when arrested was at liberty under a seven-year parole from Sing Sing Prison. He had a record of about 15 arrests on various charges, such as assault, robbery and burglary. I. had a record of 21 arrests since 1919, most of which were for burglary, and he had been convicted to five previous sentences in penitentiary. The criminal-addict, Harold N., had a record of over 90 arrests, including convictions for burglary, bootlegging, assault, carnal knowledge, robbery of a United States mail truck, and conspiracy to steal the United States mail.

Many police officers throughout the country support the observations that drug addiction shows up as one of the later phases in the criminal career of the addict. The following is quoted from a letter written by the detective sergeant in charge of the Narcotic Division of the Bureau of Police, Philadelphia, Pa., to the Commissioner of Narcotics:

I checked over the records of the last 200 white and colored, male and female prisoners arrested. We found that in those 200 records, only 22 persons commenced with being arrested for drugs. The other 178 were arrested anywhere from two to twenty times before they were eventually found to be using narcotic drugs. This, in my opinion, with seventeen years' experience at this time, proves conclusively that persons who acquire the drug habit do so after they have shown other criminal tendencies.

The following excerpts are quoted from a letter addressed to the Commissioner of Narcotics by an Inspector of Detectives at Pittsburgh, Pa.:

Careful examination of the history of the last 232 prisoners apprehended for narcotic drug offenses, consisting of male and female persons, but exclusive of juveniles, and comprising white, colored, and Chinese races, revealed that 59 of these violators were not addicts before committing crimes, and 173 had been engaged in various criminal activities on one or more occasions through periods from months to years, prior to acquiring an appetite for narcotics or becoming involved in any narcotic drug traffic.

An analysis of our records shows that virtually 75 percent were confirmed criminals before they resorted to the use of narcotic drugs.

It appears that the disclosures of our collection and tabulation of criminal facts indicates that crime cradles tolerance to addiction to narcotics.

A commanding officer of the Narcotic Detail of the Los Angeles Police Department made the statements that "at least 98 percent of all narcotic addicts are also engaged in other criminal activities"; and "a great many of the bank bandits, drug store bandits, kidnappers, etc. were found to be narcotic addicts."

The records of the members of the notorious Whittemore Gang show that they all used drugs. One was condemned to be hanged, and two to suffer forty years' imprisonment each.

A heroin addict in San Francisco, California, was convicted of murder during the early part of 1951. It was established beyond reasonable doubt that the murderer had taken an injection of heroin about one hour before the crime was committed.

In Chicago, a narcotic agent saw a narcotic drug addict take an injection of herion. About an hour later when the addict was taken into custody he violently resisted arrest and severely injured one of the arresting agents.

A gang of four armed robbers who had committed numerous robberies in Chicago and elsewhere all were addicts, and according to the signed statement of one, they all took an injection of heroin shortly prior to perpetrating their crimes.

The following paragraph is quoted from the book *Dangerous Drugs* by Arthur Woods, former Police Commissioner in New York City:

It might be said of narcotics in relation to crime that they are like weapons; they are liable to do the most damage when put in the worst hands, and as long as they are lying about there is constant danger of calamity. To the criminal-minded, they serve as a coefficient of power, heightening courage to bravado, and deftness to lightning-like rapidity. By chemistry they add further instability to those who are already by nature unstable. They induce a "state of irresponsibility which can readily suggest acts dangerous to society, and they can supply the excessive spontaneity which leads to the prompt carrying out of such suggestions. The criminal, under the steeling influence of these drugs, can become still more professional, and particularly in his earlier apprenticeship can derive from drugs the sang-froid he has not yet attained from experience.

The following excerpts are quoted from statements made by an expert on narcotics, Judge Twain Michelsen of the Municipal Court, San Francisco, California:

If the people of America are to be addressed on the admittedly vital problem of drug addiction in its relation to crime—if they are to understand the psychosis of the mental deviate who lulls himself into a false sense of well-being by the use of narcotics, then the dope fiend in his every activity should be recognized and indexed for what he is. It may be said that murder is murder, whatever the processes of its commission may be, and likewise a dope fiend is a dope fiend, whatever the source of his addiction may be. In the world of crime we find him standing in the front ranks of the most subversive and anti-social groups in the country.

Judge Michelsen, in refuting the observation that big-shot criminals are not addicts, cited some names and records of big-shot addicts as follows:

From the Los Angeles Police Department comes a staggering record of major crimes committed by opiate users: Jimmy B., burglar, hijacker bandit, (opium smoker); Verne M., gangster and killer, (hophead); this addict gunman mowed down several Federal officers with their prisoner, at the railway station in Kansas City, using machine guns and cutting down these men without warning; John J., burglar, gunman and killer (morphine addict); Hardy T., bandit, pickpocket, murderer (morphine and heroin user); Allen McN., bandit and would-be murderer (morphine addict); Joseph M., burglar and bandit (hop-head); Bert M., burglar, bank bandit (morphine addict); Peter P., burglar, bandit, bank robber and murderer (hop-head); Joe P., smuggler, bandit (morphine addict); Thomas P., bank bandit, burglar and forger (morphine addict); Tolford C., rapist, forger and bandit (morphine addict); Armando T., thief, bandit and would-be murderer (morphine addict); Phil A., gunman and two-time murderer (morphine and marihuana addict); Clarence R., robber, murderer (morphine addict); Louis P. and Montijo P., bank bandits and murderers (morphine addicts); Oscar P., bank bandit (morphine addict); Ventura R., robber, murderer (morphine and marihuana addict). Supplementing these cases are many others found in Federal records, including such addict-gunmen as Frank C., with a long record of crimes of violence; heroin was his avenue of "escape." Herbert C., with a robbery and deadly weapon record, Alfred C., with an assault and robbery record; Frank C., with a robbery, assault and gun history; Salvatore C., with an assault and robbery history; William B., a highway robber; Joe T., robber, burglar and dope fiend (morphine user) with a record dating back to 1905; Willie R., robber, would-be murderer; Henry C., alias "Kewpie," burglar, bunco artist; J. C., burglar and purveyor of knockout drops, whose record dates back to 1915, and innumerable others,—all join the vanguard of desperate criminals who found surcease of fear in narcotics.

Judge Michelsen quotes from a statement by a member of the Los Angeles Police Department:

. . . another reason for making war on the narcotic addict, is that every addict, knowing himself to be a moral and social outcast, delights in bringing others into the outcast fold; . . . it is a well known fact that they are, every one, potentially the makers of other addicts. In this respect I feel that these people are in the same category as lepers, and that the only defense society has against them is segregation and isolation whenever possible.

The ranks of both addicted and non-addicted drug peddlers are filled with persons dedicated to a life of lawlessness, and the arrest and incarceration of these people on narcotic charges has incidentally protected the public from the depredations of thieves, robbers, and other vicious criminals engaged in organized crime.

That crime and narcotics are interwoven is illustrated by the fact that narcotic drug violators are near the head on the list of all criminals in the United States having previous fingerprint records, which include crimes ranging from vagrancy to robbery, forgery, counterfeiting, burglary, and other serious offenses. Of the narcotic violators arrested during the year 1950, 70.3 percent had previous records and arrests.

Listed below are the criminal records in a few run-of-the-mill cases of individuals convicted of Federal narcotic law violations in a six-month period:

Frank C., robbery conviction

Herbert C., robbery and deadly weapon record

Alfred C., assault and robbery record

Frank C., robbery, assault and gun history

Salvatore C., assault and robbery history

Francis H., extortionist

William B., highway robber

Robert D., robbery and concealed weapons history

Herbert E., robbery and escape history

Edward D., robbery and other criminal history

Louis S., robbery and history of assault with intent to murder

Alfred B., assault and robbery history

Jacob M., burglar, horse "doper"

Don F., concealed weapons, extortion and robbery history

Philip C., who was carrying four loaded revolvers when arrested, fugitive in connection with pay roll robbery

Charles S., on parole for robbery and had a pending charge for a hold-up with a gun

Arthur R., three previous convictions for violations of Federal narcotic laws and conviction for receiving stolen property

Jerry S., robbery arrest

Glenn C., four previous convictions for violations of Federal narcotic laws, and conviction and three-year sentence for theft

Moe L., two previous convictions for violations of the Federal narcotic laws, one for carrying a concealed deadly weapon as well as for grand larceny; arrested several times for homicide, and alleged to be a professional killer.

Thomas S., two previous convictions for violations of the Federal narcotic laws, one conviction for robbery with sentence of from three to twenty years

Dewey R., six prior sentences for narcotic law violations and two for burglary

Abe C., two prior convictions for Federal narcotic law violations, and an arrest for theft

George K., criminal record extending over twenty years for offenses ranging from pick-pocketing, carnal knowledge, conspiracy to bribe, narcotic law violations

Emanuel W., fugitive under indictment for murder; considered one of most vicious and dangerous criminals in New York City.

In addition to suppressing the narcotic traffic in itself, police activity against drug addicts is a very essential part of general police operations. Addicts in the great majority are parasitic. This parasitic drug addict is a tremendous burden on the community. As Superintendent R. S. S. Wilson, the noted narcotic expert of the Royal Canadian Mounted Police points out: "The ordinary criminal may attempt to go straight, perhaps reform or the fear of punishment deter him but not so the addict; for him there is no reform, no road back. For just so long as he is an addict so is he inexorably bound to a life of crime."

The situation described below is cited as illustrating the losses suffered by the community through depredations of drug addicts.

During a three-year period, two doctors in a certain Virginia city had the reputation of supplying addicts with morphine. The news of the ease with which prescriptions could be purchased and filled there spread to cities and states nearby, and about 500 addicts flocked there from North Carolina, the District of Columbia, Tennessee and cities in Virginia, South Carolina, Georgia, and Maryland. These addicts were known not to have a medical need for narcotic drugs and the majority of them had previous criminal records. The Bureau of Narcotics was unsuccessful twice in bringing these doctors to trial. Meanwhile, their business thrived. Before cases were finally closed against the doctors, crime in that city had increased due to the presence of those addicts, as shown by the following figures:

Arrests	Increased from		
Burglary	11	to	38
Drug Addicts	58	to	155
Highway robbery	78	to	97
Petty larceny	785	to	1,025

These figures do not include arrests for shoplifting and other small thieveries.

A chief of police in a western city, in commenting on narcotics and crime stated: "I fully realize that any gain in the illegal use of narcotics has a direct relation to the increase in crime, and, conversely, where narcotic traffic is suppressed, crimes become less frequent. I have, therefore, increased the number of officers assigned to our narcotic squad in order that we might more effectively combat this evil."

In a report (1930) by the Narcotic Educational Association of Michigan, Inc., covering ten years' work in the operation of a farm for the cure of drug addiction, an analysis of 83 cases handled at the institution divulged the information that only 9 of the addicts had been gainfully employed; 2 were maintained by relatives; and 72 had been engaged in various types of crime as a means of livelihood.

In 1924, a special committee of physicians prepared a report on the ambulatory treatment for drug addiction, which was adopted by the American Medical Association and printed in its *Journal*, reading in part as follows:

Your committee desires to place on record its firm conviction that any method of treatment for narcotic drug addiction, whether private, institutional, official or governmental, which permits the addicted person to dose himself with the habit-forming narcotic drugs, placed in his hands for self-administration, begets deception, extends the abuse of habit-forming narcotic drugs, and causes an increase in crime. Therefore, your committee recommends that the American Medical Association urge both Federal and State governments to exert their full powers and authority to put an end to all manner of such so-called ambulatory methods of treatment of narcotic drug addiction, whether prescribed by the private physician or by the so-called narcotic clinics or dispensary.

The following is quoted from statements regarding "The Criminal Addict" made by an expert on narcotics, Judge William T. McCarthy, U. S. District Court, Boston, Massachusetts:

The Harrison Narcotic Act and the Narcotic Import and Export Act are very efficacious laws. They are a part of the golden treasury of laws that help to preserve our social order and we should resist with all the power at our command any attempt to interfere with their proper administration.

Both logical reasoning and demonstrable facts place the great group of narcotic addicts in the category of criminals first and addicts later. The crook and the hoodlum, the prostitute and the shoplifter are most frequently and freely exposed; therefore, their ranks logically contain a large percentage of recruits to drug addiction. . . . With few exceptions the use of narcotics is not the efficient cause of the presence of the addict in the underworld; he is usually thoroughly conversant with a dubious environment long before he becomes addicted. . . . In attempting to dispel the conception that the opiate addict is a dope fiend who is stimulated to crimes of violence, too much emphasis is placed on the soothing effects of opiates. . . . The drug that allows a patient to contemplate the surgeon's scalpel with equanimity also gives the irresponsible criminal a false sense of security and serves as an obvious explanation in many instances for the commission of very serious crimes. . . .

The statement, "The long criminal records which drug addicts sometimes accumulate must be studied carefully," implies that these records arise from addiction. I agree that the records of these people should be carefully examined, but such records usually disclose a first arrest for something other than narcotics. While it is not conclusive, it gives rise to the presumption that the man was a criminal first and an addict afterward. Even where the first arrest is for narcotics, careful examination often discloses criminal or borderline activities before the narcotic agent happened to apprehend him. . . .

Dr. J. Bouquet, the French expert, in his remarks included in the papers of the 24th Meeting of the Opium Advisory Committee at Geneva, Switzerland, referring to a North African situation, makes these trenchant comments: "Nothing, I think, can be expected from methods which liken a toxicomaniac to a sick person and not to an offender. Such methods are only applicable to the class of drug sufferers who, as the result of necessary temporary medical treatment, have become accustomed to morphine or heroin. . . . But it must not be forgotten that this class constitutes a very small group of toxicomaniacs. The majority have no desire to become cured; it consists only of depraved people who are not only useless to the community but dangerous to the public welfare because they have only one desire, that is to find a means to satisfy their vice however ignoble the means to be employed to that end may be. In my opinion, such people should be considered not as sick people worthy of pity but as delinquents who must be prevented from causing harm and who must be treated with the greatest severity."

In a report dated July 25, 1943, on "The Present Drug Addiction Situation in Tunisia" Dr. Bouquet states, "It is argued that 'the majority of the drug addicts are vicious criminals and that they deserve to be imprisoned rather than placed in hospitals.' "

Several years ago, the Canadian Government conducted a study on narcotic criminality. It showed that 93 percent of those convicted of narcotic offenses during the period under review had committed at least 1 crime prior to the first narcotic offense, and some had committed as many as 27 other crimes prior to the first narcotic offense. Two hundred persons convicted had committed a total of 2122 crimes, of which only 465 were narcotic crimes.

It was the conclusion of Canadian authorities that over 95 percent of all drug addicts are criminal addicts; and that in nearly all of these cases the addict was a criminal before becoming addicted; addiction was caused by criminal association.

The General Secretary of the Department of Public Health, Mexico, D. F., Mexico, reporting on observations made with respect to 150 drug addicts in the Federal Penitentiary, stated that "in almost all of the cases the prisoners give as the reason for their addiction having been influenced by vicious friends."

The most casual inquiry would disclose that there are among the population of Federal and State penitentiaries in the United States a large number of non-addicted drug peddlers. In those ranks one will find a substantial proportion of big-shot racketeers ranging from the arrest and conviction of persons such as Louis (Lepke) Buchalter, head of the notorious gang, Murder, Inc.*

* In that capacity, it was alleged that he had ordered the deaths of anywhere from sixty to eighty men, and had manipulated simultaneously some 250 criminal ventures, with at least 300 straw bosses and a staff of irresponsible triggermen, strongarms and industrial saboteurs. Buchalter was eventually convicted of first-degree murder and executed in 1944.

(not only an interstate but actually an intercountry and inter-continent organization which obtained its narcotic supplies in China and distributed them from New York throughout the coun-try); the Newman (Neiditch) brothers of New York City (who were important enough to have at one time corralled the entire illicit drug supply being exported from France to the United States), and extending back in the past to the capture and im-prisonment of figures like the Ezra brothers and "Black Tony" Parmagini. (In 1930, Antone Parmagini, alias "Black Tony," who had been "king" of the racketeers on the Pacific Coast, was con-victed of narcotic law violations and sentenced to serve seventeen years in the penitentiary and fined $17,000. William Levin, a confederate, was given a similar sentence and fined the same amount in 1930, when he and Parmagini were considered the largest drug smugglers on the Pacific Coast. It was then esti-mated that their drug smuggling had netted $50,000,000 an-nually.)

There is ample evidence that few of the non-addicted big shots in the narcotic traffic finally escaped the law.

DISCUSSION

AT MEETING OF THE WASHINGTON PSYCHIATRIC SOCIETY
ON THE CONTROL OF THE NARCOTIC ADDICT AND CON-
TEMPORARY PROBLEMS

December 17, 1952.
SPEAKERS: H. J. Anslinger, U. S. Commissioner of Narcotics; K. W. Chapman, M.D., Medical Officer in Charge, U. S. Public Health Service
Hospital, Lexington, Kentucky.

The Commissioner:

If our definitions were simple with relation to drug addiction and addiction-forming drugs, we would indeed be fortunate. I am going to let Dr. Chapman handle that part of the subject because we have been in much controversy in international committees over the definition of addiction.

In order to get a good understanding of the problem we are faced with today, I want to give you a run-down of addiction in various parts of the world as related to this country; it all ties together.

In England, the British Government reports annually only 350 drug addicts known to the authorities—mostly doctors and nurses. When we ask them about the statistics on seizures of opium and hashish, they say: Negroes, Indians, and Chinese are involved. In this country, we don't distinguish; we take the situation as a whole. England, during the past year, has had a surge of hashish addiction among young people. A year ago they were looking at the United States with an "it can't happen here" attitude. Suddenly hashish addiction hit the young people. Ordinarily hashish is only something for the Egyptian, the Indian. Now the British press is filled with accounts of cases of addiction of young people.

Two years ago the French said they had no problem of addiction; perhaps a little cocaine was being used. Recently we helped the French Sûreté uncover three heroin factories in France. The French admitted that probably 400 kilos of heroin were manufactured clandestinely in France last year. Incidentally, the trade in heroin has been prohibited by some fifty nations.

The nation I thought would hold out to the last against controls was Switzerland, but they have now prohibited the manufacture and consumption of heroin.

There has been a big surge of addiction in Germany since World War II. Prior to that, the Nazi regime bore down heavily on the addict, and had the situation pretty well in hand. There are signs of a great spread of addiction again. We have tried to set up an organization in West Germany to combat the narcotic traffic.

There is some cocaine addiction in Italy, and some in Czechoslovakia.

The representatives of the USSR tell us that there is no addiction in the Soviet Union. I have reminded the Russians of the eight tons of smoking opium seized along the Siberian border. That indicates addiction.

Some of the worst addiction spots are in the Near and Middle East. In Istanbul, Turkey, addiction is far higher than it is anywhere in the United States. There is uncontrolled production of opium, and no control of distribution. Almost every shop in the opium growing centers sells opium. There are many clandestine heroin laboratories operating.

Egypt has suffered most from addiction; it is a victim country. There is no production there, only consumption. General Naguib recently decreed that an addict would serve fifteen years at hard labor; a peddler would be executed. The result of this decree is, of course, as yet unknown.

Iran once had a government opium-smoking monopoly. They have introduced in their Parliament a law providing the death penalty for anyone caught smoking opium.

India has made rapid strides in controlling addiction, despite the fact that many addicts there have a quasi-medical need to eat opium. The All-India Congress has decided that by 1958 all such consumption must cease.

During World War II, we succeeded in having the British, French, Portuguese, and Dutch abandon across-the-counter selling of smoking opium in their possessions. As a result of that action the situation has greatly improved but there is still some illicit traffic.

Only one government in the whole world legalizes the sale of opium for smoking—Thailand. The opium comes from Yunnan and Burma, and is sold in government shops.

In Communist China there is a great deal of opium smoking, and a great deal of heroin used. We get some of these drugs on our Atlantic and Pacific Coasts.

Japan, strangely enough, is overrun with heroin addicts and peddlers—a situation very different from what it was before the recent war. Our agents, in cooperation with the Japanese Government, have uncovered the activities of a great many Communists engaged in smuggling.

North Korea has the largest opium production of any country in the Russian orbit.

There is relatively little addiction in South America, some use of marihuana in Brazil. Peru and Bolivia produce coca leaves from which cocaine is derived. Indians there have been chewing coca leaves for many years. A commission sent there from the United Nations to study the situation found that the practice was largely a result of malnutrition.

There is much addiction to cannabis (marihuana) in Mexico. Mexico has a large illicit production of marihuana.

Cocaine Traffic in the United States

By 1948 we could scarcely find one cocaine seizure in all those that we made in this country. Suddenly the country was flooded with cocaine. It was found to be coming from Peru. The government there had allowed seventeen factories to operate, producing cocaine. There is only one factory in this country and we manufacture for 155 million people. Your Commissioner went to the Peruvian Ambassador and succeeded in having the President of Peru close all the factories. In six months there was a phenomenal change in the prevalence of cocaine addiction—it had almost disappeared again.

Heroin

Most of the heroin smuggled into this country comes from old stocks in Italy. Italy didn't live up to her treaty obligations very well. She estimated for manufacture ten times more heroin than was needed or used. Finally we got an agreement from her suspending the further production of heroin.

Much of our heroin comes from Turkey and some from China.

Heroin is the most popular drug with addicts in this country today. As bought by addicts, the drug is from 5 to 8 percent pure. After the smuggler "cuts" it, the wholesaler and retailers all "cut" it. Users pay $3,000 an ounce for heroin here; it costs $100 an ounce in Turkey.

Addiction in the United States

In the New England States there is relatively little addiction. The big addiction centers are large cities: New York, Philadelphia, Washington, Baltimore (last year they took effective action there), Chicago, Cleveland, Detroit, Los Angeles.

We have been able to get especially good cooperation in New

Jersey. New Jersey leads the States in efforts to combat addiction. They approached the problem in a very intelligent way. The Legislature established a commission of very able men who came up with a set of recommendations, all but one of which were adopted. (The one not adopted was a plan for establishing a farm for the treatment of addicts in southern New Jersey, in an old CCC Camp). They established narcotic squads in the State Police and in local police forces in the cities where they had a problem. We matched them man for man.

It's a curious thing about the State of Pennsylvania. There is rather heavy addiction in southern Philadelphia, then none until you get to Pittsburgh. Washington has a very substantial problem. In Baltimore, a year ago, they were finding fifteen-year-old boys dead in the gutter from an overdose of heroin. The government was going to place some beds in state hospitals for addicts. Maryland adopted a very stiff penalty law for peddlers, and judges in Baltimore really gave sentences to peddlers: two, five and ten years for first, second, and third offenses. There the situation has been cleaned up by enforcement measures.

In St. Louis, Missouri, one Federal judge said, "Bring me your big peddlers." They invariably got eighteen years for peddling, and this practically wiped out the narcotic traffic in St. Louis.

Michigan has taken the problem seriously. In Detroit there was a very bad situation a couple years ago. Seventy-eight teenagers were brought before the Grand Jury. They were not school children, but were of school age. Michigan passed a law providing that first offenders—peddlers—get twenty years to life imprisonment. This had a very sobering effect on peddlers in Detroit. A peddler is an innate gambler: he will gamble on being caught, on how much of a sentence he will get, and so on.

In Chicago, some citizen groups established an advisory council in an attempt to solve their narcotic problem. They advised the family and the victim, before and after cure. They have furnished us useful information.

I almost omitted Texas. We can make more cases in Texas than in any other State in the country. Precisely why, we do not understand. One thinks of wide open spaces and healthful outdoor living in connection with Texas. But there is oil and money, and where you have these, you will have pimps and prostitutes.

Los Angeles has a police squad of twenty-eight men for narcotic investigations. The feeling was that every addict would steal $30 worth of merchandise a day to maintain his addiction; his drugs would cost about $10 a day. If there are police to bring in the peddler and addict, the crime rate would be substantially reduced. A good narcotic agent is worth three detectives.

We have a bad addiction problem in Washington, D.C. If you go across the bridge into Alexandria or Arlington, you don't find addiction. Virginia has a very stiff penalty law. Once in a while we have a few cases in Norfolk or Richmond.

Throughout the South, little addiction is found until you come to New Orleans.

On the State level in this country, we have the Uniform State Narcotic Acts. The one in the District of Columbia is not very strong. On the international level, we should thank God for the United Nations, if only for what they have done on international narcotic control. International treaties lessened the manufacture of morphine from 100 tons a year to 40 tons a year, the manufacture of heroin from 5 tons to 1½ tons, cocaine about the same.

Nearly all the traffic in drugs today, with the exception of diversion from Italy, is underground. Some years ago it thrived above ground; there was no control. Today, almost every nation observes protocols limiting manufacture and distribution. Every nation must make an estimate of its medical needs. Those estimates are added, and that amount is manufactured throughout the world. Every country is put on its honor to manufacture only for legitimate needs. Furthermore, exporting drugs involves the use of import and export certificates of various governments. All governments have adhered to the Hague Convention requiring that all persons handling narcotic drugs must be licensed. We are working now on a protocol to limit the production of opium. It has already been drawn up and will be considered in May 1953.

So far as synthetic drugs are concerned, all nations are bound by protocol to produce only for medical needs. If it weren't for that protocol, this country would be flooded with synthetic drugs.

The Michigan Medical Society in 1878 made a survey in which they found that one out of 400 was sniffing cocaine, smoking or

eating opium, or using morphine. I know a little town not far
from here where the records in the drug store show that out of
a population of 600 people, 60 used laudanum—mostly women.
The proportion in the past, by the way, was four female drug
addicts to one male. That proportion is reversed today.

It is interesting to see Army records on narcotic addiction. Here
are records you can rely on; these draftees are pretty well
screened by the doctors. During World War I, one out of 1500
was rejected for drug addiction. This was a good indicator of the
general incidence of drug addiction, both our Bureau and the
U. S. Public Health Service found. Then came all the international actions: reductions in world drug manufacturing totals.
In World War II, one out of every 10,000 was rejected for military service for drug addiction. This reduction makes us feel
pretty good.

Wardens ask us what has happened to the drug addict; they
don't see him any longer. By 1948 Congress was seriously consid-
ering closing the U. S. Hospital for the treatment of addiction.
I argued that they should maintain it; that it was the only place
in the world where research was being done. I pointed out that
we were going to get an upsurge of addiction again as it is well
known that drug addiction always increases after a war. At that
time there were only about 700 addicts in the hospital. Reason
prevailed and the hospital was kept in operation. Data on the
prevalence of drug addiction since World War II are available
only on Selective Service registrants examined during September
and part of November 1948, and represent highly depleted age
groups. They show higher prevalence rates for drug addiction
than the corresponding rates for World War II. (The total re-
jection rate for all defects during this period was over twice as
high as during World War II.)

The over-all picture doesn't look too bad because we are not
standing alone in this struggle. We have international action.
Most of the states aren't doing too good a job but many cities are
doing quite well. New York City, I think, is the only place where
they have established a hospital for teen-age addicts. The Federal
hospitals have to bear the burden of the whole country. You have
to have all these things operating. You must apprehend peddlers

and smugglers, and you must have all countries adhere to international treaties. If it weren't for the international action, we would have a million drug addicts in the United States.

We only arrest the peddlers; we don't go after addicts as such. About 70 percent of the peddlers are addicts. In the higher echelons of racketeers, addiction isn't usually found.

In the District of Columbia, there is much to be done. Experts are drafting legislation for compulsory treatment of drug addicts, but it's rather a difficult legal question to handle. It's always a serious matter to deprive persons of some freedom. I think it could be handled on a State and local basis. New Jersey has a law providing that an addict may be given one year as a disorderly person. The judge may suspend sentence if the addict submits to hospitalization. (A compulsory hospitalization Law for drug addicts in the District of Columbia was passed by the Congress in June, 1953)

Dr. Kenneth W. Chapman:

At the risk of being repetitious, I shall have to refer to some of the points already raised for the sake of coherence. I hope you will bear with me.

In 1914 the Harrison Narcotic Act was passed, after efforts on the part of numerous persons. Dr. Lawrence Kolb, for example, felt that there were about 100,000 addicts on the East Coast alone. He also supported Mr. Anslinger's point that the ratio of men to women was inverse to what it is at the present time.

I am concerned primarily with the treatment of narcotic addiction. I beg your indulgence for not answering other questions.

In the past some States have attempted to handle and treat narcotic addicts cut off from their supply. Free clinics were also tried and closed as very unsatisfactory. The Harrison Narcotic Act, by the way, is a tax act. Federal offenders against the Harrison Narcotic Act were first sent to Leavenworth, Kansas. An old army annex was used for segregating addicts. It was felt that they were an unusual breed of criminals. They desired to prevent cross contamination.

Early in the 1930's a unit developed at Leavenworth for study and treatment—research in narcotic addiction. Dr. Himmelsbach did some work there. Later he came to Lexington and did a great study on withdrawal. Also in the early 1930's Dr. Lawrence Kolb, Sr., and Dr. Walter Treadway worked to develop special institutions for hospitalizing addicts. In 1935 came the opening of the hospital at Lexington. Actually, it is only a hospital in the most general sense of the word. It is a kind of penal institution, with certain hospital aspects. In 1938 the hospital at Forth Worth, Texas, opened, with 900 beds. The Fort Worth hospital is much less like a penal institution and has more of a hospital atmosphere.

Lexington has a program for research. The National Institute of Mental Health now operates an addiction research unit. From that much of our knowledge has been obtained, largely, of course, from the pharmaceutical angle. The unit is primarily charged, with investigation of new drugs, in the unending attempt to find one which will be analgesic and non-addicting. It's surprising how close we have sometimes been to finding one. I have some doubts, though, that it will ever be obtained. There are 2,200 Federal beds available now for the treatment of narcotic addicts.

Now, to consider briefly the term "drug addiction." The Committee on Drug Addiction of the National Research Council furnishes us with this definition:

Addiction is a state of periodic intoxication detrimental to the individual and to society, produced by the repeated administration of a drug. Characteristics are compulsion to continue taking the drug and to increase the dose, with development of psychic and sometimes physiological dependence on the drug. Finally, maintenance of drug supply becomes the individual's paramount motivation.

This offers very little assistance to us in understanding why a person takes the first dose. It does emphasize the compulsion to take drugs, and has important implications.

Since there is some misunderstanding, even among those interested in the drug addict, about the drugs concerned, we might say something about them. There are two groups, the excitatory (stimulant) drugs and the depressants. Cocaine is an excitatory drug; it gives temporary sensations of ecstasy, then extreme nervousness, then paranoid delusions. This is the prototype of the drug fiend of the yellow press. Cocaine is not a truly addicting drug, although users may compulsively continue to take it. Once they cease, there is no necessity to continue to prevent withdrawal effects. However, it is interesting to talk to addicts concerning cocaine; very few use it. One addict that I spoke to said: "If you aren't nuts before you use it, you sure are after." That summarizes the feeling of most addicts.

Marihuana is a depressant, in spite of early excitatory effects: exhilaration, euphoria, release of inhibitions, visual and auditory hallucinations. There is no physical dependency. *Peyote,* used by some Indians in the West, is also in that category. Other depressants include heroin, morphine, alcohol, barbiturates.

So far as the truly addicting drugs are concerned, a tolerance is developed, and there is physical illness when abruptly ceasing prolonged use.

It is often puzzling to doctors to have an addict who is physically ill, one with cancer, far advanced, for instance. It can't be determined that he needs drugs, yet he screams for them. These are difficult people to treat; they continually pose a problem. It might be noted that narcotic agents don't bother people using drugs for bona-fide illness.

It might be thought that a study of the physiological characteristics of addiction would give us some insight into why people use drugs, but it is very difficult for you and me to interpret what a person means by "feel normal," "get a bang," and so on. It is hard for us to appreciate what is involved in these subjective descriptions.

I would like to say here that we have developed certain premises accepted by those interested in drug addiction which we think offer the most rational explanation for addiction. We take drug addiction to be a symptom of personality disturbance, of character disorder all the way from a criminal psychopath through the major psychoses. We have not as yet developed screening paraphernalia to separate. We can assume, on the basis of present knowledge and extrapolating, that there are many more addiction-prone individuals running around in the world who have not yet had contact with drugs. That is reason enough, if there were no other reason, for the existence of the Commissioner and the whole control program. We feel that the potential addict is an emotionally unstable, immature individual seeking excitement and pleasure outside the usual realms, unable to adjust to pressures of today's world, the "lone wolf." He differs from the normally adjusted person in that he has no adequate defenses to handle anxiety. Drugs seem a substitute for inadequate or pathological defenses; they make him "feel normal." Experiencing some relief, he goes down the road in the flight from everyday living. He has a psychic need for drugs. The more drugs he uses, the more money he needs for drugs. Tolerance becomes a new factor, and any prolonged abstinence makes him feel real sickness, so that all else is forgotten. He may rob, steal, deny his family, sell home furnishings to obtain drugs. He may kill anyone who stands in his way. These are extreme examples, of course, rare in our experience.

Many user-peddlers are peddlers because of lack of funds to satisfy their habit. These are dangerous, especially because of their tendency to seek out others to use drugs.

What can be eliminated from the environment to help? Control represents a herculean task. With the few people that the Commissioner has, I don't see how he does as well as he does. There is a need for even greater controls than now exist.

Can the addict be cured? In the sense that TB can be cured, or arrested, yes. No, if you expect the addict never to return to the use of drugs. Any period of time of living without drugs for an addict is a sign of success. What can we offer an addict? First, he must submit to treatment in a drug-free environment. Second, he must be withdrawn humanely and gradually from drugs. Third, after withdrawal he must be allowed to recuperate, to recover his balance. During this period we can assay personality assets, make a prognosis. A relatively short period of addiction, of course, offers the best chance of success, provided that the personality defect is not sufficiently serious. About one fourth of those using drugs for a longer period of time have no serious, deep-seated psychosis. For the rest, it is difficult to foresee. Occasionally an esoteric factor comes into play, and an old addict will suddenly cease using drugs. There are, of course, many recidivists.

What can we do for cases with a good prognosis? We can

offer them the chance to learn to work, to face their problems, to play. Incidentally, we have dropped the idea of "come to seek"; we find that those who come for psychotherapy of their own volition derive the least benefit from it.

The length of treatment has great significance, and we don't know much about it. The longer a patient stays at the hospital, the less likely he is to return. After six months, most patients seem to gain little from intramural treatment. Yet, after release from the hospital, there is very little chance for the addict to continue treatment outside. We must develop, I feel, some means to continue extramural treatment if we are to be successful in our treatment of addiction. These people need guidance, etc., for several months after release from the hospital. Many return to the same old problems, broken homes, etc. They are easily led to their old patterns of problem solving—drugs. We suspect that the more often this is repeated, the less the person is able to make the effort. Fifty-five percent of those admitted to the hospital are new cases. There is great need for cooperation between enforcement officers and medical officers. Post treatment for the addict is difficult. Society is gradually willing to forgive a prisoner, but not an addict. I think the never never land would be reached if the public could know that of the 18,000 addicts at Lexington from 1935 to 1952, 64 percent never came back, 21 percent came back once, 6 percent returned three times, and 9 percent came back four or more times. There might be increasing confidence in the possibility of restoring the addict to society.

QUESTIONS

Dr. Davison to Dr. Chapman:

So far as the clinics before World War I are concerned, why did they fail? Why do you think they are likely to fail?

Dr. Chapman:

On the "why they failed," I would like to refer you to the Commissioner, as my senior. He has been in this field longer and has some evidence on this.

The Commissioner:

You couldn't handle the marihuana smoker under a system like that. He certainly wouldn't be licensed to get prescriptions from a doctor for marihuana. Dr. Chapman told you about the cocaine addict: "If you're not crazy before, you are after." I do not think you are ever going to license a cocaine addict to get supplies from the Government.

New York State had these clinics. Dr. Royal Copeland, who established them, said only about one third of those addicted ever would apply, and a lot of those took their drugs out and sold them to non-registered addicts. Corruption and blackmail developed. New York closed those clinics, and not at the request of the American Medical Association.

Shreveport, Louisiana, had the biggest clinic of all. The citizens made such an uproar that they closed it. Every thief within a hundred miles went to Shreveport.

No government in the world conducts such clinics, no matter what is said about England. What about all the seizures there? What about the trouble doctors are having keeping their bags from being stolen?

Our Supreme Court has ruled in several cases that it is unlawful to prescribe narcotics for an addict just to keep him comfortable. That is so far as our present law is concerned, of course. If there were a new law, there would have to be a new ruling.

Japan had clinics in Formosa. Dr. Tsungming To ran those clinics. He found that of the criminals arrested in Formosa, 70 percent were opium smokers who got supplies at cost from the government; 30 percent were non-smokers.

There are many obstacles. I don't think you could devise a system whereby everybody would go to the authorities to register. They would take part of their supply and sell it to the addict who wants to stay in the background.

Dr. Chapman:

From my knowledge, no two people are at the same level, and it would take more than Solomon to decide what an optimum dose would be, from a medical standpoint. As it is, we don't decide. From experience we have determined that almost any dose will do in a brief withdrawal—five to seven days. A grain of morphine a day seems to sustain any habit. Consider the addict placed in such a situation: if he would not get what he considered enough in the clinic, he would go around the corner and get it from a peddler. If you were to hand out a day's supply at once, ten friends would come in and help out with his supply. Twenty-four hour clinics would be necessary, and clinics all over town.

The Commissioner:

The clinic idea is not a new one. It has been in print ever since the Harrison Narcotic Act was passed. When drugs could be purchased at low prices by addicts in this country, the imports in one year (1897) rose to unbelievable heights: crude opium 1,072,914 pounds; smoking opium 157,000 pounds; morphine 15,000 ounces. At that same rate of consumption—if addicts were permitted to obtain drugs similarly in clinics today—we would have to import over 3 *million pounds* of opium a year, or ten times our present imports for medical needs, 350,000 pounds. That alone should be argument enough against the establishment of clinics.

Question to The Commissioner:

You mentioned constitutional blocks to legislation for compulsory treatment of addicts. At least two States have laws for compulsory treatment of alcoholics.

The Commissioner:

An individual State can bring about compulsory treatment. I don't think the Federal Government can do it. Wisconsin and Minnesota have compulsory commitment. It is the same statute which provides commitment of insane persons. In those two states, one addict to every 25,000 of the population is the ratio. The addict doesn't want to be caught in one of those county hospitals with the insane. California had an institution for treatment of addicts. They picked up the addict as a vagrant. After a while the addict population decreased, and they abandoned the hospital. Now it's a problem again.

The problem of the compulsory commitment of addicts in the District of Columbia will be taken up tomorrow.

Question to Dr. Chapman:

I am interested in any psychological studies carried on concerning pleasure, the hedonic scale.

Dr. Chapman:

I do not know of any studies like that. We have tried, however, numerous techniques to evaluate the pleasurable aspects of narcotics, with no success. I think it is largely a problem of the difficulty in appreciating what the addict gives us in his descriptions.

Dr. Williams to Dr. Chapman:

If pure heroin were used, would there be ill effects? Has there been any experimentation at Lexington using heroin alone? We have been using calcium glucanate intravenously. We can withdraw an addict with no ill effect. All that we look for is the usual hour that they take drugs, then beat them to it. So far we have found no ill effects.

Dr. Chapman:

We have done very little experimentation with heroin. For one thing, heroin is absolutely illegal. Sometimes we get some to compare with synthetics. Heroin is a kind of super-morphine; it wears off much more rapidly than morphine. They say you take heroin for a "bang," morphine for "hold."

So far as the other question is concerned, many investigators in the past have tried various methods of substitution for narcotics, the so-called "sure cures for narcotic addiction." Many "cures" were studied by Dr. Kolb, Dr. Small, and others, and it was found that usually the drug used merely masked the symptoms of addiction. Seeing no particular value in masking the symptoms, we haven't seen any reason for substituting something else. Sometimes the "cure" has made persons nembutal addicts.

Dr. Herbst:

My interest is in advice and suggestion in regard to formulation of legislation the objective of which is, of course, cutting down drug addiction. I have presumed from what the Commissioner has said here that effective means so far add up to heavy penalties which are successfully and conscientiously carried out upon apprehension of these people. I don't know if he would want to take the responsibility of suggesting what points in legislation are the more important ones for the Medical Society of the District of Columbia to back and suggest and argue for. That would interest me very much.

The Commissioner:

Being an enforcement officer, I naturally look at the results that we have accomplished in New Jersey, Pennsylvania, and Maryland. Maryland, particularly, is an outstanding example of what Federal and local government can do if they have good penalty legislation for the peddler—to make it so unprofitable he won't gamble. The increased penalty act was enforced to such an extent in Baltimore that repeal was demanded at the last session of the legislature—a session which met only to discuss fiscal matters. The group trying to get repeal was interested in one case—a college boy, a second offender. The women of Maryland and the American Legion marched on Annapolis, and the repeal bill died in committee. It's very difficult to make a case in Baltimore now. We send undercover men in there occasionally, and they just can't buy drugs. I don't say that that is the answer to our problem here in the District. I don't think you can get tough legislation here. We have the Federal Boggs Act, and we have the Uniform State Narcotic Act which makes drug addiction a misdemeanor. We must have understanding judges, and we must have a place to send addicts.

Stiff penalty legislation has done a lot of good in many States —stiff penalties for peddlers. We give thanks every day for Lexington because we get so many cases which involve need for treatment. You need stiff penalty laws, and you need to commit the addict for treatment.

XII

A PROGRAM OF ACTION

THE MOST IMPORTANT QUESTION IS WHAT CAN BE DONE ABOUT THIS menace of drug addiction. Historically and inherently, the American people have never been faced with a difficult problem which they have been unable to surmount. Drug addiction can and will be no exception. However, like any other stubborn problem, there is no panacea, no solution which will immediately dissipate the problem before our eyes, no magic wand which can be waved to make it vanish. During the recent upsurge in drug addiction, which, as noted elsewhere in this book had been forecast by leading authorities, many solutions have been offered by well-intentioned persons as well as by "experts" of very recent vintage. Overnight, authorities seem to have sprung up whose claim to fame is that they disagree with recognized students who have devoted their lives to the problem. And it is noteworthy that none of these so-called experts has come up with a new plan. On the contrary, these new approaches have largely consisted of untested, often discredited, or otherwise unsound plans whose disinterment hasn't contributed one iota to vanquishing this evil. An example of this is the recent suggestion that the use of narcotics be legalized. This plan is commonly known as the clinic or ration plan, and its very small group of proponents hail it as the fastest and surest way to break the illegal drug racket and conquer addiction. The history of the clinic plan has been fully told elsewhere in this book in Chapter VIII.

Fundamentally, what is being sought under the guise of a solution appears to be a form of government subsidization of

294

drug addiction—a plan as fantastic as it is amoral. If drug addiction is an evil habit—and who will say that it is not—it should be rooted out and destroyed. And you don't put out a fire by feeding it. This plan which patently envisages compromise with vice would be foredoomed to failure. As the United States Supreme Court so well indicated, the issuance of a prescription to maintain an addict's customary use would be a perversion of the meaning of the very word itself.* Suffice it to say, this idea has never proved successful anywhere in the world, and the failure has not been from lack of trial.

Other suggestions have been advanced, such as increasing our customs service sufficiently to permit examination of all articles coming into the country. This idea is reminscent of Will Rogers' solution for the submarine menace during World War I, when he advocated drying up the ocean. When pressed for details, said Will, "I'm just supplying the solution; the mechanical details are up to the Navy."

The plain fact is that narcotics will somehow manage to seep into the country. By their very nature, they can easily be secreted. And this, despite the tremendous job that is being done by the government on both international and national levels, brings us to the question of what can and should be done.

FOUNDATIONS

Strong laws, good enforcement, stiff sentences, and a proper hospitalization program are the necessary foundations upon which any successful program must be predicated. These, plus an alert and determined public, will go a long way towards blotting out the problem. Probably the greatest reason for an increase in drug addiction has been the failure on the part of legislators, of police, and of other officials to observe these important fundamentals. Most important, good results can be attained by perfecting the framework of the present Federal and State laws, which are fundamentally sound.

First of all, there is no excuse for any State to have a law which is in any way weaker than the Boggs Act passed by the Congress

* Webb & Goldbaum v. U.S. 249 U.S. 96.

in 1951. That bill provides penalties for illegal sale or possession of narcotic drugs of from two to five years for the first offense, five to ten for the second, and ten to twenty for the third. This law further provides that, except in the case of a conviction for a first offense, the imposition or execution of sentence shall not be suspended and probation or parole shall not be granted, until the minimum term provided for the offense shall have been served. In other words, it is a mandatory-sentence law in all cases except first offenses. Several States have enacted laws duplicating the Boggs Act, with New Jersey providing a wider range in its penalties, i.e., two to fifteen years for the first offense, five to twenty-five for the second, and ten to life for the third, with an added provision of two years to life for any offense where a minor is involved.

A great debate has been waged about what the penalties should be, with many suggesting a mandatory death penalty or at least a life sentence for any offense. Nobody, of course, maintains that the soul-destroying peddler should get less, or that such a penalty is not commensurate with the offense. However, a good deal of this demand for extreme mandatory sentences, it might be added, has stemmed from the fact that some judges have handed out ridiculously low sentences (the peddlers call them "vacations"), and some prosecutors have accepted "bargain pleas" to lesser offenses. For example, Isaac P. was fined $25.00 and costs for possession of 17,000 grains of marihuana—enough to make over 5,000 cigarettes—enough to do irreparable harm to any community and its youth. The following year he was convicted of raping a ten year old girl while under marihuana intoxication. In one of our western states, Robert M. pleaded guilty to furnishing marihuana to two fifteen-year-old girls, and faced a five years to life sentence. However, he was permitted to retract his plea of guilty and plead to the lesser offense of possession, for which he received six months in the county jail.

An aroused citizenry has become thoroughly disillusioned and discouraged by incidents which indicate a tendency on the part of some officials to compromise on crime, particularly regarding the murderous drug peddler for whom they feel right in demanding penalties that are swift, sure, and stringent—a demand on the part of the public for mandatory laws.

The wide range and flexibility of the New Jersey law provides a good solution for the various divergent philosophies. Under it the youthful offender can get care, treatment, and rehabilitation; the destroying peddler, a severe sentence. The mandatory features applicable to second and third offenders should serve as a deterrent to those previously convicted.

BASIC REQUIREMENT FOR EFFECTIVE LAW

To make a law—such as New Jersey's—function, and to prevent any abuses, the following principles must be observed:

1. Addict violators who are placed on probation must be given a probationary period of at least five years. Control of the addict during the period of his treatment and rehabilitation is imperative.
2. The addict violator shall be required, as a condition of his probation, to submit to hospital treatment and to remain hospitalized until released by competent medical authority.
3. The addict violator shall be required, as a condition of his probation after discharge from the institution, to submit to a thorough examination each month by a public health doctor for the remainder of his probationary period. This is the only accurate way to determine whether or not an individual has commenced taking drugs again.
4. Probation authorities should be required to keep a very close check on drug violators after their discharge from the institution and to submit monthly reports to the court from which the individuals were sentenced.
5. A comprehensive program of follow-up care should be set up either by the state or local community with the cooperation of judges, doctors, probation and parole authorities, and social welfare agencies. This is of vital importance since the lack of follow-up care has been the greatest cause of recidivism.
6. Maximum sentences should be used against the professional criminal with no probation, parole, or suspension of sen-

tences being granted in any case. The minimum sentence for the narcotic peddler should be five years. To escape this punishment he may lead law enforcement officers to the source of supply.

7. Bargain pleas made with the intent to lighten sentences should not be accepted by a prosecuting attorney.

8. Every case, no matter how small the amount of narcotics involved may be, shall be presented to the Grand Jury and vigorously prosecuted.

9. In any case involving a sale of narcotic drugs by an adult to a minor, the offender will receive the maximum sentence which the particular state or federal law allows.

Minnesota and Wisconsin have excellent laws providing for the commitment of addicts for the treatment of drug addiction without giving the addict a criminal record. The following law is patterned after the commitment law in those states, where addiction has been reduced to a minimum, or about 1 addict in every 25,000 of the population:

COMMITMENT OF ADDICTS

PROPOSED STATE LAW FOR COMMITMENT OF ADDICTS FOR TREATMENT

Whenever an affidavit duly verified by a person claiming to have knowledge of the facts and setting forth that any person named or described therein is a habitual user, without bona fide medical need therefor, of a narcotic drug, as defined in (cite State Narcotic Act), shall be filed with the county attorney of any county or the city attorney of any city in which such alleged habitual user is or may be found, such county attorney or city attorney under his hand shall issue a notice requiring the person so named or described to appear before a judge of the (district) court, the county or the (corporation) court of the city, in chambers, at a time and place specified in such notice and shall cause a copy thereof to be served by the sheriff or other court officer duly qualified to serve process in civil or criminal cases upon the person so named or described no less than two days before the date specified for such appearance. Copy of such notice shall be transmitted by mail to the (State Commissioner of Public Health). The affidavit and the original notice with proof of service shall be filed with the clerk of the court at or before the time specified for such appearance, but the same and the other records and files of the proceedings shall be open for inspection only by the person named or described therein or his counsel and by a public officer.

At the time and place specified in the notice, the person named or described in such notice or his counsel being present, the judge shall hear the evidence presented, and upon being satisfied that the allegations contained in the affidavit are true, shall make and file an order requiring such habitual user forthwith to take and continue, until otherwise ordered by the court with the advice and consent of the (State Commissioner of Public Health), treatment for the cure of such habit at a public institution, other than a penal-institution, selected by the (State Commissioner of Public Health), and at the expense of the county or city. The order shall further require reports to be made to the court and to the (State Commissioner of Public Health) at stated intervals therein specified by the physician or superintendent in charge, as to the effect and progress of the treatment. A copy of the order forthwith shall be served upon said user. In no case, however, shall any habitual user of said narcotic drug be required to continue treatment under such order for a period longer than (two) years.

Any person named or described in a notice so issued by the county attorney or the city attorney and duly served upon him and who shall fail, refuse, or neglect to appear at the time and place therein specified, or any person named or specified in the order so made and served, and who shall fail, refuse, or neglect to comply with the terms and conditions of such order shall be deemed guilty of contempt of the court and shall be proceeded against accordingly.

The nature of the illegal narcotics traffic requires a combination of individuals, and this combination includes the vicious figures of the traffic, the higher-ups, the peddlers, and the pushers. Therein is found the hierarchy of the underworld, and taken together they represent a far more formidable threat to society than the individual offender. Furthermore, in all probability the greatest opportunity to convict these individuals would be under a conspiracy indictment. Therefore the penalty for conspiracy to violate the laws relating to narcotics should be made in every case a felony.

PROSELYTISM

In recent years a revision of the Mexican Penal Act established a new definition entitled "proselytism with regard to narcotic drugs," with the provision covering two basic aspects: instigating the use of narcotic drug, that is, inducing a person to begin or continue to use narcotics; and procuring the commission of acts connected with the production and manufacture of narcotic drugs. The act specifically refers to "any act of general provocation for illicit instigation, persuasion or aid to another person in the use of narcotic drugs or seeds or plants of the same character" and further provides if the person concerned is a minor or under a disability or if the offender takes advantage of his influence or authority the penalty shall be greater. Presently two states, California and New Jersey, have laws similar to the Mexican law. The California act provides for a penalty of five years to life for the first offense of dealing in narcotics with a minor and ten years to life for any subsequent offense. The New Jersey law is more closely patterned after the Mexican law and provides that "any person who induces or persuades any other person to use any narcotic drug unlawfully, or aids or contributes to such use of any narcotic drug by another person, or contributes to the addiction of any other person to the unlawful use of any narcotic drug, is guilty of a high misdemeanor." A broad law such as the New Jersey act, which carries a strong penalty, should be of immeasurable assistance to prosecutors, particularly in cases involving teenagers.

Before leaving this subject of proselytism in drug addiction, it is interesting to note that the passage of the New Jersey law was the direct result of a horrible case which occurred in a neighboring state, wherein a young mother was given an overdose of heroin, which killed her. Her body was put in a trunk and dumped on the grounds of an estate nearby. When the culprit was arrested it was found that the only thing for which he could be prosecuted was for transporting a dead body without a health permit, for which offense he received the maximum sentence of thirty days.

LEVELS OF ENFORCEMENT

In order to secure good enforcement, there must be more state activity in the field, as well as in the larger cities. The Federal Bureau of Narcotics has been the cornerstone of the fight against the illicit traffic, but it should be remembered that its force consists of only about 275 men, a force certainly insufficient in number to police the streets of any medium-sized city. By policing the streets, of course, is meant handling the consumer who is the source of many other crimes and a menace to the health and welfare of the community. If we are to make an all-out offensive it means that the states and municipalities must assume their proper responsibilities. If that is done it will leave the Federal Bureau of Narcotics free to concentrate its major efforts on large scale national and international traffickers. Some States, including California and Pennsylvania, have met their obligation and have formed excellent Bureaus of Narcotics. New Jersey, in the Spring of 1951, created the first specialized narcotic squad in their State Police organization. These men were selected, screened, and trained by the Federal Bureau of Narcotics, a training which any State may secure. With its creation the State made available the necessary funds for the purchase of the equipment essential for the task. Among other things the equipment included automobiles with 3-way radios, walkie-talkies, cameras with telescopic lens, ultra-violet light equipment, and tape recorders. It is more than interesting to note that since this squad has been active Federal violations reported in New Jersey have fallen off over 50 percent, which is far the best showing made by any State where the problem was serious.

However, the best method of combating the street peddlers and the addicts who are the principal source of contamination is by having the larger cities set up specialized narcotic squads. Los Angeles took the initiative and was the first to establish an adequate narcotic squad. Since that time, however, cities such as New York, Newark, Chicago, and other metropolitan centers have established such groups. The records of arrests bear silent witness to the splendid jobs they have done.

A further suggestion would be that some centralized agency

maintain a rogues gallery of major interstate racketeers and systematically collect, correlate, and disseminate information concerning them, a procedure similar to that of the Treasury Department, which maintains lists of major narcotic suspects. Often the operations of big-time racketeers are so diverse and so extensive geographically that few individual local officers can comprehend their magnitude or realize the significance of the small segment which is within their ken. A device of this sort which would spot-light the operations of a major criminal would prove most helpful.

Implicit in the foregoing suggestion is the very desirable element of complete cooperation between State, local, and Federal authorities. The various groups cannot afford to operate independently of each other. Sometimes that cooperation has been built on personal associations and therefore might tend to break down when the individuals concerned leave office. If that be the case, legislators should step in to insure permanent cooperation through legislation, since there can be nothing more deadly to the fight which must be waged against the illicit narcotic traffic than to have things come to a point where the various agencies instead of working in harmony are concealing information from each other and interfering with the investigation of another agency's case.

Any authority on drug addiction will agree that it is impossible for an addict to deny himself drugs, and that he must receive treatment in a drug-free environment where the addict can be kept in and the drug out. It is of vital importance, furthermore, to get the addict off the streets because as long as he is on the streets he is making other addicts. It is almost axiomatic that each addict will probably cause four other persons to become addicts and these four will make sixteen others, a progression of grave concern to any community. In addition to spreading physical destruction and moral degradation in their wake, addicts are also the source of such crimes as burglary, carrying concealed weapons, felonious assault, shoplifting, grand and petty larceny, robbery, receiving stolen property, unlawful entry, forgery, vagrancy and prostitution, and disorderly conduct. An addict is not a normal, healthy individual capable of following a legitimate occupation while addicted to narcotic drugs and must, therefore, engage in criminal activities to obtain the funds with which to supply his narcotics. Thus he maintains his habit at the expense of the community.

Accordingly, it is imperative that each state have a law that a drug addict submit to treatment, and provide the facilities for such treatment. Both are necessary because too frequently when a drug addict is arrested he is sent off to a county jail or penitentiary, a practice which experts unanimously decry. In this connection it is noteworthy that the New Jersey investigation disclosed the fact that many of the young people who were using drugs were week-end addicts, and that true addiction had not set in. All of the members of this Commission were in complete agreement that the chances of rehabilitating these young people were excellent, provided the proper hospital facilities, adequate mental health services, and a program of follow-up care were established. As the Newark (N.J.) *Evening News* so wisely editorialized, "If anyone knows of a better investment for the tax dollar than the reclamation of young people who have fallen victim to narcotics it has not yet come to our notice."

There is nothing sensational in the suggestions contained herein. Many people feel that to succeed some new and different approach must be made. Many feel that a program is valueless unless a new and different twist is added. Others have resurrected such ideas as the discredited ration plan. However, strict adherence to the fundamentals of narcotics control can and will supply the answer to the problem. The best analogy is that a well-coached football team, crisp in its blocking, sharp in its tackling and well-drilled in all the fundamentals, rarely loses a game. A strict adherence to all of these fundamentals of control, together with the complete backing of an aware and determined public, will enable this country to stamp out the narcotic traffic.

A.D. A drug addict.
ace. A marihuana cigarette.
ace in. To get into a narcotics-selling ring.
artillery, light artillery. The equipment for taking an injection of
    a drug.
bamboo. An opium pipe.
bang. The thrill in drug taking. *Also* to inject with a drug.
bang a reefer. To smoke a marihuana cigarette.
banger. A hypodermic needle. *Also* an addict who takes drugs
    by injection, a *bangster.*
bars of soap. Drugs.
hay state. A hypodermic needle.
belt. The exhilaration produced by drugs. *Also* the effect of drugs
    on their user.
bender. A drug orgy.
bendin. An addict who has taken drugs and is under their in-
    fluence.
bending and bowing. Drug-exhilarated.
big bloke. Cocaine.
bindle. A small packet of heroin, morphine, or cocaine.
bing. A dose of a drug.
bingle. A drug peddler. *Also* drugs.
bingo. An injection of a drug.
birdie powder. Morphine, cocaine, or heroin.
biz. The business: the hypodermic needle used by the addict.
black stuff. Opium.

blast. To smoke a marihuana cigarette.

block. A *bindle* of morphine.

blow. An inhalation of a drug by an addict.

blow coke, blow snow. To take cocaine by sniffing it up the nostrils.

blow one's roof. To smoke marihuana.

bluesage. A marihuana cigarette.

bo-bo-bush. Marihuana.

boot the gong. To smoke opium or marihuana.

bouncing powder. Cocaine.

bowin. An addict who has taken drugs and is under their influence.

bowler. An opium smoker.

bow-sow. Drugs.

brick gum. Gum opium.

brown rine. Heroin.

burned out. The sclerotic condition of the vein present in most conditioned addicts.

burnese. A catarrhal powder high in cocaine content.

burnie. A marihuana cigarette.

bust the main line. To take drug intravenously.

buzz. The effect of a drug.

C. Cocaine, term used generally by addicts.

cacil, cecil. Morphine or cocaine.

cadet. A new drug addict.

a Cadillac. Cocaine.

came. Cocaine.

carpet-walker. A drug addict.

carrier. A distributor of drugs to addicts.

caught in a snowstorm. To be under the influence of drugs, especially of heroin, morphine, or cocaine.

channel. The vein into which injections of a drug are made.

charley. Cocaine.

Charlie Coke. A cocaine addict.

Chinese molasses. Opium.

chino. A Chinese drug peddler.

chuck horrors. The enormous appetite for food an addict has when he is cut off from drugs.

coconut. Cocaine.

coke. Cocaine.

coke-oven. A place where cocaine is sold.

cokie. An opium addict.

cold turkey. The method of curing drug addiction whereby an addict is taken off drugs with no tapering-off period.

connect. To buy drugs.

connection. A peddler who knows an addict and will sell him drugs.

cook. An attendant in an opium den.

cooked up. To be under the influence of cocaine.

Corinne. Cocaine.

cork the air. To sniff cocaine up the nostrils.

cotics. Narcotics.

courage pills. Heroin in tablet form.

croaker. A doctor who sells narcotic prescriptions (readers).

crying weed. A marihuana cigarette.

cube. Bootleg morphine.

cubes. Morphine tablets.

cut in. To get into a narcotic ring.

D.A. Drug addict.

dealer. A drug peddler.

deck. A small packet of morphine, cocaine, or heroin.

dip. A drug addict.

dipper. An opium pipe.

do-right john. One who is not a drug addict.

Doctor White, Old Lady White. Drugs, especially cocaine, heroin, or morphine.

dodo. A drug addict.

dope. Drugs. *Also* a drug addict.

dope booster. One who incites others to drug-taking and directs them to the peddler.

dope hop. The exhilaration produced by drugs.

dope jagg. A drug orgy.

doped up, dopey. To be in a stupor from the excessive use of drugs.

drag-weed. Marihuana.

dream gum. Opium.

dream-stick. An opium pipe.

dreams. Opium pellets for chewing.

drive in. To smuggle narcotics.

dropper. The medicine dropper used by an addict as a makeshift hypodermic needle. Most addicts like the device.

dry grog. Drugs.

dust. Marihuana, heroin, morphine, or cocaine.

dynamite. Heroin or cocaine. *Also* a combination of cocaine and morphine.

dynamiter. A cocaine addict.

emergency gun. A hypodermic needle made from a medicine dropper and a safety pin.

eye-opener. The addict's first injection of a drug for the day.

factory. A hypodermic needle.

feeblo. A drug addict.

fire. To inject drugs with a hypodermic needle.

fix, fix-up. A drug which is about to be injected, or has just been injected.

flier. A drug addict.

flip. To become unconscious from an overdose of drugs.

floating. Under the influence of drugs.

flogged. Under the influence of drugs.

fold up. To take the drug cure.

foo foo dust. Morphine, cocaine, or heroin.

foolish powder. Morphine, cocaine, or heroin.

fraho. Marihuana.

fu. Marihuana.

fun. A ration of opium.

fun joint. An opium den.

G.O.M. God's Own Medicine: morphine.

gage, gauge-butt. Marihuana.

gapper. An addict who is desperate for drugs.

gazer. A Federal Government agent.

gee. Drugs, especially opium.

geezer. An injection of a drug.

ghost. An opium smoker.

ghow. An opium pipe.

giggle weed. Marihuana.

the girl. Cocaine.

give the go-by. To refuse to sell drugs to an addict.

glad stuff. Opium, morphine, or cocaine.

glass-eyes. A drug addict.

glass gun. A hypodermic needle.

go into the sewer. To inject a drug into the vein.

go on a sleigh ride. To experience the exhilaration of inhaling crystallized cocaine.

go over the hump. To attain exhilaration from using drugs.

gold dust. Cocaine.

gong, gonger, gongola. An opium pipe.

gong kicker. An opium addict.

goof. A marihuana addict.

goofed-up. Drug-exhilarated.

goofy. Crazed from the lack of a drug.

gow. Drugs, especially opium.

goynk. Opium.

grease. To use opium, especially to smoke opium.

great tobacco. Opium.

greta. Marihuana.

griefer. An addict who is habituated to marihuana or Mexican hemp.

griffo. Marihuana.

gum. Opium.

gun. A hypodermic needle.

gyve. A marihuana cigarette.

H. Heroin. *Also* a hypodermic needle; an opium pipe.

habit. Addiction to drugs.

habit smoker. A person addicted to opium smoking.

happy dust. Cocaine.

happy duster. An addict who sniffs cocaine up his nostrils. *Also* a peddler of cocaine.

happy powder. Morphine, cocaine, or heroin.

harpoon. A hypodermic needle.

Harry. Heroin.

have a habit. To suffer from the craving for drugs as a result of inability to procure them.

have a heat on. To take drugs, either once or habitually.

have a monkey on one's back. To have the drug habit. *Also* to be suffering from withdrawal distress.

have an edge. To be keyed up, just after the drug exhilaration has passed and before the craving has set in again.

hay. Marihuana.

hazel. Heroin.

head. A drug addict.

headache man. A Federal agent investigating the drug traffic.

heaven dust. Morphine, cocaine, or heroin.

heesh. Hashish.

hell dust. Drugs, especially morphine or heroin.

hero. Heroin.

high, high and light. Under the influence of a drug.

hip layer. An opium smoker.

hit. A meeting with a drug peddler.

hitch up the reindeers. To inhale cocaine. *Also* to procure drugs and prepare for indulgence.

hit it. To use a drug.

hit the ceiling. To become exhilarated through smoking opium.

hit the gong. To smoke opium.

hit the grease, hit the mud. To use opium as a drug in any way.

hit the main line. To inject a drug into the vein.

hit the needle. To be addicted to injections of a drug.

hit the stuff. To be addicted to drugs.

hog. An addict who requires the maximum dose of a drug.

hokus. Opium.

honeymoon stage. Drug-exhilaration during its most agreeable period.

hoosier fiend. An inexperienced drug addict.

hop, hops. Drugs, especially opium.

hop head. A narcotics addict; originally an opium addict.

horse. Heroin.

hot dream. A dream experienced under the influence of opium.

hot shot. Poison concealed in a drug.

hygelo. A drug addict.

hype. A hypodermic needle.

hypo. An addict who self-injects the drugs with a hypodermic needle.

ice-cream habit. The use of drugs for a day or two a week without becoming addicted.

ice-tong doctor. An illegal practitioner of medicine who also sells drugs.

in high. The peak of exhilaration produced by cocaine, heroin, or morphine.

iron cure. A cure for addiction which the addict undertakes voluntarily.

jagged up. Drug-exhilarated.

jam. An overdose of a drug.

jive. Marihuana.

joint. The equipment for taking an injection of a drug. *Also* an opium den.

joker. A hypodermic needle. *Also* a dose of morphine taken by injection.

jolt. An injection of a drug taken directly into the vein. *Also* to give or take a dose of a drug by injection.

joy. Drug-induced intoxication.

joy dust. Drugs, especially cocaine.

joy flakes, joy powder. Morphine, cocaine, or heroin.

joy-popper. One who takes drugs occasionally (generally subcutaneously) without becoming an addict.

ju-ju. A marihuana cigarette.

junk. Drugs.

junked up. Under the influence of a drug.

junkey. A drug addict.

kick-back. A relapse into addiction after a period of abstinence.

kicking off. Sleeping off drug effects.

kick the habit. To stop using drugs.

kick the mooch around. To smoke an opium pipe.

kicks. The sensations derived from using drugs.

killer. A marihuana cigarette.

knock at the door. To abstain from drugs, to be taking a cure.

kokomo. A drug addict, especially a cocaine addict.

laugh and scratch. To inject or be injected with a drug.

laughing weed. A marihuana cigarette.

lay-out. The equipment used by an opium smoker.

lay the hip. To smoke opium.

leaf. Drugs.

lean against the engine. To smoke opium.

leaper. A cocaine addict.

leapin. An addict who is under the influence of drugs.

leaps. Drug-exhilaration.

leur, luer. A hypodermic needle.

lighter. A drug addict.

load. A dose of drugs.

loco weed. Marihuana.

locus. Drugs.

log. An opium pipe.

M. and C. Marmon and Cadillac: a mixture of morphine and cocaine.

machinery. A hypodermic needle.

mahoska. Habit-forming drugs.

main line. The vein, usually in the forearm near the elbow, into which an addict *(main-liner)* injects the drug.

majonda. Drugs.

Marmon. Morphine.

Mary and Johnny. A marihuana cigarette. *Also* the marihuana plant.

Mary Ann. A marihuana cigarette.

Mary Werner. Marihuana. *Also* a marihuana cigarette.

mayo. Morphine, cocaine, or heroin.

medicine. Drugs.

megg, mezz. Marihuana. *Also* a marihuana cigarette.

midnight oil. Opium.

miggles, muggles. Marihuana cigarettes.

Miss Emma. Morphine.

Mister Fish. An addict who gives himself up to the law in order to break the habit.

Mrs. White. A drug peddler.

mojo. Drugs, especially morphine, heroin, or cocaine.

moocah, mootie, mu. Marihuana.

moota. A marihuana cigarette.

mosquitoes. Cocaine.

mud. Opium for smoking.

mule. One who sells drugs for the regular peddlers.

nail. A hypodermic needle.

narcotic bull. A Federal narcotic agent.

needle. The hypodermic needle or the substitute for one. *Also* to give someone a hypodermic injection of a drug.

needles. The nervous and muscular twitchings induced by the abstinence of an addict from cocaine.

nocks. Drugs.

noise. Heroin.

nose powder. Cocaine, heroin, or morphine, especially in a form for inhaling.

Number 3. Cocaine.

Number 8. Heroin.

Number 13. Morphine.

oil-burning habit. The drug habit.

Old Steve. Any powdered drug.

on the needle. Addicted to drug injections.

on the pipe. Addicted to opium smoking.

on the stuff. Addicted to drugs.

overcharged. In a stupor from an excessive amount of a drug.

over the hump. Drug-exhilarated.

pack of rocks. A package of marihuana cigarettes.

pad. A drug party.

panic. A scarcity of drugs, usually caused by the arrest of a big peddler.

pasty face. A drug addict.

pen yen. Opium.

piddle, pital. Hospital: a hospital or sanatorium where an addict may be treated.

piece. An ounce of morphine, heroin, or cocaine.

pill. A ration of opium prepared for smoking.

ping in wing. An injection of a drug.

pinyon. Opium.

piped. Under the influence of drugs.

pitch. To sell or smuggle drugs.

pleasure jolt. An occasional indulgence in drugs which does not lead to addiction.

poison. A doctor who will not sell drugs to an addict.

Poison Act. The Federal Narcotics Act.

pop. An injection of a drug.

pot. A marihuana cigarette.

powder. A powdered drug.

pox. An opium pill. Also a ration of opium prepared for smoking.

prod, prop. A hypodermic injection.

puff. An opium addict.

puffing. Smoking opium.

pusher. A retailer of drugs to addicts.

Racehorse Charlie. Morphine, heroin, or cocaine.

reader. A prescription for narcotics which is sold by a doctor.

rear. The exhilaration produced by the daily dose of some drug, especially cocaine.

Red Cross. Morphine.

reefer. A marihuana cigarette.

reindeer dust. Cocaine, heroin, or morphine.

riding a wave. Drugged.

right croaker. A doctor who sells narcotics illegally.

roach. A partially consumed marihuana cigarette.

rockets. Marihuana cigarettes.

rock-pile cure. A sudden forced abstinence from drugs.

roll a pill. To prepare opium for smoking.

roll the boy. To smoke opium.

runner. Teen-age contact used to recruit new addicts.

safety. A safety pin used as a makeshift hypodermic needle.

saxophone, Chinese saxophone. An opium pipe.

scat. Heroin.

score. A meeting with a drug peddler. *Also* enough money to buy a ration of drugs.

script. A prescription for drugs.

self-starter. An addict who voluntarily places himself in an institution in order to be cured.

sharp. To be elated by drugs.

shoot, shot. An injection of a drug.

shot in the arm. An injection of a drug into the bloodstream.

shot up. Under the influence of drugs.

shover. A drug peddler.

skamas. Opium for smoking.

skate. To use morphine.

skee. Opium.

skin pop, skin shot. An injection of a drug beneath the skin.

shive. An attendant in an opium den.

sky the wipe. A hypodermic needle.

Sleigh. A drug addict.

sleigh ride. A spree after indulging in drugs. *Also* a drug addict.

slum dump. An opium den. *Also* a den for cocaine- or morphine-users.

smack, smeck, schmeck. Drugs, especially powdered drugs in the form of snuff.

smoke. A bout of opium smoking.

snake. An habitual smoker of marihuana.

snaved in. Drug-exhilarated.

sneeze it out. To stop using drugs abruptly.

sniffing, snuffing. Inhaling a drug.

snort. An inhalation of cocaine or heroin.

snow. Cocaine.

snowbird. A cocaine addict.

snow fall. A bout of cocaine- or morphine-using.

snow flower. A girl addicted to morphine.

snuffy. An addict who snuffs cocaine or heroin.

speed ball. A powerful shot of a drug, usually heroin and cocaine combined.

spike. A drug. *Also* a hypodermic needle; an injection of a drug.

spread. To smoke opium.

stem. An opium pipe.

stick. A marihuana cigarette. *Also* a home-made opium pipe.

stink weed. Marihuana.

stoned. Under the influence of drugs.

stuff. Drugs.

sugar, sweet stuff. Cocaine, heroin, or morphine.

swing-man. A drug peddler.

take a sweep. To inhale a drug.

tar. Opium.

tea. Marihuana.

tea-pad. A marihuana smoking den.

teo. A marihuana smoker.

Texas tea. Marihuana.

toy. A measure of opium.

turkey. A substance which does not contain narcotics or marihuana; not connected with *cold turkey.*

twist. A marihuana cigarette.

twist up a few. To smoke opium.

twitcher. A drug addict.

uncle. A Federal narcotic agent.

viper. A marihuana smoker.

wash up. To take the drug cure.

weed, viper's weed. Marihuana.

week-end habit. The use of narcotics irregularly without becoming addicted.

Whiskers. A Federal Government officer.

white silk. Morphine in crystal form.

white stuff. Any powdered drug, especially morphine, heroin, or
cocaine.

whiz-bang. A mixture of, or the injection of a mixture of cocaine,
heroin, or morphine.

wing-ding. A feigned fit or spasm thrown by an addict in an attempt to obtain drugs.

Wings, witch. Cocaine, morphine, or heroin.

yen-hok. A long steel needle upon which an opium pill is cooked.

yen pock. A ration of opium prepared for smoking.

yen-pop. Marihuana.

yen-shee. The residue left in the opium pipe's bowl and stem after
the opium has been smoked.

yen shee doy. Chinese: a Chinese drug addict.

yen-shee gow. A scraper for removing *yen-shee* from the opium
pipe.

yen shee suey. Opium wine: *yen-shee* mixed with water or
whiskey.

WHAT THE UNIFORM NARCOTIC DRUG ACT
WILL ACCOMPLISH

1. Aid the United States in carrying out its international obligations under the Hague Convention.

2. Arrest the growth and spread of the traffic in illicit narcotics by replacing the present inadequate and conflicting state laws.

3. Utilize and call in to full exercise the powers that reside in the states alone, permitting prosecution in such cases as illegal possession, over which the Federal courts have no jurisdiction.

4. Make a necessary division of responsibility in narcotic law enforcement between the Federal and the several state governments, if the general welfare of the citizens of each state is to be maintained.

5. Coordinate enforcement machinery through mandatory cooperation of state with Federal officers.

6. Prohibit sales or transfers of narcotic drugs except under state licenses, to include manufacturers and wholesalers; a requirement solely within the power of the states.

7. Prohibit production of narcotic drugs within state borders, except by specific license and under strict regulation.

8. Include within the definition of narcotic drugs those narcotics which may be prepared synthetically (such as tropococaine) as well as those directly derived from opium and coca leaves.

9. Provide for revocation of licenses for violations of the state

narcotic law, direct control of this phase of enforcement being beyond the power of the Federal Government.

10. Strengthen enforcement by making admissible as evidence what are normally privileged communications, when they are used to procure unlawfully a narcotic drug.

11. Require the return of the unused portion of a narcotic drug to the practitioner from whom received, when no longer required as a medicine by the patient.

12. Permit of prosecution in all cases of persons obtaining narcotic drugs by fraud or deceit, and particularly in those cases where narcotics are obtained by means of false or altered prescriptions. These cases are difficult, if not impossible, to handle satisfactorily under the present Federal law.

UNIFORM NARCOTIC DRUG ACT

PREFATORY NOTE

THE UNIFORM NARCOTIC DRUG ACT, ADOPTED BY THE NATIONAL Conference of Commissioners on Uniform State Laws, in 1932, is an act which has received the study of the committee in charge and many experts for the past five years.

It is difficult for one not familiar with the subject to understand how many different organizations and associations have an interest in the provisions of this act. The fact was recognized in drafting that a social problem, as well as an economic question, was involved, and that the act must protect those using narcotic drugs legally, as well as provide punishment for those using such drugs illegally. Manufacturers, wholesalers, retailers, apothecaries, doctors, dentists, nurses, internes, and attendants had to be protected in their legitimate use of the substances known as narcotic drugs. The idea was never absent, however, that those who were protected in the use of drugs by the act might in some cases use such drugs illegally. The committee also had to learn something of the medical effects of opium, coca leaves, cannabis, and their derivatives, in order better to frame an act that would be enforceable.

Provisions in regard to addiction and search and seizure were omitted from this act, so that each state might provide its own method for the care and cure of addicts, and methods by which drugs used in illegal traffic might be forfeited. In consideration of the subject of addiction, it was evident that each state, in order to care for its addicts, must expend quite a large amount of money for hospital service. The subject of addiction and its cure, however, is so important that no state should delay in making immediate and thorough study of this great social problem. As each state now has in its laws some provisions for search, seizure and forfeiture, it was deemed best that each state provide such methods for search, seizure and forfeiture as would best harmonize with its constitution and laws already enacted.

The committee took into consideration the fact that the federal government had already passed the Harrison Act and the Federal Import and Export Act. Many persons have assumed that the Harrison Act was all that was necessary. The Harrison Act, however, is a revenue-producing act, and while it provides penalties for violation, it does not give the states themselves authority to exercise police power in regard to seizure of drugs used in illicit trade, or in regard to punishment of those responsible therefor. Every provision which would cause duplication of records was omitted from the act, and a section was inserted providing against double jeopardy.

Great care had to be exercised not to violate the provisions of any treaties between the United States and foreign countries in regard to traffic in narcotic drugs.

The demand for uniform state legislation on this subject was very extensive. It was argued that the traffic in narcotic drugs should have the same safeguards and the same regulation in all of the states. This act is recommended to the states for that purpose.

UNIFORM NARCOTIC DRUG ACT

AN ACT DEFINING AND RELATING TO NARCOTIC DRUGS AND TO MAKE UNIFORM THE LAW WITH REFERENCE THERETO

[*Note: Title should be worded to comply with the requirements of the constitution and laws of the State adopting.*]

Be it enacted. [Insert here the proper enacting clause for the State.]

SECTION 1. [*Definitions.*] The following words and phrases, as used in this act, shall have the following meanings, unless the context otherwise requires:

(1) "Person" includes any corporation, association, co-partnership, or one or more individuals.

(2) "Physician" means a person authorized by law to practice medicine in this state and any other person authorized by law to treat sick and injured human beings in this state and to use narcotic drugs in connection with such treatment.

(3) "Dentist" means a person authorized by law to practice dentistry in this state.

(4) "Veterinarian" means a person authorized by law to practice veterinary medicine in this state.

(5) "Manufacturer" means a person who by compounding, mixing, cultivating, growing, or other process, produces or prepares narcotic drugs, but does not include an apothecary who compounds narcotic drugs to be sold or dispensed on prescriptions.

(6) "Wholesaler" means a person who supplies narcotic drugs that he himself has not produced nor prepared, on official written orders, but not on prescriptions.

(7) "Apothecary" means a licensed pharmacist as defined by the laws of this state and, where the context so requires, the owner of a store or other place of business where narcotic drugs are compounded or dispensed by a licensed pharmacist; but nothing in this act shall be construed as conferring on a person who is not registered nor licensed as a pharmacist any authority, right, or privilege, that is not granted to him by the pharmacy laws of this state.

(8) "Hospital" means an institution for the care and treatment of the sick and injured, approved by [Insert here proper official designation of state officer or board] as proper to be entrusted with the custody of narcotic drugs and the professional use of narcotic drugs under the direction of a physician, dentist, or veterinarian.

(9) "Laboratory" means a laboratory approved by [Insert here proper official designation of state officer or board] as proper to be entrusted with the custody of narcotic drugs and the use of narcotic drugs for scientific and medical purposes and for purposes of instruction.

(10) "Sale" includes barter, exchange, or gift, or offer therefor, and each such transaction made by any person, whether as principal, proprietor, agent, servant, or employee.

(11) "Coca leaves" includes cocaine and any compound, manufacture, salt, derivative, mixture, or preparation of coca leaves, except

derivatives of coca leaves which do not contain cocaine, ecgonine, or substances from which cocaine or ecgonine may be synthesized or made.

(12) "Opium" includes morphine, codeine, and heroin, and any compound, manufacture, salt, derivative, mixture, or preparation of opium, but does not include apomorphine or any of its salts.

(13) "Cannabis" includes all parts of the plant Cannabis sativa L., whether growing or not; the seeds thereof; the resin extracted from any part of such plant; and every compound, manufacture, salt, derivative, mixture, or preparation of such plant, its seeds, or resin; but shall not include the mature stalks of such plant, fiber produced from such stalks, oil or cake made from the seeds of such plant, any other compound, manufacture, salt, derivative, mixture or preparation of such mature stalks (except the resin extracted therefrom), fiber, oil, or cake, or the sterilized seed of such plant which is incapable of germination.

(14) "Narcotic drugs" means coca leaves, opium, cannabis, and every other substance neither chemically nor physically distinguishable from them; any other drugs to which the Federal laws relating to narcotic drugs may now apply; and any drug found by the (State Commissioner of Health or other competent state officer) after reasonable notice and opportunity for hearing, to have an addiction-forming or addiction-sustaining liability similar to morphine or cocaine, from the date of publication of such finding by said (State Commissioner of Health or other competent state officer).

(15) "Federal Narcotic Laws" means the laws of the United States relating to opium, coca leaves, and other narcotic drugs.

(16) "Official written order" means an order written on a form provided for that purpose by the United States Commissioner of Narcotics, under any laws of the United States making provision therefor, if such order forms are authorized and required by federal law, and if no such order form is provided, then on an official form provided for that purpose by [Insert here proper official designation of state officer or board.]

(17) "Dispense" includes distribute, leave with, give away, dispose of, or deliver.

(18) "Registry number" means the number assigned to each person registered under the Federal Narcotic Laws.

SECTION 2. [Acts Prohibited.] It shall be unlawful for any person to manufacture, possess, have under his control, sell, prescribe, administer, dispense, or compound any narcotic drug, except as authorized in this act.

SECTION 3. [*Manufacturers and Wholesalers.*] No person shall manufacture, compound, mix, cultivate, grow, or by any other process produce or prepare narcotic drugs, and no person as a wholesaler shall supply the same, without having first obtained a license so to do from the [Insert here proper official designation of state officer or board.]

SECTION 4. [*Qualification for Licenses.*] No license shall be issued under the foregoing section unless and until the applicant therefor has furnished proof satisfactory to [Insert here proper official designation of state officer or board.]

(a) That the applicant is of good moral character or, if the applicant be an association or corporation, that the managing officers are of good moral character.

(b) That the applicant is equipped as to land, buildings, and paraphernalia properly to carry on the business described in his application.

No license shall be granted to any person who has within five years been convicted of a willful violation of any law of the United States, or of any state, relating to opium, coca leaves, or other narcotic drugs, or to any person who is a narcotic drug addict.

The [Insert here proper official designation of state officer or board] may suspend or revoke any license for cause.

SECTION 5. [*Sale on Written Orders.*]

(1) A duly licensed manufacturer or wholesaler may sell and dispense narcotic drugs to any of the following persons, but only on official written orders:

a) To a manufacturer, wholesaler, or apothecary.

b) To a physician, dentist, or veterinarian.

c) To a person in charge of a hospital, but only for use by or in that hospital.

d) To a person in charge of a laboratory, but only for use in that laboratory for scientific and medical purposes.

(2) A duly licensed manufacturer or wholesaler may sell narcotic drugs to any of the following persons:

a) On a special written order accompanied by a certificate of exemption, as required by the Federal Narcotic Laws, to a person in the employ of the United States Government or of any state, territorial, district, county, municipal, or insular government, purchasing, receiving, possessing, or dispensing narcotic drugs by reason of his official duties.

b) To a master of a ship or a person in charge of any aircraft upon which no physician is regularly employed, or to a physician or surgeon duly licensed in some State, Territory, or the District of Columbia to practice his profession, or to a retired commissioned medical officer of the United States Army, Navy, or Public Health Service employed upon such ship or aircraft, for the actual medical needs of persons on board such ship or aircraft, or to a physician, surgeon, or retired commissioned medical officer of the United States Army, Navy, or Public Health Service employed upon such ship or aircraft when not in port. Provided: Such narcotic drugs shall be sold to the master of such ship or person in charge of such aircraft only in pursuance of a special order form approved by a commissioned medical officer or acting assistant surgeon of the United States Public Health Service.

c) To a person in a foreign country if the provisions of the Federal Narcotic Laws are complied with.

(3) [*Use of Official Written Orders.*] An official written order for any narcotic drug shall be signed in duplicate by the person giving said order or by his duly authorized agent. The original shall be presented to the person who sells or dispenses the narcotic drug or drugs named therein. In event of the acceptance of such order by said person, each party to the transaction shall preserve his copy of such order for a period of two years in such a way as to be readily accessible for inspection by any public officer or employee engaged in the enforcement of this act. It shall be deemed a compliance with this subsection if the parties to the transaction have complied with the Federal Narcotic Laws, respecting the requirements governing the use of order forms.

(4) [*Possession Lawful.*] Possession of or control of narcotic drugs obtained as authorized by this section shall be lawful if in the regular course of business, occupation, profession, employment, or duty of the possessor.

(5) A person in charge of a hospital or of a laboratory, or in the employ of this state or of any other state, or of any political subdivision thereof, or a master of a ship or a person in charge of any aircraft upon which no physician is regularly employed, or a physician or surgeon duly licensed in some State, Territory, or the District of Columbia, to practice his profession, or a retired commissioned medical officer of the United States Army, Navy, or Public Health Service

employed upon such ship or aircraft, who obtains narcotic drugs under the provisions of this section or otherwise, shall not administer, nor dispense, nor otherwise use such drugs, within this state, except within the scope of his employment or official duty, and then only for scientific or medicinal purposes and subject to the provisions of this act.

SECTION 6. [*Sales by Apothecaries.*]

(1) An apothecary, in good faith, may sell and dispense narcotic drugs to any person upon a written prescription of a physician, dentist, or veterinarian, dated and signed by the person prescribing on the day when issued and bearing the full name and address of the patient for whom, or of the owner of the animal for which, the drug is dispensed, and the full name, address, and registry number under the Federal Narcotic Laws of the person prescribing, if he is required by those laws to be so registered. If the prescription be for an animal, it shall state the species of animal for which the drug is prescribed. The person filling the prescription shall write the date of filling and his own signature on the face of the prescription. The prescription shall be retained on file by the proprietor of the pharmacy in which it is filled for a period of two years, so as to be readily accessible for inspection by any public officer or employee engaged in the enforcement of this act. The prescription shall not be refilled.

(2) The legal owner of any stock of narcotic drugs in a pharmacy, upon discontinuance of dealing in said drugs, may sell said stock to a manufacturer, wholesaler, or apothecary, but only on an official written order.

(3) An apothecary, only upon an official written order, may sell to a physician, dentist, or veterinarian, in quantities not exceeding one ounce at any one time, aqueous or oleaginous solutions of which the content of narcotic drugs does not exceed a proportion greater than twenty percent of the complete solution, to be used for medical purposes.

SECTION 7. [*Professional Use of Narcotic Drugs.*]

(1) [*Physicians and Dentists.*] A physician or a dentist, in good faith and in the course of his professional practice only, may prescribe, administer, and dispense narcotic drugs, or he may cause the same to be administered by a nurse or interne under his direction and supervision.

(2) [*Veterinarians.*] A veterinarian, in good faith and in the course of his professional practice only, and not for use by a human being,

may prescribe, administer, and dispense narcotic drugs, and he may cause them to be administered by an assistant or orderly under his direction and supervision.

(3) [*Return of Unused Drugs.*] Any person who has obtained from a physician, dentist, or veterinarian any narcotic drug for administration to a patient during the absence of such physician, dentist, or veterinarian, shall return to such physician, dentist, or veterinarian any unused portion of such drug, when it is no longer required by the patient.

SECTION 8. [*Preparations exempted.*] Except as otherwise in this act specifically provided, this act shall not apply to the following cases:

Administering, dispensing, or selling at retail of any medicinal preparation that contains in one fluid ounce, or if a solid or semi-solid preparation, in one avoirdupois ounce, not more than one grain of codeine or of any of its salts, or not more than 1/6 grain of dihydrocodeinone or any of its salt.

The exemption authorized by this section shall be subject to the following conditions: (1) that the medicinal preparation administered, dispensed, or sold, shall contain, in addition to the narcotic drug in it, some drug or drugs conferring upon it medicinal qualities other than those possessed by the narcotic drug alone; and (2) that such preparation shall be administered, dispensed, and sold in good faith as a medicine, and not for the purpose of evading the provisions of this act.

Nothing in this section shall be construed to limit the quantity of codeine, dihydrocodeinone or any of their salts that may be prescribed, administered, dispensed, or sold, to any person or for the use of any person or animal, when it is prescribed, administered, dispensed, or sold, in compliance with the general provisions of this act.

SECTION 9. [*Record to Be Kept.*]

(1) [*Physicians, Dentists, Veterinarians, and Other Authorized Persons.*] Every physician, dentist, veterinarian, or other person who is authorized to administer or professionally use narcotic drugs, shall keep a record of such drugs received by him, and a record of all such drugs administered, dispensed, or professionally used by him otherwise than by prescription. It shall, however, be deemed a sufficient compliance with this subsection if any such person using small quantities of solutions or other preparations of such drugs for local application, shall keep a record of the quantity, character, and potency of such solutions or other preparations purchased or made up by him, and of the dates when purchased or made up, without keeping a

record of the amount of such solution or other preparation applied by him to individual patients.

Provided, That no record need be kept of narcotic drugs administered, dispensed, or professionally used in the treatment of any one patient, when the amount administered, dispensed, or professionally used for that purpose does not exceed in any forty-eight consecutive hours, (a) four grains of opium, or (b) one-half of a grain of morphine or of any of its salts, or (c) two grains of codeine or of any of its salts, or (d) one-fourth of a grain of heroin or of any of its salts, or (e) a quantity of any other narcotic drug or any combination of narcotic drugs that does not exceed in pharmacologic potency any one of the drugs named above in the quantity stated.

(2) [*Manufacturers and Wholesalers.*] Manufacturers and wholesalers shall keep records of all narcotic drugs compounded, mixed, cultivated, grown, or by any other process produced or prepared, and of all narcotic drugs received and disposed of by them, in accordance with the provisions of subsection 5 of this section.

(3) [*Apothecaries.*] Apothecaries shall keep records of all narcotic drugs received and disposed of by them, in accordance with the provisions of subsection 5 of this section.

(4) [*Vendors of Exempted Preparations.*] Every person who purchases for resale, or who sells narcotic drug preparations exempted by Section 8 of this act, shall keep a record showing the quantities and kinds thereof received and sold, or disposed of otherwise, in accordance with the provisions of subsection 5 of this section.

(5) [*Form and Preservation of Records.*] The form of records shall be prescribed by the [Insert here proper official designation of state officer or board.] The record of narcotic drugs received shall in every case show the date of receipt, the name and address of the person from whom received, and the kind and quantity of drugs received; the kind and quantity of narcotic drugs produced or removed from process of manufacture, and the date of such production or removal from process of manufacture; and the record shall in every case show the proportion of morphine, cocaine, or ecgonine contained in or producible from crude opium or coca leaves received or produced and the proportion of resin contained in or producible from the plant Cannabis sativa L., received or produced. The record of all narcotic drugs sold, administered, dispensed, or otherwise disposed of, shall show the date of selling, administering, or dispensing, the name and address of the person to whom, or for whose use, or the owner and species of animal for which the drugs were sold, administered or dis-

pensed, and the kind and quantity of drugs. Every such record shall be kept for a period of two years from the date of the transaction recorded. The keeping of a record required by or under the Federal Narcotic Laws, containing substantially the same information as is specified above, shall constitute compliance with this section, except that every such record shall contain a detailed list of narcotic drugs lost, destroyed, or stolen, if any, the kind and quantity of such drugs, and the date of the discovery of such loss, destruction, or theft.

SECTION 10. [*Labels.*]

(1) Whenever a manufacturer sells or dispenses a narcotic drug, and whenever a wholesaler sells or dispenses a narcotic drug in a package prepared by him, he shall securely affix to each package in which that drug is contained a label showing in legible English the name and address of the vendor and the quantity, kind, and form of narcotic drug contained therein. No person, except an apothecary for the purpose of filling a prescription under this act, shall alter, deface, or remove any label so affixed.

(2) Whenever an apothecary sells or dispenses any narcotic drug on a prescription issued by a physician, dentist, or veterinarian, he shall affix to the container in which such drug is sold or dispensed, a label showing his own name, address, and registry number, or the name, address, and registry number of the apothecary for whom he is lawfully acting; the name and address of the patient or, if the patient is an animal, the name and address of the owner of the animal and the species of the animal; the name, address, and registry number of the physician, dentist, or veterinarian, by whom the prescription was written; and such directions as may be stated on the prescription. No person shall alter, deface, or remove any label so affixed.

SECTION 11. [*Authorized Possession of Narcotic Drugs by Individuals.*] A person to whom or for whose use any narcotic drug has been prescribed, sold, or dispensed, by a physician, dentist, apothecary, or other person authorized under the provisions of Section 5 of this act, and the owner of any animal for which any such drug has been prescribed, sold, or dispensed, by a veterinarian, may lawfully possess if only in the container in which it was delivered to him by the person selling or dispensing the same.

Note: It is recommended by the committee that each State provide its own method of search, seizure, and forfeiture, of narcotic drugs.

SECTION 12. [*Persons and Corporations Exempted.*]

The provisions of this act restricting the possession and having control of narcotic drugs shall not apply to common carriers or to warehousemen, while engaged in lawfully transporting or storing such drugs, or to any employee of the same acting within the scope of his employment; or to public officers or their employees in the performance of their official duties requiring possession or control of narcotic drugs; or to temporary incidental possession by employees or agents of persons lawfully entitled to possession, or by persons whose possession is for the purpose of aiding public officers in performing their official duties.

SECTION 13. [*Common Nuisances.*] Any store, shop, warehouse, dwelling house, building, vehicle, boat, aircraft, or any place whatever, which is resorted to by narcotic drug addicts for the purpose of using narcotic drugs or which is used for the illegal keeping or selling of the same, shall be deemed a common nuisance. No person shall keep or maintain such a common nuisance.

SECTION 14. [*Narcotic Drugs to be Delivered to State Official, Etc.*] All narcotic drugs, the lawful possession of which is not established or the title to which cannot be ascertained, which have come into the custody of a peace officer, shall be forfeited, and disposed of as follows:

a) Except as in this section otherwise provided, the court or magistrate having jurisdiction shall order such narcotic drugs forfeited and destroyed. A record of the place where said drugs were seized, of the kinds and quantities of drugs so destroyed, and of the time, place, and manner of destruction, shall be kept, and a return under oath, reporting said destruction, shall be made to the court or magistrate and to the United States Commissioner of Narcotics, by the officer who destroys them.

b) Upon written application by the State [Commissioner of Public Health], the court or magistrate by whom the forfeiture of narcotic drugs has been decreed may order the delivery of any of them, except heroin and its salts and derivatives, to said State [Commissioner of Public Health], for distribution or destruction, as hereinafter provided.

c) Upon application by any hospital within this State, not operated for private gain, the State [Commissioner of Public Health] may in his discretion deliver any narcotic drugs that have come into his custody by authority of this section to the applicant for medicinal use. The

State [Commission of Public Health] may from time to time deliver excess stocks of such narcotic drugs to the United States Commissioner of Narcotics, or may destroy the same.

d) The State [Commissioner of Public Health] shall keep a full and complete record of all drugs received and of all drugs disposed of, showing the exact kinds, quantities, and forms of such drugs; the persons from whom received and to whom delivered; by whose authority received, delivered, and destroyed; and the dates of the receipt, disposal, or destruction, which record shall be open to inspection by all Federal or State officers charged with the enforcement of Federal and State narcotic laws.

SECTION 15. [*Notice of Conviction to Be Sent to Licensing Board.*] On the conviction of any person of the violation of any provision of this act, a copy of the judgment and sentence, and of the opinion of the court or magistrate, if any opinion be filed, shall be sent by the clerk of the court, or by the magistrate, to the board or officer, if any, by whom the convicted defendant has been licensed or registered to practice his profession or to carry on his business. On the conviction of any such person, the court may, in its discretion, suspend or revoke the license or registration of the convicted defendant to practice his profession or to carry on his business. On the application of any person whose license or registration has been suspended or revoked, and upon proper showing and for good cause, said board or officer may reinstate such license or registration.

SECTION 16. [*Records, Confidential.*] Prescriptions, orders and records, required by this act, and stocks of narcotic drugs, shall be open for inspection only to federal, state, county, and municipal officers, whose duty it is to enforce the laws of this state or of the United States relating to narcotic drugs. No officer having knowledge by virtue of his office of any such prescription, order, or record shall divulge such knowledge, except in connection with a prosecution or proceeding in court or before a licensing or registration board or officer, to which prosecution or proceeding the person to whom such prescriptions, orders, or records relate is a party.

SECTION 17. [*Fraud or Deceit.*]

(1) No person shall obtain or attempt to obtain a narcotic drug, or procure or attempt to procure the administration of a narcotic drug, (a) by fraud, deceit, misrepresentation, or subterfuge; or (b) by the forgery or alteration of a prescription or of any written order; or (c)

by the concealment of a material fact; or (d) by the use of a false name or the giving of a false address.

(2) Information communicated to a physician in an effort unlawfully to procure a narcotic drug, or unlawfully to procure the administration of any such drug, shall not be deemed a privileged communication.

(3) No person shall wilfully make a false statement in any prescription, order, report, or record, required by this act.

(4) No person shall, for the purpose of obtaining a narcotic drug, falsely assume the title of, or represent himself to be, a manufacturer, wholesaler, apothecary, physician, dentist, veterinarian, or other authorized person.

(5) No person shall make or utter any false or forged prescription or false or forged written order.

(6) No person shall affix any false or forged label to a package or receptacle containing narcotic drugs.

(7) The provisions of this section shall apply to all transactions relating to narcotic drugs under the provisions of Section 8 of this act, in the same way as they apply to transactions under all other sections.

SECTION 18. [*Exceptions and Exemptions Not Required to be Negatived.*] In any complaint, information, or indictment, and in any action or proceeding brought for the enforcement of any provision of this act, it shall not be necessary to negative any exception, excuse, proviso, or exemption, contained in this act, and the burden of proof of any such exception, excuse, proviso or exemption, shall be upon the defendant.

SECTION 19. [*Enforcement and Cooperation.*] It is hereby made the duty of the [Insert here proper official designation of state officer or board], its officers, agents, inspectors, and representatives, and of all peace officers within the state, and of all county attorneys, to enforce all provisions of this act, except those specifically delegated, and to cooperate with all agencies charged with the enforcement of the laws of the United States, of this state, and of all other states, relating to narcotic drugs.

SECTION 20. [*Penalties.*] * [*Proposed Amendment to Penalty Provisions of the Uniform State Narcotic Drug Act.*]

Whoever violates any provision of this act shall upon conviction be

* This penalty provision has been passed by West Virginia, Tennessee, Maryland, Alabama, Alaska, Colorado, Georgia, Indiana, Kentucky, Oklahoma, and New Jersey.

fined not more than ($) and be imprisoned not less than two or more than five years. For a second offense, or if, in case of a first conviction of violation of any provision of this act, the offender shall previously have been convicted of any violation of the laws of the United States or of any other state, territory or district relating to narcotic drugs or marihuana, the offender shall be fined not more than ($) and be imprisoned not less than five or more than ten years. For a third or subsequent offense, or if the offender shall previously have been convicted two or more times in the aggregate of any violation of the law of the United States or of any other state, territory or district relating to narcotic drugs or marihuana, the offender shall be fined not more than ($) and be imprisoned not less than ten or more than twenty years.

Except in the case of conviction for a first offense for violation of the provisions of this act, the imposition or execution of sentence shall not be suspended and probation or parole shall not be granted until the minimum imprisonment herein provided for the offense shall have been served.

Section 21. [*Effect of Acquittal or Conviction under Federal Narcotic Laws.*] No person shall be prosecuted for a violation of any provision of this act if such person has been acquitted or convicted under the Federal Narcotic Laws of the same act or omission which, it is alleged, constitutes a violation of this act.

Section 22. [*Constitutionality.*] If any provision of this act or the application thereof to any person or circumstances is held invalid, such invalidity shall not affect other provisions or applications of the act which can be given effect without the invalid provision or application, and to this end the provisions of this act are declared to be severable.

Section 23. [*Interpretation.*] This act shall be so interpreted and construed as to effectuate its general purpose, to make uniform the laws of those states which enact it.

Section 24. [*Inconsistent Laws Repealed.*] All acts or parts of acts which are inconsistent with the provisions of this act are hereby repealed.

Section 25. [*Name of Act.*] This act may be cited as the Uniform Narcotic Drug Act.

Section 26. [*Time of Taking Effect.*] This act shall take effect [Insert here statement of time when the act is to take effect.]

NATIONAL RESEARCH COUNCIL

THE COMMITTEE ON DRUG ADDICTION AND NARCOTICS OF
THE DIVISION OF MEDICAL SCIENCES, NATIONAL RESEARCH
COUNCIL

IN JANUARY, 1929, THE BUREAU OF SOCIAL HYGIENE, INC., OFFERED
to the National Research Council a sum of money to defray the
expenses incidental to the conduct of research studies of cause
and effect, prevention, and cure of drug addiction. The Council accepted the funds and appointed in its Division of Medical
Sciences, to draft and supervise a plan of research work, a
Committee on Drug Addiction (later denominated the Committee
on Drug Addiction and Narcotics). In addition to the Chairman
who was a Consulting Pathologist to the National Institute of
Health, the Committee was composed of two experts representing chemistry, five experts representing pharmacology, the
Commissioner of Narcotics, the Assistant Surgeon General and
the former Assistant Surgeon General, respectively, of the then
Division of Mental Hygiene of the U. S. Public Health Service,
and the Chairman of the Division of Medical Sciences, *ex officio*.
Although the membership of the Committee, with one exception,
has changed since it was originally established, the Committee
continues to have expert representation of the sciences of patho-
logy, chemistry and pharmacology, and of the government
agencies mentioned.

In the first report of the Committee on Drug Addiction, covering the period from January 1, 1929 to April 30, 1930, it set forth its objectives as follows:

First, the reduction of the legitimate uses of habit-forming drugs to be obtained through the decrease of physicians' prescriptions and proprietary remedies containing such drugs.

Second, the replacement of each use of habit-forming drugs with a substance non-habit-forming but capable of producing the medicinal action required of the habit-forming product.

Third, in this way to reduce to a minimum the legitimate production of alkaloids and thus to lessen the problem of police authority necessary to control the situation.

To accomplish these three results the Committee concluded that it would be necessary to proceed in the following ways in laying out the program of its work:

1. To prepare for general educational purposes by means of the lay and scientific press monographs on the indispensable uses of morphine and other alkaloids.

2. To seek to prepare by synthesis and analysis compounds without addiction fractions that would perform in medical practice the functions now obtained by those with addiction properties.

3. To study the effects of the compounds thus obtained on animals and later to test the value of these compounds as replacement substances in human therapy.

At the request of the Committee, the American Medical Association in 1931 caused several articles to be prepared by various physicians under the general subject "The Indispensable Use of Narcotics," these articles being published in issues of the Association's *Journal* of that year. These articles were designed to educate physicians to reduce to the minimum the use of opium and its derivatives. Along the lines of Items 2 and 3 of its plan of procedure, the Committee directed the performance of a vast amount of research work. The nature and extent of this work is shown in publications by the investigators: *Chemistry of the*

Opium Alkaloids, by Small and Lutz, (*Supplement No. 103* to the Public Health *Reports*); *The Pharmacology of the Opium Alkaloids,* by Krueger, Eddy, and Sumwalt, (*Supplement No. 165* to the Public Health *Reports*); and *Studies on Drug Addiction,* by Small, Eddy, Mosettig, and Himmelsbach, (*Supplement No 138* to the Public Health *Reports*).

The Committee, however, has not restricted its research activity to that concerning the various opium derivatives, whether new or old. In 1939, dolantin (also known as pethidine or Demerol) was discovered, and the discovery of amidone (also known as methadon, Dolophine or Adanon) followed shortly thereafter, with the subsequent development of a number of variant forms of these two new drugs. Still later, another new drug in this class was discovered and given the name of Dromoran. All of these new drugs and some of their variant forms were prepared synthetically and bore no close chemical relationship to morphine, yet they were found to have analgesic properties similar to morphine which would indicate their importance as substitutes for morphine for pain-relief. To determine the status of any such new drug, particularly with reference to the possible application of the Federal narcotic laws, it is necessary to ascertain whether it also possesses addiction-forming or addiction-sustaining liability similar to morphine. The Committee undertakes to determine, on the basis of clinical studies, whether the new drug possesses sufficient merit for analgesic use in comparison with morphine or other analgesics already available to justify further study and, if this finding is favorable, it recommends that addiction-liability tests be made. It receives the full cooperation of interested government agencies such as the Public Health Service, the Bureau of Narcotics, and the Food and Drug Administration, but its decision is based upon an unbiased scientific analysis of the facts and is respected alike by the government agencies concerned and the producers of the new drugs.

The Committee acts as scientific adviser to any government agency or to a professional association, on any important question within its competency relating to narcotic drugs or narcotic drug addiction. It also acts as the unofficial but highly-respected clearing house for proposals for privately-conducted scientific projects involving the use of narcotic drugs or synthetic substitutes, and its approval is usually accepted as a guaranty that the project as submitted is technically adequate, practically worth while, and is probably not being duplicated elsewhere.

Chart showing the results of a mortality study made by **Dr.** Tsungming To, Pharmacological Institute, faculty of Medicine, National Taiwan University, Taipeh, Formosa.

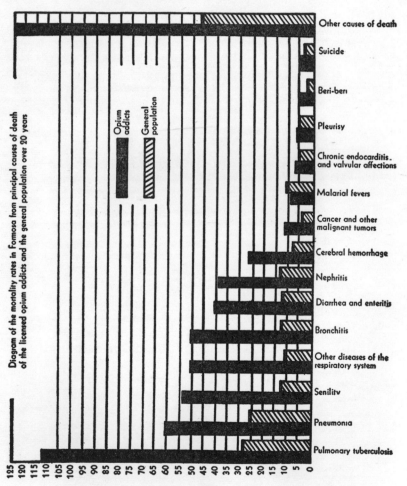

Diagram of the mortality rates in Formosa from principal causes of death of the licensed opium addicts and the general population over 20 years

Opium addicts

General population

Other causes of death
Suicide
Beri-beri
Pleurisy
Chronic endocarditis and valvular affections
Malarial fevers
Cancer and other malignant tumors
Cerebral hemorrhage
Nephritis
Diarrhea and enteritis
Bronchitis
Other diseases of the respiratory system
Senility
Pneumonia
Pulmonary tuberculosis

342

INDEX

Expert Committee on Drugs
Liable to Produce Ad-
diction, 64-65
definition of addiction-forming drugs, 67-68
definition of drug addiction,
67
definition of habit-forming
drugs, 68
Ezzat, Ibrahim (Egypt UN representative), 101, 103,
104

famine, opium and, 2
federal jurisdiction, 117-154
Fishbein, Dr. Morris, 130
follow-up treatment, 228, 240,
297
Food and Drug Administration,
334
Foreign Policy Association, 55
Formosa, 114, 189, 190, 267,
290
opium smoking in, 54, 189,
190, 267
Formosa plan, the, 189-190
France, addiction in, 279, 280
illicit traffic driven from, 51
member of United Nations
Commission on Narcotic
Drugs, 61
Opium Advisory Committee,
50
opium smoking suppressed
by, 56
Shanghai conference (1909),
29
French Indochina, opium smoking in, 54

ganja, 19
Gardeke, 17
Geilen, 224
General Federation of Women's
Clubs, 222
Geneva Convention (1925), 33-
34, 35, 36, 39, 40, 41, 43,
51, 52, 53, 57, 64, 65,
140, 143, 257
provisions of, 43-44
Germany, drug addiction in,
11, 279
estimates on narcotic drugs,
47
Permanent Central Board
and, 43
Shanghai conference (1909),
29
gil, 1
Gilmartin, Peter F., 201
Gioffredi, 245
Goodman, Judge Louis E., 154
Great Britain, drug addiction
in, 11, 279, 280
Indian hemp in, 18
member of United Nations
Commission on Narcotic
Drugs, 61
Opium Advisory Committee,
50
opium smoking suppressed
by, 56
Opium War, 4, 7-8
Shanghai conference (1909),
29
Greece, chira in, 19
hemp plant grown in, 18
heroin in, 63
knowledge of poppy's medicinal properties in, 1
Griffin, Dr. Clifford, 201